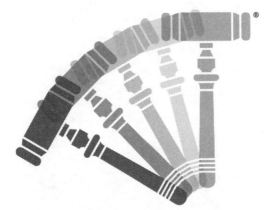

Casenote™ *Legal Briefs*

CIVIL PROCEDURE

Keyed to
Yeazell's
Civil Procedure
Sixth Edition

PUBLISHERS

1185 Avenue of the Americas, New York, NY 10036
·www.aspenpublishers.com

This publication is designed to provide accurate and authoritative information in regard to the subject matter covered. It is sold with the understanding that the publisher is not engaged in rendering legal, accounting, or other professional services. If legal advice or other expert assistance is required, the services of a competent professional person should be sought.

— From a *Declaration of Principles* adopted jointly by
a Committee of the American Bar Association and a
Committee of Publishers and Associates

© 2004 Aspen Publishers, Inc.
A WoltersKluwer Company
www.aspenpublishers.com

Permissions
Aspen Publishers
1185 Avenue of the Americas
New York, NY 10036

Printed in the United States of America.

ISBN 0-7355-4523-5

1 2 3 4 5 6 7 8 9 0

FORMAT FOR THE CASENOTE LEGAL BRIEF

PARTY ID: Quick identification of the relationship between the parties.

NATURE OF CASE: This section identifies the form of action (e.g., breach of contract, negligence, battery), the type of proceeding (e.g., demurrer, appeal from trial court's jury instructions) or the relief sought (e.g., damages, injunction, criminal sanctions).

FACT SUMMARY: This is included to refresh the student's memory and can be used as a quick reminder of the facts.

CONCISE RULE OF LAW: Summarizes the general principle of law that the case illustrates. It may be used for instant recall of the court's holding and for classroom discussion or home review.

FACTS: This section contains all relevant facts of the case, including the contentions of the parties and the lower court holdings. It is written in a logical order to give the student a clear understanding of the case. The plaintiff and defendant are identified by their proper names throughout and are always labeled with a (P) or (D).

ISSUE: The issue is a concise question that brings out the essence of the opinion as it relates to the section of the casebook in which the case appears. Both substantive and procedural issues are included if relevant to the decision.

HOLDING AND DECISION: This section offers a clear and in-depth discussion of the rule of the case and the court's rationale. It is written in easy-to-understand language and answers the issue(s) presented by applying the law to the facts of the case. When relevant, it includes a thorough discussion of the exceptions to the case as listed by the court, any major cites to other cases on point, and the names of the judges who wrote the decisions.

CONCURRENCE / DISSENT: All concurrences and dissents are briefed whenever they are included by the casebook editor.

EDITOR'S ANALYSIS: This last paragraph gives the student a broad understanding of where the case "fits in" with other cases in the section of the book and with the entire course. It is a hornbook-style discussion indicating whether the case is a majority or minority opinion and comparing the principal case with other cases in the casebook. It may also provide analysis from restatements, uniform codes, and law review articles. The editor's analysis will prove to be invaluable to classroom discussion.

QUICKNOTES: Conveniently defines legal terms found in the case and summarizes the nature of any statutes, codes, or rules referred to in the text.

PALSGRAF v. LONG ISLAND R.R. CO.
Injured bystander (P) v. Railroad company (D)
N.Y. Ct. App., 248 N.Y. 339, 162 N.E. 99 (1928).

NATURE OF CASE: Appeal from judgment affirming verdict for plaintiff seeking damages for personal injury.

FACT SUMMARY: Helen Palsgraf (P) was injured on R.R.'s (D) train platform when R.R.'s (D) guard helped a passenger aboard a moving train, causing his package to fall on the tracks. The package contained fireworks which exploded, creating a shock that tipped a scale onto Palsgraf (P).

CONCISE RULE OF LAW: The risk reasonably to be perceived defines the duty to be obeyed.

FACTS: Helen Palsgraf (P) purchased a ticket to Rockaway Beach from R.R. (D) and was waiting on the train platform. As she waited, two men ran to catch a train that was pulling out from the platform. The first man jumped aboard, but the second man, who appeared as if he might fall, was helped aboard by the guard on the train who had kept the door open so they could jump aboard. A guard on the platform also helped by pushing him onto the train. The man was carrying a package wrapped in newspaper. In the process, the man dropped his package, which fell on the tracks. The package contained fireworks and exploded. The shock of the explosion was apparently of great enough strength to tip over some scales at the other end of the platform, which fell on Palsgraf (P) and injured her. A jury awarded her damages, and R.R. (D) appealed.

ISSUE: Does the risk reasonably to be perceived define the duty to be obeyed?

HOLDING AND DECISION: (Cardozo, C.J.) Yes. The risk reasonably to be perceived defines the duty to be obeyed. If there is no foreseeable hazard to the injured party as the result of a seemingly innocent act, the act does not become a tort because it happened to be a wrong as to another. If the wrong was not willful, the plaintiff must show that the act as to her had such great and apparent possibilities of danger as to entitle her to protection. Negligence in the abstract is not enough upon which to base liability. Negligence is a relative concept, evolving out of the common law doctrine of trespass on the case. To establish liability, the defendant must owe a legal duty of reasonable care to the injured party. A cause of action in tort will lie where harm, though unintended, could have been averted or avoided by observance of such a duty. The scope of the duty is limited by the range of danger that a reasonable person could foresee. In this case, there was nothing to suggest from the appearance of the parcel or otherwise that the parcel contained fireworks. The guard could not reasonably have had any warning of a threat to Palsgraf (P), and R.R. (D) therefore cannot be held liable. Judgment is reversed in favor of R.R. (D).

DISSENT: (Andrews, J.) The concept that there is no negligence unless R.R. (D) owes a legal duty to take care as to Palsgraf (P) herself is too narrow. Everyone owes to the world at large the duty of refraining from those acts that may unreasonably threaten the safety of others. If the guard's action was negligent as to those nearby, it was also negligent as to those outside what might be termed the "danger zone." For Palsgraf (P) to recover, R.R.'s (D) negligence must have been the proximate cause of her injury, a question of fact for the jury.

EDITOR'S ANALYSIS: The majority defined the limit of the defendant's liability in terms of the danger that a reasonable person in defendant's situation would have perceived. The dissent argued that the limitation should not be placed on liability, but rather on damages. Judge Andrews suggested that only injuries that would not have happened but for R.R.'s (D) negligence should be compensable. Both the majority and dissent recognized the policy-driven need to limit liability for negligent acts, seeking, in the words of Judge Andrews, to define a framework "that will be practical and in keeping with the general understanding of mankind." The Restatement (Second) of Torts has accepted Judge Cardozo's view.

QUICKNOTES
FORESEEABILITY – The reasonable anticipation that damage is a likely result from certain acts or omissions.
NEGLIGENCE - Failure to exercise that degree of care which a person of ordinary prudence would exercise under similar circumstances.
PROXIMATE CAUSE – Something which in natural and continuous sequence, unbroken by any new intervening cause, produces an event, and without which the injury would not have occurred.

NOTE TO STUDENTS

Aspen Publishers is proud to offer *Casenote Legal Briefs*—continuing thirty years of publishing America's best-selling legal briefs.

Casenote Legal Briefs are designed to help you save time when briefing assigned cases. Organized under convenient headings, they show you how to abstract the basic facts and holdings from the text of the actual opinions handed down by the courts. Used as part of a rigorous study regime, they can help you spend more time analyzing and critiquing points of law than on copying out bits and pieces of judicial opinions into your notebook or outline.

Casenote Legal Briefs should never be used as a substitute for assigned casebook readings. They work best when read as a follow-up to reviewing the underlying opinions themselves. Students who try to avoid reading and digesting the judicial opinions in their casebooks or on-line sources will end up shortchanging themselves in the long run. The ability to absorb, critique, and restate the dynamic and complex elements of case law decisions is crucial to your success in law school and beyond. It cannot be developed vicariously.

Casenote Legal Briefs represent but one of the many offerings in Aspen's Study Aid Timeline, which includes:

- Casenotes *Legal Briefs*
- Emanuel *Outlines*
- *Examples & Explanations* Series
- *Introduction to Law* Series
- Emanuel *Law in a Flash* Flashcards
- Emanuel *CrunchTime* Series

Each of these series is designed to provide you with easy-to-understand explanations of complex points of law. Each volume offers guidance on the principles of legal analysis and, consulted regularly, will hone your ability to spot relevant issues. We have titles that will help you prepare for class, prepare for your exams, and enhance your general comprehension of the law along the way.

To find out more about Aspen Study Aid publications, visit us on-line at www.aspenpublishers.com or e-mail us at legaledu@aspenpubl.com. We'll be happy to assist you.

Free access to Briefs on-line!

Download the cases you want in your notes or outlines using the full cut-and-paste feature accompanying our on-line briefs. Please fill out this form for full access to this useful feature. No photocopies of this form will be accepted.

① Name: _____ Phone: (___) _____

    Address: _____ Apt.: _____

    City: _____ State: _____ ZIP Code: _____

    Law School: _____ Year (circle one): 1st 2nd 3rd

② Cut out the UPC found on the lower left-hand corner of the back cover of this book. Staple the UPC inside this box. Only the original UPC from the book cover will be accepted. (No photocopies or store stickers are allowed.)

> **Attach UPC inside this box.**

③ E-mail:_____ (Print LEGIBLY or you may not get access!)

④ Title (course subject) of this book _____

⑤ Used with which casebook (provide author's name): _____

⑥ Mail the completed form to:

    Aspen Publishers, Inc.
    Legal Education Division
    Casenote On-line Access
    675 Massachusetts Ave., 11th floor
    Cambridge, MA 02139

I understand that on-line access is granted solely to the purchaser of this book for the academic year in which it was purchased. Any other usage is not authorized and will result in immediate termination of access. Sharing of codes is strictly prohibited.

_____
Signature

Upon receipt of this completed form, you will be e-mailed codes so that you may access the Briefs for this Casenote Legal Brief. On-line Briefs may not be available for all titles. For a full list of available titles please check www.aspenpublishers.com/casenotes.

HOW TO BRIEF A CASE

A. DECIDE ON A FORMAT AND STICK TO IT

Structure is essential to a good brief. It enables you to arrange systematically the related parts that are scattered throughout most cases, thus making manageable and understandable what might otherwise seem to be an endless and unfathomable sea of information. There are, of course, an unlimited number of formats that can be utilized. However, it is best to find one that suits your needs and stick to it. Consistency breeds both efficiency and the security that when called upon you will know where to look in your brief for the information you are asked to give.

Any format, as long as it presents the essential elements of a case in an organized fashion, can be used. Experience, however, has led *Casenotes* to develop and utilize the following format because of its logical flow and universal applicability.

NATURE OF CASE: This is a brief statement of the legal character and procedural status of the case (e.g., "Appeal of a burglary conviction").

There are many different alternatives open to a litigant dissatisfied with a court ruling. The key to determining which one has been used is to discover *who is asking this court for what.*

This first entry in the brief should be kept as *short as possible.* The student should use the court's terminology if the student understands it. But since jurisdictions vary as to the titles of pleadings, the best entry is the one that apprises the student of who wants what in this proceeding, not the one that sounds most like the court's language.

CONCISE RULE OF LAW: A statement of the general principle of law that the case illustrates (e.g., "An acceptance that varies any term of the offer is considered a rejection and counteroffer").

Determining the rule of law of a case is a procedure similar to determining the issue of the case. Avoid being fooled by red herrings; there may be a few rules of law mentioned in the case excerpt, but usually only one is *the* rule with which the casebook editor is concerned. The techniques used to locate the issue, described below, may also be utilized to find the rule of law. Generally, your best guide is simply the chapter heading. It is a clue to the point the casebook editor seeks to make and should be kept in mind when reading every case in the respective section.

FACTS: A synopsis of only the essential facts of the case, i.e., those bearing upon or leading up to the issue.

The facts entry should be a short statement of the events and transactions that led one party to initiate legal proceedings against another in the first place. While some cases conveniently state the salient facts at the beginning of the decision, in other instances they will have to be culled from hiding places throughout the text, even from concurring and dissenting opinions. Some of the "facts" will often be in dispute and should be so noted. Conflicting evidence may be briefly pointed up. "Hard" facts must be included. Both must be *relevant* in order to be listed in the facts entry. It is impossible to tell what is relevant until the entire case is read, as the ultimate determination of the rights and liabilities of the parties may turn on something buried deep in the opinion.

The facts entry should never be longer than one to three *short* sentences.

It is often helpful to identify the role played by a party in a given context. For example, in a construction contract case the identification of a party as the "contractor" or "builder" alleviates the need to tell that that party was the one who was supposed to have built the house.

It is always helpful, and a good general practice, to identify the "plaintiff" and the "defendant." This may seem elementary and uncomplicated, but, especially in view of the creative editing practiced by some casebook editors, it is sometimes a difficult or even impossible task. Bear in mind that the *party presently* seeking something from this court may not be the plaintiff, and that sometimes only the cross-claim of a defendant is treated in the excerpt. Confusing or misaligning the parties can ruin your analysis and understanding of the case.

ISSUE: A statement of the general legal question answered by or illustrated in the case. For clarity, the issue is best put in the form of a question capable of a "yes" or "no" answer. In reality, the issue is simply the Concise Rule of Law put in the form of a question (e.g., "May an offer be accepted by performance?").

The major problem presented in discerning what is *the* issue in the case is that an opinion usually purports to raise and answer several questions. However, except for rare cases, only one such question is really the issue in the case. Collateral issues not necessary to the resolution of the matter in controversy are handled by the court by language known as *"obiter dictum"* or merely *"dictum."* While dicta may be included later in the brief, it has no place under the issue heading.

To find the issue, the student again asks *who wants what* and then goes on to ask *why did that party succeed or fail in getting it.* Once this is determined, the "why" should be turned into a question.

The complexity of the issues in the cases will vary, but in all cases a single-sentence question should sum up the issue. *In a few cases,* there will be two, or even more rarely, three issues of equal importance to the resolution of the case. Each should be expressed in a single-sentence question.

Since many issues are resolved by a court in coming to a final disposition of a case, the casebook editor will reproduce the portion of the opinion containing the issue or issues most relevant to the area of law under scrutiny. A noted law professor gave this advice: "Close the book; look at the title on the cover." Chances are, if it is Property, the student need not concern himself with whether, for example, the federal government's treatment of the plaintiff's land really raises a federal question sufficient to support jurisdiction on this ground in federal court.

The same rule applies to chapter headings designating sub-areas within the subjects. They tip the student off as to what the text is designed to teach. The cases are arranged in a casebook to show a progression or development of the law, so that the preceding cases may also help.

It is also most important to remember to *read the notes and questions* at the end of a case to determine what the editors wanted the student to have gleaned from it.

HOLDING AND DECISION: This section should succinctly explain the rationale of the court in arriving at its decision. In capsulizing the "reasoning" of the court, it should always include an application of the general rule or rules of law to the specific facts of the case. Hidden justifications come to light in this entry; the reasons for the state of the law, the public policies, the biases and prejudices, those considerations that influence the justices' thinking and, ultimately, the outcome of the case. At the end, there should be a short indication of the disposition or procedural resolution of the case (e.g., "Decision of the trial court for Mr. Smith (P) reversed").

The foregoing format is designed to help you "digest" the reams of case material with which you will be faced in your law school career. Once mastered by practice, it will place at your fingertips the information the authors of your casebooks have sought to impart to you in case-by-case illustration and analysis.

B. BE AS ECONOMICAL AS POSSIBLE IN BRIEFING CASES

Once armed with a format that encourages succinctness, it is as important to be economical with regard to the time spent on the actual reading of the case as it is to be economical in the writing of the brief itself. This does not mean "skimming" a case. Rather, it means reading the case with an "eye" trained to recognize into which "section" of your brief a particular passage or line fits and having a system for quickly and precisely marking the case so that the passages fitting any one particular part of the brief can be easily identified and brought together in a concise and accurate manner when the brief is actually written.

It is of no use to simply repeat everything in the opinion of the court; the student should only record enough information to trigger his or her recollection of what the court said. Nevertheless, an accurate statement of the "law of the case," i.e., the legal principle applied to the facts, is absolutely essential to class preparation and to learning the law under the case method.

To that end, it is important to develop a "shorthand" that you can use to make margin notations. These notations will tell you at a glance in which section of the brief you will be placing that particular passage or portion of the opinion.

Some students prefer to underline all the salient portions of the opinion (with a pencil or colored underliner marker), making marginal notations as they go along. Others prefer the color-coded method of underlining, utilizing different colors of markers to underline the salient portions of the case, each separate color being used to represent a different section of the brief. For example, blue underlining could be used for passages relating to the concise rule of law, yellow for those relating to the issue, and green for those relating to the holding and decision, etc. While it has its advocates, the color-coded method can be confusing and time-consuming (all that time spent on changing colored markers). Furthermore, it can interfere with the continuity and concentration many students deem essential to the reading of a case for maximum comprehension. In the end, however, it is a matter of personal preference and style. Just remember, whatever method you use, underlining must be used sparingly or its value is lost.

For those who take the marginal notation route, an efficient and easy method is to go along underlining the key portions of the case and placing in the margin alongside them the following "markers" to indicate where a particular passage or line "belongs" in the brief you will write:

N   (NATURE OF CASE)
CR   (CONCISE RULE OF LAW)
I   (ISSUE)
HC   (HOLDING AND DECISION, relates to the CONCISE RULE OF LAW behind the decision)
HR   (HOLDING AND DECISION, gives the RATIONALE or reasoning behind the decision)
HA   (HOLDING AND DECISION, APPLIES the general principle(s) of law to the facts of the case to arrive at the decision)

Remember that a particular passage may well contain information necessary to more than one part of your brief, in which case you simply note that in the margin. If you are using the color-coded underlining method instead of margin notation, simply make asterisks or checks in the margin next to the passage in question in the colors that indicate the additional sections of the brief where it might be utilized.

The economy of utilizing "shorthand" in marking cases for briefing can be maintained in the actual brief writing process itself by utilizing "law student shorthand" within the brief. There are many commonly used words and phrases for which abbreviations can be substituted in your briefs (and in your class notes also). You can develop abbreviations that are personal to you and which will save you a lot of time. A reference list of briefing abbreviations will be found elsewhere in this book.

C. USE BOTH THE BRIEFING PROCESS AND THE BRIEF AS A LEARNING TOOL

Now that you have a format and the tools for briefing cases efficiently, the most important thing is to make the time spent in briefing profitable to you and to make the most advantageous use of the briefs you create. Of course, the briefs are invaluable for classroom reference when you are called upon to explain or analyze a particular case. However, they are also useful in reviewing for exams. A quick glance at the fact summary should bring the case to mind, and a rereading of the concise rule of law should enable you to go over the underlying legal concept in your mind, how it was applied in that particular case, and how it might apply in other factual settings.

As to the value to be derived from engaging in the briefing process itself, there is an immediate benefit that arises from being forced to sift through the essential facts and reasoning from the court's opinion and to succinctly express them in your own words in your brief. The process ensures that you understand the case and the point that it illustrates, and that means you will be ready to absorb further analysis and information brought forth in class. It also ensures you will have something to say when called upon in class. The briefing process helps develop a mental agility for getting to the *gist* of a case and for identifying, expounding on, and applying the legal concepts and issues found there. Of most immediate concern, that is the mental process on which you must rely in taking law school examinations. Of more lasting concern, it is also the mental process upon which a lawyer relies in serving his clients and in making his living.

ABBREVIATIONS FOR BRIEFING

acceptance	acp	offer	O
affirmed	aff	offeree	OE
answer	ans	offeror	OR
assumption of risk	a/r	ordinance	ord
attorney	atty	pain and suffering	p/s
beyond a reasonable doubt	b/r/d	parol evidence	p/e
bona fide purchaser	BFP	plaintiff	P
breach of contract	br/k	prima facie	p/f
cause of action	c/a	probable cause	p/c
common law	c/l	proximate cause	px/c
Constitution	Con	real property	r/p
constitutional	con	reasonable doubt	r/d
contract	K	reasonable man	r/m
contributory negligence	c/n	rebuttable presumption	rb/p
cross	x	remanded	rem
cross-complaint	x/c	res ipsa loquitur	RIL
cross-examination	x/ex	respondeat superior	r/s
cruel and unusual punishment	c/u/p	Restatement	RS
defendant	D	reversed	rev
dismissed	dis	Rule Against Perpetuities	RAP
double jeopardy	d/j	search and seizure	s/s
due process	d/p	search warrant	s/w
equal protection	e/p	self-defense	s/d
equity	eq	specific performance	s/p
evidence	ev	statute of limitations	S/L
exclude	exc	statute of frauds	S/F
exclusionary rule	exc/r	statute	S
felony	f/n	summary judgment	s/j
freedom of speech	f/s	tenancy in common	t/c
good faith	g/f	tenancy at will	t/w
habeas corpus	h/c	tenant	t
hearsay	hr	third party	TP
husband	H	third party beneficiary	TPB
in loco parentis	ILP	transferred intent	TI
injunction	inj	unconscionable	uncon
inter vivos	I/v	unconstitutional	unconst
joint tenancy	j/t	undue influence	u/e
judgment	judgt	Uniform Commercial Code	UCC
jurisdiction	jur	unilateral	uni
last clear chance	LCC	vendee	VE
long-arm statute	LAS	vendor	VR
majority view	maj	versus	v
meeting of minds	MOM	void for vagueness	VFV
minority view	min	weight of the evidence	w/e
Miranda warnings	Mir/w	weight of authority	w/a
Miranda rule	Mir/r	wife	W
negligence	neg	with	w/
notice	ntc	within	w/i
nuisance	nus	without prejudice	w/o/p
obligation	ob	without	w/o
obscene	obs	wrongful death	wr/d

TABLE OF CASES

CHAPTER 1
AN OVERVIEW OF PROCEDURE

QUICK REFERENCE RULES OF LAW

1. **Subject Matter Jurisdiction.** For purposes of determining diversity jurisdiction, a person is a "citizen" of the state in which he or she is "domiciled," which for adults is established by physical presence in a place in connection with the intent to remain there. (Hawkins v. Masters Farms, Inc.)

2. **The Lawyer's Responsibility.** Federal Rule of Civil Procedure 11 imposes an obligation on counsel and client to stop, think, investigate and research before filing papers either to initiate the suit or to conduct the litigation. (Bridges v. Diesel Service, Inc.)

3. **The Complaint.** A complaint which alleges only that a defendant negligently drove a motor vehicle and thereby injured the plaintiff is sufficient under Federal Rule of Civil Procedure 8. (Bell v. Novick Transfer Co.)

4. **Permissive and Compulsory Joinder.** Permissive joinder requires transactional relatedness—parties must assert rights, or have rights asserted against them, that rise from related activities. (Bridgeport Music, Inc. v. 11C Music)

5. **Factual Development — Discovery.** Lists of past and current patients are privileged from discovery. (Butler v. Rigby)

6. **Pretrial Disposition — Summary Judgment.** Under Federal Rule of Civil Procedure 56, a federal court must enter summary judgment if after complete discovery a party fails to show that the evidence, viewed in the light most favorable to that party, is sufficient to establish the existence of an essential element on which that party has the burden of proof. (Houchens v. American Home Assurance Co.)

7. **Trial.** A judgment notwithstanding the verdict should only be granted where the evidence so strongly points in favor of a moving party that reasonable people could not arrive at a contrary verdict. (Norton v. Snapper Power Equipment)

8. **Former Adjudication.** Where a person suffers both personal injuries and property damage as a result of the same wrongful act, only a single cause for action arises, the different injuries occasioned thereby being separate items of damages from such act. (Rush v. City of Maple Heights)

9. **Appeals.** An order of the court made under Federal Rule of Civil Procedure 34 for discovery and production of documents is interlocutory and therefore not appealable. (Apex Hosiery Co. v. Leader)

HAWKINS v. MASTERS FARMS, INC.
Representative of estate (P) v. Tractor driver (D)
2003 WL 21555767 (D.Kan 2003).

NATURE OF CASE: Motion to dismiss for lack of subject matter jurisdiction.

FACT SUMMARY: James Creal was killed when his automobile was struck by a tractor owned by Masters Farms, Inc. (D). Creal's estate (P) brought suit against Masters Farms, Inc. (D) in federal court alleging diversity subject matter jurisdiction. Masters Farms, Inc. (D) moved to dismiss on grounds of incomplete diversity among the parties.

CONCISE RULE OF LAW: For purposes of determining diversity jurisdiction, a person is a "citizen" of the state in which he or she is "domiciled," which for adults is established by physical presence in a place in connection with the intent to remain there.

FACTS: On December 8, 2000, James Creal (P) was killed in an automobile accident just south of Troy, Kansas, when his car was struck by a tractor driven by Masters (D), a citizen of Kansas. At the time of his death, James Creal (P) was living in Kansas with his wife and her children. James Creal (P) had lived in Missouri most of his life, while Mrs. Creal had resided in Kansas the majority of her life. When Mrs. Creal moved into an apartment in Troy, Kansas, in March 2000, James Creal brought his clothes, furniture and many other items and moved to the new apartment. The Creals were married in July 2000. In November, the Creals moved into a house in Troy, Kansas. His death certificate listed Kansas as his residence. The representatives of James Creal (P) brought suit against Masters (D) in the federal district court for Kansas, alleging the existence of diversity jurisdiction under 28 U.S.C. § 1332. Masters (D) moved to dismiss, disputing that there was complete diversity among the parties.

ISSUE: For purposes of determining diversity jurisdiction, is a person a "citizen" of the state in which he or she is "domiciled," which for adults is established by physical presence in a place in connection with the intent to remain there?

HOLDING AND DECISION: (Van Bebber, Sr. J.) Yes. For purposes of determining diversity jurisdiction, a person is a "citizen" of the state in which he or she is "domiciled," which for adults is established by physical presence in a place in connection with the intent to remain there. Here, at the time of his death, Creal (P) had not only established a physical presence in the state of Kansas, but also displayed an intent to remain there. Although he lived the majority of his life in Missouri, he had been living in Kansas with his wife of five months for nearly one year at the time he died. Among other things, he had moved household items into the Kansas home; he contributed to household costs; and he purchased a new

bedroom set with his wife. Any non-specific so-called "floating intention" of Creal (P) to return to his former Missouri domicile would be insufficient to overcome the evidence that he was domiciled in Kansas at the time of his death. Masters' (D) motion to dismiss is granted.

EDITOR'S ANALYSIS: In *Hawkins*, the court noted that the party seeking to invoke federal jurisdiction bears the burden of proving that jurisdiction is proper. Because federal courts are courts of limited jurisdiction, the presumption is against federal jurisdiction.

QUICKNOTES
DIVERSITY JURISDICTION - The authority of a federal court to hear and determine cases involving $10,000 or more and in which the parties are citizens of different states, or in which one party is an alien.

FEDERAL JURISDICTION - The authority of federal courts to hear and determine cases of a particular nature derived from the United States Constitution and rules promulgated by Congress pursuant thereto.

NOTES:

BRIDGES v. DIESEL SERVICE INC.
Disabled employee (P) v. Employer (D)
1994 U.S. Dist. LEXIS 9429 (E.D. Pa. 1994).

NATURE OF CASE: Motion for sanctions pursuant to Federal Rule of Civil Procedure 11.

FACT SUMMARY: Bridges (P) commenced this action against Diesel Service Inc. (D) under the Americans with Disabilities Act (ADA) alleging that his employer dismissed him from his job as a result of a disability.

CONCISE RULE OF LAW: Federal Rule of Civil Procedure 11 imposes an obligation on counsel and client to stop, think, investigate and research before filing papers either to initiate the suit or to conduct the litigation.

FACTS: Bridges (P) commenced this action against Diesel Service Inc. (D) under the Americans with Disabilities Act (ADA) alleging that his employer dismissed him from his job as a result of a disability. By Order dated June 29, 1994, the court dismissed Bridges' (P) complaint without prejudice for failure to exhaust administrative remedies. In particular, Bridges (P) did not file a charge with the Equal Employment Opportunity Commission (EEOC) until after commencement of this action. Diesel Service, Inc. (D) then moved for sanctions pursuant to Federal Rule of Civil Procedure 11.

ISSUE: Does Federal Rule of Civil Procedure 11 impose an obligation on counsel and client to stop, think, investigate and research before filing papers either to initiate the suit or to conduct the litigation?

HOLDING AND DECISION: (Huyett, J.) Yes. Federal Rule of Civil Procedure 11 imposes an obligation on counsel and client to stop, think, investigate and research before filing papers either to initiate the suit or to conduct the litigation. The court is not convinced that Plaintiff's lawyer displayed a competent level of legal research. A brief review of case law would have revealed the EEOC filing requirement. Further, an award of sanctions for failure to exhaust administrative remedies is not unprecedented. However, the court will not grant sanctions. The prime goal of Rule 11 sanctions is deterrence of improper conduct. In this case, monetary sanctions are not necessary to deter future misconduct, since plaintiff's counsel immediately acknowledged his error and attempted to rectify the situation.

EDITOR'S ANALYSIS: It is possible that the court treated plaintiff's counsel with lenience in this case, since the action was brought under the Americans with Disabilities Act. As the court states in its decision, "The Court is aware of the need to avoid 'chilling' Title VII litigation." Generally, Rule 11 sanctions are awarded where the complaint filed asserts patently unmeritorious or frivolous allegations.

BELL v. NOVICK TRANSFER CO.
Automobile passenger (P) v. Trucking company (D)
17 F.R.D. 279 (1955).

NATURE OF CASE: Motion to dismiss for failure to state a claim.

FACT SUMMARY: Bell (P) filed a tort complaint in federal court after removal which stated only that Novick's (D) agent drove a truck which negligently collided with the car in which Bell (P) was riding, causing injury to Bell (P).

CONCISE RULE OF LAW: A complaint which alleges only that a defendant negligently drove a motor vehicle and thereby injured the plaintiff is sufficient under Federal Rule of Civil Procedure 8.

FACTS: After Bell's (P) tort action arising out of an automobile-truck accident was removed to federal court, Bell (P) filed a complaint there, which alleged only that an agent of Novick (D) drove a truck negligently so as to collide with a car in which Bell (P) was riding, causing injury to Bell (P). Novick (D) moved to dismiss the complaint for failure to state a cause of action.

ISSUE: Is a complaint which alleges only that defendant negligently drove a motor vehicle and thereby injured the plaintiff sufficient under Fed. R. Civ. P. 8?

HOLDING AND DECISION: (Thompsen, J.) Yes. This tort action was originally filed in Court of Common Pleas of Baltimore City but was removed to federal court. After such a removal, the Fed. R. Civ. P. applies rather than the laws of the State of Maryland. Thus, while Maryland law might regard the complaint here as insufficient for failure to state a cause of action, the inquiry here is to be made in light of the Fed. R. Civ. P. Rule 8 controls the sufficiency of complaints, and requires only "a short and plain statement of the claim showing the pleader is entitled to relief." The complaint in this case contains such a statement and sufficiently states a cause of action under Rule 8. A complaint which alleges only that a defendant negligently drove a motor vehicle and thereby injured the plaintiff is sufficient under Rule 8. Motion denied.

EDITOR'S ANALYSIS: A complaint is designed to apprise the defendant of the claim against which he is to defend. The argument against sufficiency in this case is that the defendant is not told what negligent acts he has allegedly committed, giving rise to liability save the general allegation of "negligence." However, the policy of granting everyone access to the courts militates toward permitting generalized allegations and forcing the defendant to move for a more particularized statement under Fed. R. Civ. P. 12(e).

BRIDGEPORT MUSIC, INC. v. 11C MUSIC
Music publishers (P) v. Alleged copyright infringers (D)
202 F.R.D. 229 (M.D. Tenn., Nashville Division 2001).

NATURE OF CASE: Motion to dismiss for failure of complaint to set forth a short and plain statement of claims, and for improper joinder of defendants.

FACT SUMMARY: When Bridgeport (P), music publishers, brought suit in federal district court against over 770 music and entertainment companies, its 901 page complaint included 486 counts, each representing a separate alleged music infringement. 11C Music (D) and all defendants moved to dismiss, arguing the complaint failed to provide a "short and plain statement" of its claims, and because defendants are not properly joined.

CONCISE RULE OF LAW: Permissive joinder requires transactional relatedness—parties must assert rights, or have rights asserted against them, that rise from related activities.

FACTS: Bridgeport (P), music publishers, brought suit in federal district court against over 770 music and entertainment companies, including 11C Music (D), alleging copyright infringement. The 901-page complaint included 486 counts. 11C Music (D) and all defendants moved to dismiss on the grounds that Bridgeport (P) violated Rules 8 and 20 of the Federal Rules of Civil Procedure because the complaint failed to provide a "short and plain statement" of its claims, and because the 770 alleged infringers (D) were not properly joined.

ISSUE: Does permissive joinder require transactional relatedness—parties must assert rights, or have rights asserted against them, that rise from related activities?

HOLDING AND DECISION: (Campbell, Dist.J.) Yes. Permissive joinder requires transactional relatedness—parties must assert rights, or have rights asserted against them, that rise from related activities. Bridgeport's (P) 477 counts of alleged infringement are really 477 separate lawsuits rolled into one enormous pleading, each allegedly infringing song representing a separate transaction or occurrence. Each infringement count will require a unique set of proof. Each song represents a discrete occurrence. The fact that certain defendants were involved in the production, publishing, and distribution of more than one allegedly offending song does not, in itself, cause these songs to be related occurrences in the manner contemplated by Rule 20(a). Even if the counts in Bridgeport's (P) complaint arose from the same series of occurrences, the court would exercise the discretion afforded it to order a severance to avoid causing unreasonable prejudice and expense to the many defendants and to avoid a great inconvenience in the administration of justice. As a practical matter, the case is unmanageable in its current form. The severed copyright infringement counts should proceed separately as 477 individual cases.

EDITOR'S ANALYSIS: In *Bridgeport Music*, the court noted that, from a practical standpoint, its courtroom would seat only a small fraction of defendants and their attorneys. If joined in one action, hundreds of defendants would be subject to an overwhelming onslaught of materials and information unrelated to the specific claims against them, all of which they must pay their attorneys to review.

QUICKNOTES
FED. R. CIV. P. 8 - Sets forth the general rules of pleading a claim for relief.

JOINDER - The joining of claims or parties in one lawsuit.

NOTES:

BUTLER v. RIGBY
Parties not identified.
1998 U.S. Dist. Lexis 4618 (E.D. La. 1998).

NATURE OF CASE: Appeal from denial of protective order in personal injury action.

FACT SUMMARY: AMG and MHC, two groups of doctors, sought a protective order against having to produce certain documents for a lawsuit in which they were not a party.

CONCISE RULE OF LAW: Lists of past and current patients are privileged from discovery.

FACTS: After an automobile accident, the plaintiffs hired attorneys who may have had some connection to American Medical Group (AMG) and Midtown Health Care (MHC), two medical care providers. The defendants filed identical notices of depositions on AMG and MHC and sought past and current patient lists, as well as the total number of patients treated over a significant period of time. AMG and MHC moved for a protective order on the grounds that the information was not relevant, was protected by the health care provider-patient privilege and was overly burdensome. However, the magistrate judge disagreed and ordered that most of the information was discoverable. AMG and MHC appealed.

ISSUE: Are lists of past and current patients privileged from discovery?

HOLDING AND DECISION: (Vance, J.) Yes. Lists of past and current patients are privileged from discovery. The Federal Rules provide for liberal discovery and broad treatment of relevance. The discovery sought need not be admissible at trial if the information appears reasonably calculated to lead to the discovery of admissible evidence. However, discovery may be limited by the court if it determines that the discovery sought is unreasonably cumulative or duplicative or if the burden and expense outweighs its likely benefit. Privileged information also is not discoverable. In the present case, the number of total patients treated by AMG and MHC could be relevant in demonstrating that their connection with the plaintiff's attorneys shows bias. Thus, the magistrate was not clearly wrong in ordering this information discoverable despite the significant expense and burden of compiling the information. However, as to the patient lists sought, Louisiana law construes the health care provider-patient privilege broadly. Thus, the lists are not discoverable and an order should have been granted to AMG and MHC on that issue. Affirmed in part, reversed in part.

EDITOR'S ANALYSIS: The court also made two related points in this case. Acknowledging that there was some expense involved in compiling the number of patients, the court ordered that the defendants pay half the cost. Also, the court noted that the patient lists sought were probably not relevant even if they hadn't been privileged.

QUICKNOTES
FED. R. CIV. P. 26(b)(1) - Provides for a broad scope of discovery.

NOTES:

HOUCHENS v. AMERICAN HOME ASSURANCE CO.

Decedents' spouse (P) v. Life insurance company (D)
927 F.2d 163 (4th Cir. 1991).

NATURE OF CASE: Appeal of dismissal of action for damages for breach of contract.

FACT SUMMARY: On American's (D) summary judgment motion, the court dismissed Houchens' (P) suit for payment on two accidental death policies because of insufficient evidence that Houchens' (P) husband died accidentally.

CONCISE RULE OF LAW: Under Federal Rule of Civil Procedure 56, a federal court must enter summary judgment if after complete discovery a party fails to show that the evidence, viewed in the light most favorable to that party, is sufficient to establish the existence of an essential element on which that party has the burden of proof.

FACTS: Houchens' (P) husband disappeared in Thailand in August, 1980, and was not heard from since. Under Virginia law, a person who is missing for seven years is presumed dead. In 1988, Houchens (P) had her husband declared legally dead. Houchens (P) attempted to collect on two life insurance policies issued by American (D), under which the proceeds would only be paid upon proof that the insured's death was accidental. American (D) refused to pay and Houchens (P) sued in federal court for breach of contract. American (D) moved for summary judgment, arguing there was no evidence that the insured had died or that he had died accidentally. The district court granted the motion and dismissed the case, and Houchens (P) appealed.

ISSUE: Under Fed. R. Civ. P. 56, must a federal court enter summary judgment if a party fails to show that the evidence, viewed in the light most favorable to that party, is sufficient to establish the existence of an essential element on which that party has the burden of proof?

HOLDING AND DECISION: (Ervin, C.J.) Yes. Under Fed. R. Civ. P. 56, a federal court must enter summary judgment if a party fails to show that the evidence, viewed in the light most favorable to that party, is sufficient to establish the existence of an essential element on which that party has the burden of proof. Under Rule 56(c), a summary judgment motion must be granted where there is "no genuine issue as to any material fact." Here, Houchens (P) is entitled to the Virginia presumption that her husband is dead. However, for recovery on the policy it still must be shown that her husband's death was accidental. The meager circumstances surrounding his disappearance do not provide sufficient evidence to allow a reasonable jury to conclude that he died accidentally. Under Virginia law, Houchens (D) had the burden of proof as to accident, a necessary element of her case. She had insufficient evidence to meet this burden. Thus, as there was no genuine issue as to a material fact, the summary judgment motion was properly granted. Affirmed.

EDITOR'S ANALYSIS: Houchens (P) cited two cases where the issue was the same and a summary judgment motion by the insurance company defendant was denied. In *Valley National Bank of Arizona v. J. C. Penney Ins. Co.*, Ariz. Ct. App., 129 Ariz. 108, 628 P.d. 991 (1981), the insured disappeared, and his skeletal remains were later found with bullet casings nearby. In *Martin v. Insurance Co. of America*, 1 Wash. App. 218, 460 P.d. 682 (1969), the insured disappeared in fog and snow on a steep and wooded mountainside after having last been seen without a compass at the 3,000-foot level, asking for directions. In each of these cases, the court found that there was a genuine issue of material fact because there was sufficient evidence, unlike in the Houchens case, for a jury to find that the insured died accidentally.

QUICKNOTES

BURDEN OF PROOF - The duty of a party to introduce evidence to support a fact that is in dispute in an action.

FED. R. CIV. P. 56(c) - Provides that a court arrive at a pre-verdict disposition on the case at bar when one party fails to prove an a\essential element of its case.

SUMMARY JUDGMENT - Judgment rendered by a court in response to a motion by one of the parties, claiming that the lack of a question of material fact in respect to an issue warrants disposition of the issue without consideration by the jury.

NOTES:

CASENOTE LEGAL BRIEFS — CIVIL PROCEDURE

NORTON v. SNAPPER POWER EQUIPMENT

Gardener (P) v. Lawn mower manufacturer (D)
806 F.d. 1545 (11th Cir. 1987).

NATURE OF CASE: Appeal from judgment notwithstanding the verdict denying damages for personal injuries.

FACT SUMMARY: In Norton's (P) suit for damages against Snapper Power Equipment (D), Snapper (D) moved for and was granted a judgment notwithstanding the verdict, contending that since a reconstruction of Norton's (P) accident with a Snapper (D) riding mower was impossible, the jury could not determine whether a blade-stopping device would have eliminated or lessened Norton's (P) injury.

CONCISE RULE OF LAW: A judgment notwithstanding the verdict should only be granted where the evidence so strongly points in favor of a moving party that reasonable people could not arrive at a contrary verdict.

FACTS: Norton (P), a commercial gardener, was injured while riding a lawn mower manufactured by Snapper Power Equipment (D). Norton (P) sued Snapper (D) for damages based on strict liability. At the close of Norton's (P) case, and against the close of all evidence, Snapper (D) moved for a directed verdict. The court left the strict liability claim for the jury, and the jury returned a verdict for Norton (P), holding Snapper (D) liable for 80% of the injuries. After dismissing the jury, the court indicated that it would enter a judgment notwithstanding the verdict based on Snapper's (D) contention that since a reconstruction of Norton's (P) accident with the mower was impossible, the jury could not determine whether a blade-stopping device would have eliminated or lessened Norton's (P) injury. Norton (P) appealed.

ISSUE: Should a judgment notwithstanding the verdict only be granted where the evidence so strongly points in favor of a moving party that reasonable people could not arrive at a contrary verdict?

HOLDING AND DECISION: (Clark, J.) Yes. A judgment notwithstanding the verdict should only be granted where the evidence so strongly points in favor of a moving party that reasonable people could not arrive at a contrary verdict. The issues here were whether the failure to install "dead man" devices rendered the mower defective, and if the mower was defective, whether the lack of a "dead man" control caused the injury. Snapper (D) claims that there was little or no evidence to support the jury's verdict. The jury is, however, permitted to reconstruct the series of events by drawing an inference upon an inference. The causation evidence here, although circumstantial, was far more impressive than Snapper (D) contends, and Snapper (D) was given every opportunity to point out the weaknesses in Norton's (P) proof, but was unpersuasive to the jury. Reversed and remanded.

EDITOR'S ANALYSIS: Within 10 days of an adverse verdict, the loser may move for a judgment notwithstanding the verdict. This motion asserts that even if all the winner's evidence is true, the loser is entitled to a verdict as a matter of law. A motion for a new trial may be based either on an error of law or an erroneous charge.

QUICKNOTES

DIRECTED VERDICT - A verdict ordered by the court in a jury trial.

JUDGMENT N.O.V. - A judgment entered by the trial judge reversing a jury verdict if the jury's determination has no basis in law or fact.

STRICT LIABILITY - Liability for all injuries proximately caused by a party's conducting of certain inherently dangerous activities without regard to negligence or fault.

NOTES:

RUSH v. CITY OF MAPLE HEIGHTS
Motorcycle passenger (P) v. Municipality (D)
Ohio Ct. App., 147 N.E.2d 599, cert. denied, 358 U.S. 814 (1958).

NATURE OF CASE: Action for damages for personal injuries.

FACT SUMMARY: In Rush's (P) action against the City of Maple Heights (D) to recover damages for personal injuries suffered in a motorcycle accident, Rush (P) claimed that she should be permitted to split her cause of action, filing a claim for property damage in one court and a separate action for personal injuries in another court.

CONCISE RULE OF LAW: Where a person suffers both personal injuries and property damage as a result of the same wrongful act, only a single cause for action arises, the different injuries occasioned thereby being separate items of damages from such act.

FACTS: Rush (P) was riding on a motorcycle operated by her husband and was injured when the cycle ran into a hole in the road, throwing her to the ground. Rush (P) brought suit against the City of Maple Heights (D) for damage to the cycle. The lower court found that the City (D) was negligent in not repairing the road and awarded Rush (P) $100. That judgment was affirmed by the court of appeals and the Ohio supreme court. Then, Rush (P) brought the present suit to recover damages for personal injuries suffered in the same accident, contending that she should be permitted to split her cause of action and file separate claims for property damage and personal injuries in separate courts. The trial court held that the issues of negligence and proximate cause had been determined in the prior action against the City (D) and were binding. The jury awarded Rush (P) $12,000 solely on the question of damages, and the court of appeals affirmed this judgment. The City (D) appealed.

ISSUE: Where a person suffers both personal injuries and property damage as a result of the same wrongful act, does only a single cause of action arise, the different injuries occasioned thereby being separate items of damage from such act?

HOLDING AND DECISION: (Herbert, J.) Yes. Where a person suffers both personal injuries and property damage as a result of the same wrongful act, only a single cause of action arises, the different injuries occasioned thereby being separate items of damage from such act. This is the majority rule in this country, and the reasoning behind it is that a single tort can be the basis of but one action. It is not improper to declare in different counts for damages to the person and property when both result from the same tort; it is the better practice to do so where there is any difference in the measure of damages, and all damages must be sued for in one suit. This is necessary to prevent multiplicity of suits, burdensome expense, delay, and vexatious litigation. Here, Rush (P) suffered both personal injuries and property damage as a result of the same wrongful act—nonrepair of the road. The different injuries occasioned by the wrongful act were separate items of damage from such act, but the actions of the City (D) constituted but one tort. A single tort can be the basis of but one suit. Reversed and remanded.

CONCURRENCE: (Stewart, J.) The rule at common law and in a majority of the states of the union is that damages resulting from a single wrongful act, even though they include both property and personal injury damages, are, when suffered by the same person, the subject of only one action against the wrongdoer.

DISSENT: (Zimmerman, J.) Established law should remain undisturbed in order to insure a stability on which the lower courts and the legal profession generally may rely with some degree of confidence.

EDITOR'S ANALYSIS: Former adjudication can be divided into claim preclusion and issue preclusion. Two requirements must be met before the rules of claim preclusion apply: (1) the claim must be the same in the first and second action; and (2) the first decision must be "on the merits." Issue preclusion prevents a litigant from basing a claim, in a second suit, on the same events as those in the first suit if the same issues were determined in the first litigation between the parties.

QUICKNOTES
CAUSE OF ACTION - A fact or set of facts the occurrence of which entitle a party to seek judicial relief.

COLLATERAL ESTOPPEL - A doctrine whereby issues litigated and determined in a prior proceeding are binding upon all subsequent litigation between the parties regarding that issue.

RES JUDICATA - The rule of law that a final judgment by a court precludes subsequent litigation between the parties regarding the same cause of action.

APEX HOSIERY CO. v. LEADER
Hosiery company (P) v. Appellant (D)
102 F.2d 702 (3d Cir. 1939).

NATURE OF CASE: Appeal from a court order to produce, for inspection, documents for trial in antitrust action.

FACT SUMMARY: Leader (D) appealed from an order of the court for the discovery and production of documents for inspection, copying, and photographing by Apex Hosiery Co. (P) for use at trial.

CONCISE RULE OF LAW: An order of the court made under Federal Rule of Civil Procedure 34 for discovery and production of documents is interlocutory and therefore not appealable.

FACTS: Leader (D), in an action for treble damages under the Sherman Anti-Trust Act note, appealed from an order of the district court made under Fed. R. Civ. P. 34 for the discovery and production by it of documents for inspection, copying, and photographing by Apex Hosiery (D) for use at the trial of the action.

ISSUE: Is an order of the court made under Fed. R. Civ. P. 34 for discovery and production of documents interlocutory and therefore not appealable?

HOLDING AND DECISION: (Per curiam) Yes. An order of the court made under Fed. R. Civ. P. 34 for discovery and production of documents is interlocutory and therefore not appealable. In this case, the disposition made of the motion will necessarily determine the conduct of the trial and may vitally affect the result. In essence, the motion resembles others made before or during a trial to secure or to suppress evidence, such as applications to suppress a deposition, to compel the production of books or documents, or to physically examine a plaintiff. The orders made upon such applications, so far as they affect the rights only of parties to the litigation, are interlocutory. Appeal denied.

EDITOR'S ANALYSIS: The above doctrine is known as the "final judgment" rule. Its application prevents endless litigation of interim rulings that may ultimately be mooted anyway by resolution or settlement of a case. However, some jurisdictions permit appeal of nonfinal rulings at the trial court level, provided they are judged to be sufficiently "significant."

QUICKNOTES

FED. R. CIV. P. 24 - Governs discovery and the production of documents at trial.

FINAL JUDGMENT - A decision by the court settling a dispute between the parties on its merits and which is appealable to a higher court.

INTERLOCUTORY (ORDER) - An order entered by the court determining an issue that does not resolve the disposition of the case, but is essential to a proper adjudication of the action.

NOTES:

CHAPTER 2
PERSONAL JURISDICTION

QUICK REFERENCE RULES OF LAW

1. **The Origins.** Where the object of an action is to determine the personal rights and obligations of the parties, service by publication against a nonresident is ineffective to confer jurisdiction upon the court. (Pennoyer v. Neff)

2. **Redifining Constitutional Power.** For a state to subject a nonresident defendant to in personam jurisdiction, due process requires that he have certain minimum contacts with it such that the maintenance of the suit does not offend traditional notions of fair play and substantial justice. (International Shoe Co. v. Washington)

3. **Absorbing In Rem Jurisdiction.** Due process requires only that in order to subject a nonresident defendant to the personal jurisdiction of the forum, the suit be based on a contract which has substantial connection with the forum. (McGee v. International Life Insurance Co.)

4. **Absorbing In Rem Jurisdiction.** For there to be "minimal contacts" sufficient to support in personam jurisdiction, it is essential that there be some act by which the defendant purposefully avails itself of the privilege of conducting activities within the forum state, thus invoking the benefits and protections of its laws. (Hanson v. Denckla)

5. **Absorbing In Rem Jurisdiction.** Jurisdiction cannot be founded on property within a state unless there are sufficient contacts within the meaning of the test developed in International Shoe. (Shaffer v. Heitner)

6. **Specific Jurisdiction: The Modern Cases.** A state court may exercise personal jurisdiction over a nonresident defendant only so long as there exist sufficient "minimum contacts" between him and the forum state such that maintenance of the suit does not offend "traditional notions of fair play and substantial justice." (World-Wide Volkswagen Corp. v. Woodson)

7. **Specific Jurisdiction: The Modern Cases.** Minimum contacts sufficient to sustain jurisdiction are not satisfied simply by the placement of a product into the stream of commerce coupled with an awareness that its product would reach the forum state. (Asahi Metal Industry Co. v. Superior Court)

8. **Specific Jurisdiction: The Modern Cases.** Direct and continuous contacts by a franchisee with the franchisor may lead to the franchisee being subject to the jurisdiction of the franchisor's home forum. (Burger King Corp. v. Rudzewicz)

9. **Specific Jurisdiction: The Modern Cases.** Personal jurisdiction may not necessarily be acquired over a defendant based on a posting on a passive Internet Web site. (Pavlovich v. Superior Court)

10. **General Jurisdiction.** A party who maintains a Web site with a high degree of interactivity with sales generated in the forum state may be subject to the forum state's general jurisdiction. (Coastal Video Communications Corp. v. The Staywell Corp.)

11. **General Jurisdiction.** State courts have jurisdiction over nonresidents who are physically present in the state. (Burnham v. Superior Court)

12. **Consent as a Substitute for Power.** Reasonable forum selection clauses contained in passenger tickets are presumptively valid. (Carnival Cruise Lines, Inc. v. Shute)

13. **The Constitutional Requirement of Notice.** In order to satisfy due process challenges, notice must be by means calculated to inform the desired parties, and, where they reside outside of the state and their names and addresses are available, notice by publication is insufficient. (Mullane v. Central Hanover Bank & Trust Co.)

14. **Long-Arm Statutes as a Restraint on Jurisdiction.** A prior decision to file a lawsuit in a state does not qualify as sufficient activity in the state to confer personal jurisdiction. (Gibbons v. Brown)

15. **Venue as a Further Localizing Principle.** The general venue statute, providing that aliens may be sued in any district, overrides special venue laws that place venue more specifically. (Dee-K Enterprises, Inc. v. Heveafil Sdn. Bhd.)

16. **Declining Jurisdiction: Forum Non Conveniens.** A plaintiff may not defeat a motion to dismiss for forum non conveniens merely by showing that the substantive law that would be applied in the alternative forum is less favorable to him than that of the present forum. (Piper Aircraft v. Reyno)

PENNOYER v. NEFF
Purchaser of property (D) v. Real property owner (P)
95 U.S. 714 (1877).

NATURE OF CASE: Action to recover possession of land.

FACT SUMMARY: Neff (P) attacked the validity of a sheriff's sale of his property to satisfy a personal judgment obtained against him where service was by publication.

CONCISE RULE OF LAW: Where the object of an action is to determine the personal rights and obligations of the parties, service by publication against a nonresident is ineffective to confer jurisdiction upon the court.

FACTS: Neff (P) owned real property in Oregon. Mitchell brought suit in Oregon to recover legal fees allegedly owed him by Neff (P). Neff (P), a nonresident, was served by publication and Mitchell obtained a default judgment. The court ordered Neff's (P) land sold at a sheriff's sale to satisfy the judgment. Pennoyer (D) purchased the property. Neff (P) subsequently learned of the sale and brought suit in Oregon to recover possession of the property. Neff (P) alleged that the court ordering the sale had never acquired in personam jurisdiction over him. Therefore, the court could not adjudicate the personal rights between Neff (P) and Mitchell and the default judgment had been improperly entered.

ISSUE: Where an action involves the adjudication of personal rights and obligations of the parties, is service by publication against a nonresident sufficient to confer jurisdiction?

HOLDING AND DECISION: (Field, J.) No. Substituted service of process in actions against nonresidents of a state is effective only in proceedings in rem. Where an action involves the determination of personal rights and obligations of the parties, service by publication is ineffective to confer jurisdiction over the nonresident defendant. No state can exercise direct jurisdiction and authority over persons or property outside of its boundaries. The validity of every judgment depends upon the jurisdiction of the court rendering judgment. Thus, Mitchell could not obtain a personal judgment against Neff (P) without first obtaining in personam jurisdiction. Substituted service by publication is ineffective to confer personal jurisdiction over a nonresident. The sale was therefore void. A different result could have been reached if Mitchell had first obtained in rem jurisdiction by seizing the property at the time suit was commenced. Affirmed.

EDITOR'S ANALYSIS: Although no state can exercise direct jurisdiction and authority over people or property outside the state, the state may exercise jurisdiction over persons and property inside the state in ways that will affect persons and property outside the state. *Pennoyer v. Neff* established that every state had the power to regulate the way in which property within the state is acquired, enjoyed, and transferred. But a state cannot bring a person or property outside the stale into its jurisdiction simply by using substituted service.

QUICKNOTES
IN PERSONAM JURISDICTION - The jurisdiction of a court over a person as opposed to his interest in property.

IN REM JURISDICTION - A court's authority over a thing so that its judgment is binding in respect to the rights and interests of all parties in that thing.

SERVICE OF PROCESS - The communication of reasonable notice of a court proceeding to a defendant in order to provide him with an opportunity to be heard.

NOTES:

INTERNATIONAL SHOE CO. v. WASHINGTON
Delaware corporation (D) v. State (P)
326 U.S. 310 (1945).

NATURE OF CASE: Proceedings to recover unemployment contributions.

FACT SUMMARY: A state statute authorized the mailing of notice of assessment of delinquent contributions for unemployment compensation to nonresident employers. International Shoe Co. (D) was a nonresident corporation. Notice of assessment was served on one of its salespersons within the state and was mailed to International's (D) office.

CONCISE RULE OF LAW: For a state to subject a nonresident defendant to in personam jurisdiction, due process requires that he have certain minimum contacts with it such that the maintenance of the suit does not offend traditional notions of fair play and substantial justice.

FACTS: A Washington statute set up a scheme of unemployment compensation which required contributions by employers. The statute authorized the commissioner, Washington (P), to issue an order and notice of assessment of delinquent contributions by mailing the notice to nonresident employers. International (D) was a Delaware corporation having its principal place of business in Missouri. International employed 11 to 13 salespersons under the supervision of managers in Missouri. These salespeople resided in Washington, did most of their work there, and had no authority to enter into contracts or make collections. International (D) did not have an office in Washington and made no contracts there. Notice of assessment was served upon one of International's (D) Washington salespersons and a copy of the notice was sent by registered mail to International's (D) Missouri address.

ISSUE: For a state to subject a nonresident defendant to in personam jurisdiction, does due process require only that he have certain minimum contacts with it, such that the maintenance of the suit does not offend notions of fair play and substantial justice?

HOLDING AND DECISION: (Stone, C.J.) Yes. Historically the jurisdiction of courts to render judgment in personam is grounded on their power over the defendant's person, and his presence within the territorial jurisdiction of a court was necessary to a valid judgment. But now, due process requires only that in order to subject a defendant to a judgment in personam, if he is not present within the territorial jurisdiction, he have certain minimum contacts with the territory such that the maintenance of the suit does not offend traditional notions of fair play and substantial justice. The contacts must be such as to make it reasonable, in the context of our federal system, to require a defendant corporation to defend the suit brought there. An estimate of the inconveniences which would result to the corporation from a trial away from its "home" is relevant. To require a corporation to

defend a suit away from home where its contact has been casual or isolated activities has been thought to lay too unreasonable a burden on it. However, even single or occasional acts may, because of their nature, quality and circumstances, be deemed sufficient to render a corporation liable to suit. Hence, the criteria to determine whether jurisdiction is justified is not simply mechanical or quantitative. Satisfaction of due process depends on the quality and nature of the activity in relation to the fair and orderly administration of the laws. In this case International's (D) activities were neither irregular nor casual. Rather, they were systematic and continuous. The obligation sued upon here arose out of these activities. They were sufficient to establish sufficient contacts or ties to make it reasonable to permit Washington (P) to enforce the obligations International (D) incurred there. Affirmed.

DISSENT: (Black, J.) The U.S. Constitution leaves to each state the power to tax and to open the doors of its courts for its citizens to sue corporations who do business in the state. It is a judicial deprivation to condition the exercise of this power on this court's notion of "fair play."

EDITOR'S ANALYSIS: Before this decision three theories had evolved to provide for suits by and against foreign corporations. The first was the consent theory. It rested on the proposition that since a foreign corporation could not carry on its business within a state without the permission of that state, the state could require a corporation to appoint an agent to receive service of process within the state. However, it soon became established law that a foreign corporation could not be prevented by a state from carrying on interstate commerce within its borders. The presence doctrine required that the corporation was "doing business" and "present" in the state. The third theory used either the present or consent doctrine, and it was necessary to determine whether the corporation was doing business within the state either to decide whether its consent could properly be implied or to discover whether the corporation was present.

QUICKNOTES

CONSENT JURISDICTION - The forum having jurisdiction over a lawsuit as agreed upon by the parties prior to litigation.

IN PERSONAM JURISDICTION - The jurisdiction of a court over a person as opposed to his interest in property.

MINIMUM CONTACTS - The minimum degree of contact necessary in order to sustain a cause of action within a particular forum, consistent with the requirements of due process.

McGEE v. INTERNATIONAL LIFE INSURANCE CO.
Beneficiary (P) v. Insurance company (D)
355 U.S. 220 (1957).

NATURE OF CASE: Suit to enforce payment of life insurance proceeds.

FACT SUMMARY: McGee (P) was the beneficiary of a life insurance policy on a California resident who had purchased the policy from an insurer who was subsequently bought by International Life Insurance Co. (International Life) (D). McGee obtained a judgment for the proceeds in California and attempted to enforce the judgment in Texas.

CONCISE RULE OF LAW: Due process requires only that in order to subject a nonresident defendant to the personal jurisdiction of the forum, the suit be based on a contract which has substantial connection with the forum.

FACTS: Lowell Franklin, a resident of California, purchased a life insurance policy from an insurer. The reinsurer, International Life (D), mailed a reinsurance certificate to the California resident offering to insure him. Franklin accepted this offer and paid all premiums by mail from his California home to the reinsurer's Texas office. The insured died, and the beneficiary, McGee (P), notified the insurer (D) of the death. The insurer (D) refused to make payment, and McGee (P) sued the insurer in California, obtaining a judgment.

ISSUE: Does due process require only that in order to subject a nonresident defendant to the personal jurisdiction of the forum, the suit be based on a contract which has substantial connection with the forum?

HOLDING AND DECISION: (Black, J.) Yes. Due process requires only that in order to subject a nonresident defendant to the personal jurisdiction of the forum, the suit be based on a contract which has substantial connection with the forum. Here, the insurance contract was delivered to California, and the premiums were payable there. The beneficiary and policyholders are California residents. It cannot be denied that California has a manifest interest in providing effective means of redress for its residents when their insurers refuse to pay claims. These residents would be at a severe disadvantage if forced to follow the insurance company to a distant state in order to hold it legally accountable.

EDITOR'S ANALYSIS: The fact of solicitation of the policy in California was a key element of this decision. That solicitation, albeit a single incident, could reasonably be thought to have put International Life (D) on notice that it might be sued in California. If, on the other hand, the insured had taken out the policy in Texas and then moved to California, where he was the sole policyholder, this foreseeability argument would be greatly diluted. However, if the insured was one of a number of California policyholders, the exercise of personal jurisdiction there could be expected.

QUICKNOTES
FULL FAITH AND CREDIT - Doctrine that a judgment by a court of one state shall be given the same effect in another state.

MINIMUM CONTACTS - The minimum degree of contact necessary in order to sustain a cause of action within a particular forum, consistent with the requirements of due process.

NOTES:

HANSON v. DENCKLA
Will legatees (P) v. Trust beneficiaries (D)
357 U.S. 235 (1958).

NATURE OF CASE: Appeal from disposition of property in a trust.

FACT SUMMARY: Mrs. Donner, mother of three daughters, established a trust in Delaware and later moved to Florida where she died.

CONCISE RULE OF LAW: For there to be "minimal contacts" sufficient to support in personam jurisdiction, it is essential that there be some act by which the defendant purposefully avails itself of the privilege of conducting activities within the forum state, thus invoking the benefits and protections of its laws.

FACTS: Mrs. Donner established a trust in Delaware and later moved to Florida where she died. A will contest ensued among her three daughters: if Florida could acquire jurisdiction over the Delaware trust, two daughters would get the entire estate; if the Delaware courts had jurisdiction, all three daughters would share equally.

ISSUE: For there to be "minimal contacts" sufficient to support in personam jurisdiction, is it essential that there be some act by which the defendant purposefully avails itself of the privilege of conducting activities within the forum state?

HOLDING AND DECISION: (Warren, C.J.) Yes. For there to be "minimal contacts" sufficient to support in personam jurisdiction, it is essential that there be some act by which the defendant purposefully avails itself of the privilege of conducting activities with the forum state, thus invoking the benefits and protections of its laws. In this case, no such contacts could be found. The Delaware trustee had no office in Florida and conducted no business there. No trust assets were ever held in Florida or administered there, and there was no solicitation of business in that state either in person or by mail. Consequently, this suit was not one to enforce an obligation that arose from a privilege exercised in Florida. However minimal the burden of defending in a foreign tribunal, a defendant may not be called upon to do so unless he has had the minimum contacts with that state that are a prerequisite to its exercise of power over him. Reversed and remanded.

EDITOR'S ANALYSIS: The case really revolves around the validity of the inter vivos trust. The trust was created in Delaware, and the corpus remains there. The fact that some Florida residents are beneficiaries thereunder, or that they wish to defeat the trust, is not a compelling state interest. It certainly is not a more substantial interest than is Delaware's right to construe the validity of a trust created under its laws and the corpus of which is within its jurisdiction. The fact that the settlor was a Florida resident is immaterial. She was not a resident when the trust was created, nor was she attempting to have the trust set aside.

QUICKNOTES

IN PERSONAM JURISDICTION - The jurisdiction of a court over a person as opposed to his interest in property.

INTER VIVOS TRUST - Property that is held by one person for the benefit of another and which is created by an instrument that takes effect during the life of the grantor.

MINIMUM CONTACTS - The minimum degree of contact necessary in order to sustain a cause of action within a particular forum, consistent with the requirements of due process.

RESIDUARY CLAUSE (OF WILL) - A clause contained in a will disposing of the assets remaining following distribution of the estate.

NOTES:

SHAFFER v. HEITNER
Corporation (D) v. Shareholder (P)
433 U.S. 186 (1977).

NATURE OF CASE: Appeal from a finding of state jurisdiction.

FACT SUMMARY: Heitner (P) brought a derivative suit against Greyhound (D) directors for antitrust losses it had sustained in Oregon. The suit was brought in Delaware, Greyhound's (D) state of incorporation.

CONCISE RULE OF LAW: Jurisdiction cannot be founded on property within a state unless there are sufficient contacts within the meaning of the test developed in *International Shoe.*

FACTS: Heitner (P) owned one share of Greyhound (D) stock. Greyhound (D) had been subjected to a large antitrust judgment in Oregon. Heitner (P), a nonresident of Delaware, brought a derivative suit in Delaware, the state of Greyhound's (D) incorporation. Jurisdiction was based on sequestration of Greyhound (D) stock which was deemed to be located within the state of incorporation. The Delaware sequestration statute allowed property within the state to be seized ex parte to compel the owner to submit to the in personam jurisdiction of the court. None of the stock was actually in Delaware, but a freeze order was placed on the corporate books. Greyhound (D) made a special appearance to challenge the court's jurisdiction to hear the matter. Greyhound (D) argued that the sequestration statute was unconstitutional under the line of case's beginning with Snidatch. Greyhound (D) also argued that there were insufficient contacts with Delaware to justify an exercise of jurisdiction. The Delaware courts found that the sequestration statute was valid since it was not a per se seizure of the property and was merely invoked to compel out-of-state residents to defend actions within the state. Little or no consideration was given to the "contact" argument based on a finding that the presence of the stock within the state conferred quasi-in-rem jurisdiction.

ISSUE: May a state assume jurisdiction over an issue merely because defendant's property happens to be within the state?

HOLDING AND DECISION: (Marshall, J.) No. Mere presence of property within a state is insufficient to confer jurisdiction on a court absent independent contacts within the meaning of *International Shoe*, which would make acceptance constitutional. We expressly disapprove that line of cases represented by *Harris v. Balk*, which permits jurisdiction merely because the property happens to be within the state. If sufficient contacts do not exist to assume jurisdiction absent the presence of property within the state, it cannot be invoked on the basis of property within the court's jurisdiction. We base this decision on the fundamental concepts of justice and fair play required under the

due process and equal protection clauses of the Fourteenth Amendment. Here, the stock is not the subject of the controversy. There is no claim to ownership of it or injury caused by it. The defendants do not reside in Delaware or have any contacts there. The injury occurred in Oregon. No activities complained of were done within the forum. Finally, Heitner (P) is not even a Delaware resident. Jurisdiction was improperly granted. Reversed.

CONCURRENCE: (Powell, J.) I would only disagree as to cases involving property permanently within the state, *e.g.*, real property. Such property should confer jurisdiction.

CONCURRENCE: (Stevens, J.) I concur in the result since purchase of stock in the marketplace should not confer in rem jurisdiction in the state of incorporation. I also concur with Mr. Justice Powell's statements.

CONCURRENCE AND DISSENT: (Brennan, J.) A state may exercise jurisdiction over a party only on the basis of the minimum contacts among the parties, the contested transaction and the forum state. In this case, however, the assertion of jurisdiction was based on the presence of property, in the form of capital stock, in Delaware. This is quasi-in-rem jurisdiction and is not based upon minimum contacts. However, even under the minimum contacts analysis that the majority requires today, jurisdiction should not be denied in this case. The state of Delaware has a strong interest in adjudicating claims as to corporations chartered by it. It must provide restitution for its corporations, it has a regulatory interest, and an interest in providing a convenient forum for the entity which is a creature of its law. Thus, jurisdiction should attach.

EDITOR'S ANALYSIS: While the corporation could be sued in its state of incorporation under the dissent's theory, the suit is against the directors and neither the site of the wrong nor the residence of a defendant is in Delaware. The decision will only have a major impact in cases such as herein where the state really has no reason to want to adjudicate the issue. Of course, real property would still be treated as an exception.

QUICKNOTES

EX PARTE - A proceeding commenced by one party without providing any opposing parties with notice or which is uncontested by an adverse party.

IN REM JURISDICTION - A court's authority over a thing so that its judgment is binding in respect to the rights and interests of all parties in that thing.

QUASI-IN REM JURISDICTION - A court's authority over the defendant's property within a specified geographical area.

WORLD-WIDE VOLKSWAGEN CORP. v. WOODSON
Automobile distributor (P) v. Court (D)
444 U.S. 286 (1980).

NATURE OF CASE: Petition for a writ prohibiting the exercise of in personam jurisdiction.

FACT SUMMARY: World-Wide (P) sought a writ of prohibition to keep district court Judge Woodson (D) from exercising in personam jurisdiction over it, alleging it did not have sufficient "contacts" with the forum state of Oklahoma to render it subject to such jurisdiction.

CONCISE RULE OF LAW: A state court may exercise personal jurisdiction over a nonresident defendant only so long as there exist sufficient "minimum contacts" between him and the forum state such that maintenance of the suit does not offend "traditional notions of fair play and substantial justice."

FACTS: World-Wide (P) was the regional distributor of Audi automobile for the tri-state area of New York, New Jersey, and Connecticut. It was the distributor of the particular Audi that the Robinsons purchased from a New York dealer and drove to Oklahoma, where three family members were severely burned when another car struck their Audi in the rear. The Robinsons brought a products liability action in an Oklahoma district court, suing the New York dealership and World-Wide (a New York corporation). Claiming that no evidence showed it had any connection with Oklahoma whatsoever, World-Wide (P) sought a writ of prohibition to keep district court Judge Woodson (D) from exercising in personam jurisdiction. World-Wide (P) argued that a lack of sufficient contacts with the forum state made assertion of such jurisdiction improper under the Due Process Clause. The Supreme Court of Oklahoma denied the writ, noting that World-Wide (P) could foresee that the automobiles it sold would be taken into other states, including Oklahoma. The United States Supreme Court granted certiorari.

ISSUE: Must a defendant have "minimum contacts" with the forum state before it can exercise in personam jurisdiction over him?

HOLDING AND DECISION: (White, J.) Yes. Under the Due Process Clause, the exercise of in personam jurisdiction over a defendant is not constitutional unless he has sufficient "minimum contacts" with the forum state so that maintenance of the suit does not offend "traditional notions of fair play and substantial justice." Here, World-Wide (P) had no "contacts, ties, or relations" with Oklahoma, so personal jurisdiction could not be exercised. As for the notion that it was foreseeable that cars sold in New York would wind up in Oklahoma, the foreseeability that is critical to due process analysis is not the mere likelihood that a product will find its way into the forum state. Rather, it is that the defendant's conduct and connection with the forum state are such that he should reasonably anticipate being hauled into court there. Such conduct and connection are simply missing in this case. Reversed.

DISSENT: (Brennan, J.) The automobile is designed specifically to facilitate travel from place to place, and the sale of one purposefully injects it into the stream of interstate commerce. Thus, this case is not unlike those where in personam jurisdiction is properly exercised over one who purposefully places his product into the stream of interstate commerce with the expectation it will be purchased by consumers in other states. Furthermore, a large part of the value of automobiles is the extensive, nationwide network of highways. State maintenance of such roads contributes to the value of World-Wide's (P) business. World-Wide (P) also participates in a network of related dealerships with nationwide service facilities. Having such facilities in Oklahoma also adds to the value of World-Wide's (P) business. Thus, it has the required minimum contacts with Oklahoma to render this exercise of personal jurisdiction constitutional.

EDITOR'S ANALYSIS: Over the years, modern transportation and communication have made foreign state suits much less of a burden to defendants. This resulted in a relaxing of the due process limits placed on state jurisdiction down to the "minimum contacts" concept. However, even if there were no inconvenience to the defendant, a state could not exercise personal jurisdiction over him if he had no "contacts, ties, or relations." This is true even if that state had a strong interest in applying its law to the controversy, it was the most convenient location for litigation, etc. The reason is that the Due Process Clause serves two distinct functions: the first is as a guarantor against inconvenient litigation but the second is as a guardian of interstate federalism. It is in this second capacity that the Due Process Clause would prevent assumption of jurisdiction in the aforementioned instance by recognizing the "territorial limitations on the power of the respective states."

QUICKNOTES
IN PERSONAM JURISDICTION - The jurisdiction of a court over a person as opposed to his interest in property.

MINIMUM CONTACTS - The minimum degree of contact necessary in order to sustain a cause of action within a particular forum, consistent with the requirements of due process.

ASAHI METAL INDUSTRY CO. v. SUPERIOR COURT
Japanese tire corporation (P) v. Court (D)
480 U.S. 102 (1987).

NATURE OF CASE: Appeal from discharge of writ quashing service of summons.

FACT SUMMARY: Asahi (P) appealed from a decision of the California Supreme Court discharging a peremptory writ issued by the appeals court quashing service of summons in Cheng Shin's indemnity action, contending that there did not exist minimum contacts between California and Asahi (P) sufficient to sustain jurisdiction.

CONCISE RULE OF LAW: Minimum contacts sufficient to sustain jurisdiction are not satisfied simply by the placement of a product into the stream of commerce coupled with an awareness that its product would reach the forum state.

FACTS: Asahi (P), a Japanese corporation, manufactured tire valve assemblies in Japan, selling some of them to Cheng Shin, a Taiwanese company who incorporated them into the motorcycles it manufactured. Zurcher was seriously injured in a motorcycle accident, and a companion was killed. He sued Cheng Shin, alleging the motorcycle tire manufactured by Cheng Shin was defective. Cheng Shin sought indemnity from Asahi (P), and the main action settled. Asahi (P) moved to quash service of summons, contending that jurisdiction could not be maintained by California, the state in which Zurcher filed his action, consistent with the Due Process Clause of the Fourteenth Amendment. The evidence indicated that Asahi's (P) sales to Cheng Shin took place in Taiwan, and shipments went from Japan to Taiwan. Cheng Shin purchased valve assemblies from other manufacturers. Sales to Cheng Shin never amounted to more than 1.5% of Asahi's (P) income. Approximately 20% of Cheng Shin's sales in the United States are in California. In declaration, an attorney for Cheng Shin stated he made an informal examination of tires in a bike shop in Solano County, where Zurcher was injured, finding approximately 20% of the tires with Asahi's (P) trademark (25% of the tires manufactured by Cheng Shin). The superior court (D) denied the motion to quash, finding it reasonable that Asahi (P) defend its claim of defect in their product. The court of appeals issued a peremptory writ commanding the superior court (D) to quash service of summons. The state supreme court reversed and discharged the writ, finding that Asahi's (P) awareness that some of its product would reach California by placing it in the stream of commerce satisfied minimum contacts sufficient to sustain jurisdiction. From this decision, Asahi (P) appealed.

ISSUE: Are minimum contacts sufficient to sustain jurisdiction satisfied by the placement of a product into the stream of commerce, coupled with the awareness that its product would reach the forum state?

HOLDING AND DECISION: (O'Connor, J.) No. Minimum contacts sufficient to sustain jurisdiction are not satisfied by the placement of a product in the stream of commerce, coupled with the awareness that its product would reach the forum state. To satisfy minimum contacts, there must be some act by which the defendant purposefully avails itself of the privilege of conducting activities within the forum state. Although the courts that have squarely addressed this issue have been divided, the better view is that the defendant must do more than place a product in the stream of commerce. The unilateral act of a consumer bringing the product to the forum state is not sufficient. Asahi (P) has not purposefully availed itself of the California market. It does not do business in the state, conduct activities, maintain offices or agents, or advertise. Nor did it have anything to do with Cheng Shin's distribution system, which brought the tire valve assembly to California. Assertion of jurisdiction based on these facts exceeds the limits of due process. [The Court went on to consider the burden of defense on Asahi (P) and the slight interests of the state and Zurcher, finding the assertion of jurisdiction unreasonable and unfair.] Reversed and remanded.

CONCURRENCE: (Brennan, J.) The state supreme court correctly concluded that the stream of commerce theory, without more, has satisfied minimum contacts in most courts which have addressed the issue, and it has been preserved in the decision of this Court.

CONCURRENCE: (Stevens, J.) The minimum contacts analysis is unnecessary; the Court has found by weighing the appropriate factors that jurisdiction under these facts is unreasonable and unfair.

EDITOR'S ANALYSIS: The Brennan concurrence is quite on point in criticizing the plurality for its characterization that this case involves the act of a consumer in bringing the product within the forum state. The argument presented in *World-Wide Volkswagen Corp. v. Woodson*, 444 U.S. 286 (1980), cited by the plurality, seems more applicable to distributors and retailers than to manufacturers of component parts.

QUICKNOTES
PEREMPTORY WRIT - Writ directing the sheriff to have the defendant appear before the court so long as the plaintiff has provided adequate security in order to prosecute the action.

PURPOSEFUL AVAILMENT - An element in determining whether a defendant had the required minimum contacts in a forum necessary in order for a court to exercise jurisdiction over the party, whereby the court determines whether the defendant intentionally conducted activities in the forum and thus knows, or could reasonably expect, that such conduct could give rise to litigation in that forum.

BURGER KING CORP v. RUDZEWICZ
Fast food corporation (P) v. Franchisee (D)
471 U.S. 462 (1985).

NATURE OF CASE: Appeal from reversal of award of damages and injunctive relief for breach of contract.

FACT SUMMARY: Burger King Corp. (P) brought an action against Rudzewicz (D), a defaulting franchisee, in Burger King's (P) home forum.

CONCISE RULE OF LAW: Direct and continuous contacts by a franchisee with the franchisor may lead to the franchisee being subject to the jurisdiction of the franchisor's home forum.

FACTS: Rudzewicz (D) contracted for a Burger King franchise in Michigan with Burger King Corp. (P), a Florida corporation. A franchise was granted. The terms of the contract called for substantial supervision of the franchise's operations by Burger King (P), and also for the laws of Florida to apply. Despite the fact that Rudzewicz (D) was a sophisticated businessman, the business failed, and Burger King (P) brought suit for unpaid rent. The Florida district court granted damages and injunctive relief, but the Eleventh Circuit reversed, holding that Rudzewicz (D) was not amenable to Florida jurisdiction. Burger King Corp. (P) appealed.

ISSUE: May direct and continuous contacts by a franchisee with the franchisor lead to the franchisee being subject to the jurisdiction of the franchisor's home forum?

HOLDING AND DECISION: (Brennan, J.) Yes. Direct and continuous contacts by a franchisee with the franchisor may lead to the franchisee being subject to the jurisdiction of the franchisor's home forum. The main test for personal jurisdiction is whether a defendant's actions were such that he should have been put on notice of the possibility of becoming subject to the subject forum's jurisdiction. The yardstick here is the nature of that defendant's contacts with that forum. Here, Rudzewicz (D) contracted with a Florida franchisor and entered into a contract providing for a continuous relationship with that franchisor and constant monitoring by that franchisor. Further, the contract stated that it was to be construed a Florida contract. Considering the nature of Rudzewicz's (D) contacts with Florida, an ample basis for jurisdiction existed. Reversed.

DISSENT: (Stevens, J.) The typical franchise is a large operation connected with the franchisor's home office only in name. Since the business is purely local, only local jurisdiction should apply.

EDITOR'S ANALYSIS: Part of the rationale for the Court's opinion was the clause making the contract a Florida one. Most contracts involving parties in different states have such clauses.

Exactly how much weight was given this was not spelled out by the Court, but the opinion did say that such a clause is not determinative.

QUICKNOTES

INJUNCTIVE RELIEF - A count order issued as a remedy, requiring a person to do, or prohibiting that person from doing, a specific act.

MINIMUM CONTACTS - The minimum degree of contact necessary in order to sustain a cause of action within a particular forum, consistent with the requirements of due process.

PERSONAL JURISDICTION - The court's authority over a person or parties to a law suit.

NOTES:

PAVLOVICH v. SUPERIOR COURT
Web site creator (P) v. Superior Court (D)
29 Cal.4th 262, 58 P.3d 2 (2002).

NATURE OF CASE: Appeal of finding of personal jurisdiction over defendant.

FACT SUMMARY: When the trial court found specific personal jurisdiction over Pavlovich (P) based solely on his passive Internet Web site, Pavlovich (P) argued that personal jurisdiction may not be acquired over a defendant simply based on a posting on a passive Internet Web site.

CONCISE RULE OF LAW: Personal jurisdiction may not necessarily be acquired over a defendant based on a posting on a passive Internet Web site.

FACTS: Matthew Pavlovich (P), a computer systems and network administrator, was a Texas resident who did not reside or work in California and never had a place of business, telephone listing, or bank account in California, and never owned property in California. Neither Pavlovich (P) nor his company (LiVid) ever solicited any business in California nor had any business contacts in California. Pavlovich (P) opened and operated a single page passive Web site which only provided information, but did not solicit or transact any business and permitted no interactive exchange of information between its operators and visitors. The site sought to defeat certain DVD technology and enable the decryption and copying of DVDs containing motion pictures. LiVid posted the source code of a program named DeCSS on its Web site to allow users to circumvent the DVD technology and copy motion pictures. Real party in interest, DVD Copy Control Association, brought suit against Pavlovich (P) for posting this proprietary information, and the California Superior Court exercised specific personal jurisdiction over Pavlovich (P) based on his Web site. The California Court of Appeal affirmed the finding of jurisdiction, and Pavlovich (P) appealed.

ISSUE: May personal jurisdiction necessarily be acquired over a defendant based on a posting on a passive Internet Web site?

HOLDING AND DECISION: (Brown, J.) No. Personal jurisdiction may not necessarily be acquired over a defendant based on a posting on a passive Internet Web site. A court may exercise specific jurisdiction over a nonresident defendant only if (1) the defendant has purposefully availed itself of forum benefits, (2) the controversy arises out of the defendant's contacts with the forum, and (3) the assertion of personal jurisdiction would comport with fair play and substantial justice. Here, Pavlovich's (P) sole contact with California was LiVid's posting of a DVD source code containing proprietary information on an Internet Web site accessible to any person with Internet access. A passive Web site, as here, that does little more than make information available to those who are interested in it is not grounds for the exercise of

personal jurisdiction. In such case, the exercise of jurisdiction is determined by examining the level of interactivity and commercial nature of the exchange of information that occurs on the Web site. Here, LiVid's Web site merely posts information and has no interactive features. There is no evidence suggesting that the site targeted California. Indeed, there is no evidence that any California resident ever visited, much less downloaded the DeCSS source code from, the LiVid Web site. Pavlovich's (P) mere knowledge that his tortious conduct may harm industries centered in California, while relevant to the determination of personal jurisdiction, *alone* is insufficient to establish express aiming at the forum state as required to establish personal jurisdiction in the forum state. Hence, Pavlovich's (P) conduct was not, by itself, sufficient to subject him to California jurisdiction. Reversed.

DISSENT: (Baxter, J) The intended targets of Pavlovich (P) were entire businesses. He knew at least two of the targets: the movie industry and the computer industry, and both industries were centered in California. Thus, for purposes of specific personal jurisdiction, Pavlovich's (P) intentional act, even if committed outside California, was "expressly aimed" at California. In these particular circumstances, it cannot matter that Pavlovich (P) may not have known or cared about the *exact identities* or *precise locations* of each individual target, or that he happened to employ a so-called passive Internet Web site, or whether any California resident visited the site.

EDITOR'S ANALYSIS: In *Pavlovich*, the court made clear that creating a Web site, like placing a product into the stream of commerce, may be felt nationwide, or even worldwide, but, without more, is not an act purposely directed toward the forum state. Otherwise, personal jurisdiction in Internet-related cases would almost always be found in any forum in the country. Such a result would violate long-held and inviolate principles of personal jurisdiction.

QUICKNOTES
FORUM - A court or other location in which a legal remedy may be sought.

PERSONAL JURISDICTION - The court's authority over a person or parties to a law suit.

COASTAL VIDEO COMMUNICATIONS CORP. v. THE STAYWELL CORP.

Virginia corporation(P) v. Delaware publisher (D)
59 F.Supp.2d 562 (E.D. Va. 1999).

NATURE OF CASE: Defense motion to dismiss for lack of personal jurisdiction and plaintiff's motion for discovery on issue of personal jurisdiction.

FACT SUMMARY: When Coastal Video Communications Corporation (P) sought a declaratory judgment to establish that its handbook did not infringe on copyrighted material contained in a handbook produced by the Krames/Staywell Corporation (D), Krames (D) moved to dismiss for lack of personal jurisdiction.

CONCISE RULE OF LAW: A party who maintains a Web site with a high degree of interactivity with sales generated in the forum state may be subject to the forum state's general jurisdiction.

FACTS: Coastal Video Communications Corporation (P), a Virginia corporation, filed suit in the federal district court of Virginia, seeking a declaration that its handbook, "Defending Your Safety Zone: Back Protection," did not infringe on copyrighted material contained in "Safety Zone," a handbook produced by the Krames/Staywell Corporation (D), a Delaware corporation. Although Krames (D) sold its products in Virginia, as well as nationally and internationally over its interactive Web site, it had never sold any copies of its handbook in Virginia. Krames (D) moved to dismiss for lack of personal jurisdiction. Coastal Video (P) moved for discovery on the issue of personal jurisdiction over Krames (D).

ISSUE: May a party who maintains a Web site with a high degree of interactivity with sales generated in the forum state be subject to the forum state's general jurisdiction?

HOLDING AND DECISION: (Smith, Dist. J.) Yes. A party who maintains a Web site with a high degree of interactivity with sales generated in the forum state may be subject to the forum state's general jurisdiction. Krames (D), although a Delaware corporation, sells its products to more than seventy percent of hospitals in the United States, as well as to customers in fifty countries on six continents. Krames (D) has also sold products in Virginia in the past and currently. While there was no indication that copies of Krames' (D) "Safety Zone" publication were actually sold in Virginia, Krames (D) was qualified to do business in Virginia and maintains a registered agent in Virginia. Krames' (D) Web site advertises over 850 Krames (D) products and allows customers to order products directly over the Web by completing order forms online. The Web site also provides an "Ask Krames" service by which potential customers may e-mail questions about products and services. Krames (D), furthermore, offers the

"Safety Zone" product over its Web site. Even if Coastal Video (P) were able to demonstrate that Krames (D) sold the "Safety Zone" publication in Virginia, the court would still not have specific personal jurisdiction over Krames (D) because the declaratory judgment action does not "arise from" the sale of Krames' (D) publication. However, because its Web site allows the on-line visitor to purchase all of its products, Krames (D) "in essence" has established an "on-line storefront" that is readily accessible to every person in Virginia with a computer, a modem, and access to the World Wide Web. Given significant gaps in the record as to the nature and extent of both Krames' (D) traditional business contacts with Virginia and also its Internet-based contacts with Virginia, Coastal Video's (P) motion for discovery on the issue of general jurisdiction over Krames (D) is granted. Defendant's motion to dismiss is taken under advisement pending outcome of discovery.

EDITOR'S ANALYSIS: In *Coastal Video*, the court observed that, as with traditional business contacts, the most reliable indicator of the nature and extent of a defendant's Internet contact with the forum state will be the amount of sales generated in the state by and through the interactive website. In addition, it may also be possible to determine how many times a website has been accessed by residents or businesses located in a specific state. Such information, if available, would also be relevant to the determination of general personal jurisdiction.

QUICKNOTES

FORUM STATE - The state in which a court, or other location in which a legal remedy may be sought, is located.

PERSONAL JURISDICTION - The court's authority over a person or parties to a law suit.

NOTES:

BURNHAM v. SUPERIOR COURT
Husband and father (P) v. Court (D)
495 U.S. 604 (1990).

NATURE OF CASE: Appeal from denial of motion to quash service of process in dissolution action on the grounds that the court lacked personal jurisdiction.

FACT SUMMARY: Dennis Burnham (P) and his wife were living in New Jersey when they decided to separate. Mrs. Burnham moved with the children to California, filed for divorce in that state and served Mr. Burnham (P) while he was visiting.

CONCISE RULE OF LAW: State courts have jurisdiction over nonresidents who are physically present in the state.

FACTS: Dennis Burnham (P) and his wife were living in New Jersey when they decided to separate. Mrs. Burnham moved with the children to California and filed for divorce in that state. Mr. Burnham (P) visited his children in January of 1988, at which time he was served with a California court summons and a copy of his wife's divorce petition. He made a special appearance in the California Superior Court (D) moving to quash the service of process on the ground that the Court (D) lacked personal jurisdiction over him because his only contacts with California were a few short visits to the state for the purpose of conducting business and visiting his children. The Superior Court (D) denied the motion, and the California Court of Appeal denied mandamus relief. The court held it to be a valid jurisdictional predicate for in personam jurisdiction that Mr. Burnham (P) was present in the forum state and personally served with process. The U.S. Supreme Court granted certiorari.

ISSUE: Do state courts have jurisdiction over nonresidents who are physically present in the state?

HOLDING AND DECISION: (Scalia, J.) Yes. State courts have jurisdiction over nonresidents who are physically present in the state. Jurisdiction based on physical presence alone constitutes due process because it is one of the continuing traditions of our legal system that define the due process standard of traditional notions of fair play and substantial justice. That standard was developed by analogy to physical presence, and it would be perverse to say it could now be turned against that touchstone of jurisdiction. Affirmed.

CONCURRENCE: (Brennan, J.) History is an important factor in establishing whether a jurisdictional rule satisfies due process requirements, but it is not the only factor such that all traditional rules of jurisdiction are, ipso facto, forever constitutional.

CONCURRENCE: (Stevens, J.) It is sufficient to note that the historical evidence and consensus identified by Justice Scalia, the considerations of fairness identified by Justice Brennan, and the common sense displayed by Justice White, all combine to demonstrate that this is, indeed, a very easy case.

EDITOR'S ANALYSIS: In a footnote to the above case, Justice Scalia explained that in *Helicopteros Nacionales de Columbia v. Hall*, 466 U.S. at 414 (1984) the U.S. Supreme Court held that due process is not offended by a state's subjecting a corporation to its jurisdiction when there are sufficient contacts between the state and the foreign corporation. However, the only holding supporting that statement involved regular service of summons upon a corporate president while in the forum state acting in that capacity. See *Perkins v. Benguet Consolidated Mining Co.*, 342 U.S. 437 (1952). It may be that whatever special rule exists permitting continuous and systematic contacts to support jurisdiction with respect to matters unrelated to activity in the forum applied only to corporations, which have never fitted comfortably within a jurisdictional regime based primarily upon de facto power over the defendant's person.

QUICKNOTES
PERSONAL JURISDICTION - The court's authority over a person or parties to a law suit.

SERVICE OF PROCESS - The communication of reasonable notice of a court proceeding to a defendant in order to provide him with an opportunity to be heard.

NOTES:

CARNIVAL CRUISE LINES, INC. v. SHUTE
Cruise company (D) v. Customers (P)
499 U.S. 585 (1991)

NATURE OF CASE: Review of denial of defense motion for summary judgment in personal injury action.

FACT SUMMARY: Shute (P), an injured cruise ship passenger, filed suit in her home state despite a stipulation in her passenger ticket requiring all suits to be filed in Florida.

CONCISE RULE OF LAW: Reasonable forum selection clauses contained in passenger tickets are presumptively valid.

FACTS: The Shutes (P), residents of Washington State, purchased passage for a seven-day cruise on a ship owned by Carnival Cruise Lines (D). The cruise tickets they received contained a forum-selection clause setting the State of Florida as the forum where any disputes arising from the cruise would be litigated. Carnival Cruise (D) had its principal place of business in Florida, and many of its cruises departed from there. During the cruise, Mrs. Shute (P) was injured in a slip-and-fall accident. The Shutes (P) filed a negligence action in Washington. Carnival Cruise (D) moved for summary judgment, contending that the forum clause in the Shutes's (P) ticket required them to bring their suit in a Florida court. The Ninth Circuit denied its motion on the ground that the clause was not a product of negotiation, and the Supreme Court granted certiorari.

ISSUE: Are reasonable forum selection clauses contained in passenger tickets presumptively valid?

HOLDING AND DECISION: (Blackmun, J.) Yes. Reasonable forum selection clauses contained in passenger tickets are presumptively valid. They are permissible because a cruise line has a special interest in limiting the fora in which it potentially could be subject to suit. Such a clause also dispels any confusion about where a suit must be brought, thereby sparing litigants and courts the time and expense of litigating the issue. Finally, the passengers themselves benefit from forum clauses because fares are reduced commensurate with the money saved by the cruise line in limiting the fora where it may be sued. Since in this case there is no bad faith motive apparent in Carnival Cruise's (D) forum provision, and the Shutes (P) have conceded that they had notice of the provision, the Ninth Circuit erred in refusing to enforce the clause. Reversed.

DISSENT: (Stevens, J.) The prevailing rule is that forum selection clauses are not enforceable if they were not freely bargained for, create additional expense for one party, or deny one party a remedy.

EDITOR'S ANALYSIS: Besides forum selection clauses, a contract may contain a choice of law clause, stipulating which jurisdiction's substantive law will govern, or an arbitration clause, requiring parties to use arbitration as their exclusive forum. The most extreme example of a contract provision limiting a defendant's right to appeal or to even raise a defense to an action is the "cognovit." A cognovit note is written authority of a debtor for entry of a judgment against him if the obligation set forth in the note is not paid when due. Such agreements are prohibited in many states.

QUICKNOTES

COGNOVIT NOTE - A note signed by a debtor authorizing an attorney to enter judgment against him if payment is not made thereon.

FORUM SELECTION CLAUSE - Provision contained in a contract setting forth the particular forum in which the parties would resolve a matter if a dispute were to arise.

NOTES:

MULLANE v. CENTRAL HANOVER BANK AND TRUST CO.
Guardian of trust beneficiaries (P) v. Bank (D)
339 U.S. 306 (1950).

NATURE OF CASE: Constitutional challenge of the sufficiency of the notice provision of the New York Banking Law relating to beneficiaries of common trust funds.

FACT SUMMARY: Central Hanover Bank (D) pooled a number of small trust funds, and beneficiaries (some of whom lived out of state) were notified by publication in a local newspaper.

CONCISE RULE OF LAW: In order to satisfy due process challenges, notice must be by means calculated to inform the desired parties, and, where they reside outside of the state and their names and addresses are available, notice by publication is insufficient.

FACTS: A New York statute allowed corporate trustees to pool the assets of numerous small trusts administered by them. This allowed more efficient and economical administration of the funds. Each participating trust shared ratably in the common fund, but the trustees held complete control of all assets. A periodic accounting of profits, losses, and assets were to be submitted to the courts for approval. Beneficiaries were to be notified of the accounting so that they might object to any irregularities in the administration of the common fund. Once approved by the court, their claims would be barred. A guardian would be appointed to protect the interests of principal and income beneficiaries. Central Hanover Bank (D) established a common fund by consolidating the corpus of 113 separate trusts under their control. Notice of the common fund was sent to all interested parties along with the relevant portions of the statute. Notice of accountings were by publication in a local New York newspaper. Mullane (P) was the appointed guardian for all parties known and unknown who had an interest in the trust's income. He objected to the sufficiency of the statutory notice provisions claiming that they violated the Due Process Clause of the Fourteenth Amendment. Notice by publication was not a reasonable method of informing interested parties that their rights were being affected, especially with regard to out-of-state beneficiaries. Mullane's (P) objections were overruled in state courts and the present federal appeal was brought by him.

ISSUE: Is notice by publication sufficient to satisfy due process challenges where the parties to be informed reside out of state and an alternative means, better calculated to give actual notice, is available?

HOLDING AND DECISION: (Jackson, J.) No. The purpose of a notice requirement is to inform parties that their rights are being affected. Therefore, the method chosen should, if at all possible, be reasonably designed to accomplish this end. Notice in a New York legal paper is not reasonably calculated to provide out-of-state residents with the desired information. While the state has a right to discharge trustees of their liabilities through the acceptance of their accounting, it must also provide beneficiaries with adequate notice so that their rights to contest the accounting are not lost. In cases where the identity or whereabouts of beneficiaries or future interest holders is unknown, then publication is the most viable alternate means available for giving notice. Publication is only a supplemental method of giving notice. However, the Court will approve its use where alternative methods are not reasonably possible or practical. Where alternative methods, better calculated to give actual notice, are available, publication is an impermissible means of providing notice. Notice to known beneficiaries via publication is inadequate, not because it in fact fails to inform everyone, but, because under the circumstances, it is not readily calculated to reach those who could easily be informed by other means at hand. Since publication to known beneficiaries is ineffective, the statutory requirement violates the Due Process Clause of the Fourteenth Amendment. These parties have, at least potentially, been deprived of property without due process of law. With respect to remote future interest holders and unknown parties, publication is permissible. Reversed and remanded.

EDITOR'S ANALYSIS: Ineffective notice provisions violate procedural due process rights. As in all due process challenges, there must be a legitimate state interest and the means selected must be reasonably adapted to accomplish the state's purpose. While in Mullane the state's ends were permissible, the method of giving notice was unreasonable as it pertained to known parties. As has been previously stated, publication is only a supplementary method for giving notice. It is normally used in conjunction with other means when personal service by hand is unavailable or impractical. Mullane has been applied to condemnation cases where a known owner of property was never personally served. *Schroeder v. City of New York*, 371 U.S. 208. Factors considered by the Court involve the nature of the action, whether the party's whereabouts or identity are known or unknown, whether he is a resident and whether or not he has attempted to avoid personal service. If an attempt to avoid service is made, then constructive service by publication in conjunction with substitute service by mail is permitted. Finally, foreign corporations are generally required to appoint resident agents authorized to accept service of process.

GIBBONS v. BROWN
Automobile passenger (D) v. Fellow passenger (P)
716 So.2d 868 (Fl. Dist. Ct. App. 1998).

NATURE OF CASE: Appeal from dismissal of a personal injury action.

FACT SUMMARY: Mrs. Brown (P) filed a suit against Gibbons (D), a Texas resident, in Florida two years after Gibbons (D) had sued Mr. Brown in a Florida case involving the same auto accident.

CONCISE RULE OF LAW: A prior decision to file a lawsuit in a state does not qualify as sufficient activity in the state to confer personal jurisdiction.

FACTS: Mr. Brown was driving a car in Canada, in which Mrs. Brown (P) and Gibbons (D) were passengers. After a collision, Gibbons (D), a Texas resident, sued Mr. Brown in Florida. Two years later, Mrs. Brown (P) filed suit against Gibbons (D) in Florida for allegedly causing the accident by giving faulty directions. The trial court dismissed the action based on a lack of personal jurisdiction over Gibbons (D). Mrs. Brown (P) appealed.

ISSUE: Does a prior decision to file a lawsuit in a state qualify as sufficient activity in the state to confer personal jurisdiction?

HOLDING AND DECISION: (Per curiam) No. A prior decision to file a lawsuit in a state does not qualify as sufficient activity in the state to confer personal jurisdiction. Obtaining personal jurisdiction over a non-resident defendant requires a two-pronged showing. First, there must be sufficient jurisdictional facts to bring the defendant within the long-arm statute. Then, there must be sufficient minimum contacts between the defendant and forum state that jurisdiction would not violate due process. Florida requires that non-resident defendants engage in substantial and not isolated activity within the state in order to be subject to personal jurisdiction. There is no doubt that when a out-of-state plaintiff brings an action in Florida, she is subject to jurisdiction in subsequent actions regarding the same subject matter. However, in the present case, there were two years separating Gibbons' (D) suit against Mr. Brown and Mrs. Brown's (P) current action. Additionally, Mrs. Brown (P) was not a party to the first suit. Given these facts, and the lack of any other contact between Gibbons (D) and Florida, the grounds for personal jurisdiction do not meet the state's requirements. Affirmed.

EDITOR'S ANALYSIS: The court acknowledged that Florida does not allow jurisdiction to the full range allowed by the U.S. Constitution. Thus, in the present case, it is possible that another state would have allowed the case against Gibbons (D) to proceed. However, the court never reached the issue of whether the minimum contacts required by due process had been met.

QUICKNOTES

LONG-ARM STATUTE - A state statute conferring personal jurisdiction to state courts over a defendant not residing in the state, when the cause of action arises as a result of activities conducted within the state or affecting state residents.

PERSONAL JURISDICTION - The court's authority over a person or parties to a law suit.

PROCEDURAL DUE PROCESS - The constitutional mandate that if the state or federal government acts so as to deny a citizen of a life, liberty or property interest the individual is first entitled to notice and the right to be heard.

NOTES:

DEE-K ENTERPRISES, INC. v. HEVEAFIL SDN. BHD.
Domestic purchaser (P) v. Foreign seller (D)
982 F.Supp. 1138 (E.D. Va. 1997).

NATURE OF CASE: Motion to dismiss antitrust action.

FACT SUMMARY: Heveafil (D), a Malaysian corporation, challenged jurisdiction and venue of Dee-K's antitrust action in U.S. federal court.

CONCISE RULE OF LAW: The general venue statute, providing that aliens may be sued in any district, overrides special venue laws that place venue more specifically.

FACTS: Dee-K (P), a Virginia corporation, bought rubber thread from Heveafil (D), a Malaysian company, and other companies for making bungee cords. Dee-K (P) alleged that Heveafil (D) and other corporations, both foreign and domestic, were involved in a conspiracy to fix prices. Dee-K (P) brought an antitrust action in the Eastern District federal court. Heveafil (D) argued that there was no basis for jurisdiction and venue and moved to dismiss the suit.

ISSUE: Does the general venue statute, providing that aliens may be sued in any district, override special venue laws that place venue more specifically?

HOLDING AND DECISION: (Ellis, J.) Yes. The general venue statute, providing that aliens may be sued in any district, overrides special venue laws that place venue more specifically. Section 12 of the Clayton Act provides for worldwide service of process when the antitrust defendant is a corporation. Thus, jurisdiction is proper if does not offend the requirements of due process. Since Heveafil (D) appointed an exclusive sales agent for the United States and customized its product for the U.S. market, personal jurisdiction does not offend notions of fair play and substantial justice. Section 12 also lays venue in any district where the defendant is found or where it transacts business. Heveafil (D) does not meet these requirements. However, 28 USC §1391 provides that aliens may be sued in any district. This overrides the special venue statute of the Clayton Act and eliminates the venue impediment. Thus, venue is proper for Heveafil (D) in Virginia district court. However, with regard to the American defendants, venue is proper only in a district where the events occurred or where the defendant resides. The allegations of the complaint are not specific enough to make this determination at this time.

EDITOR'S ANALYSIS: The court noted that there were indications that venue might have been proper in the Western District of Virginia. The plaintiffs only had to show that one of the American defendants had enough connection to the Eastern District in order to keep the case there. If they were unable to, the case could be transferred.

QUICKNOTES

28 U.S.C. § 1391 - Permits venue to be placed where a substantial part of the events giving rise to the claim occurred.

NOTES:

PIPER AIRCRAFT v. REYNO
Aircraft company (D) v. Crash victims' representative (P)
454 U.S. 235 (1982).

NATURE OF CASE: Appeal from dismissal on the basis of forum non conveniens.

FACT SUMMARY: Reyno (P), the representative of five victims of an air crash, brought suit in California even though the location of the crash and the homes of the victims were in Scotland.

CONCISE RULE OF LAW: A plaintiff may not defeat a motion to dismiss for forum non conveniens merely by showing that the substantive law that would be applied in the alternative forum is less favorable to him than that of the present forum.

FACTS: Reyno (P) was the representative of five air crash victims' estates and brought suit for wrongful death in United States district court in California, even though the accident occurred and all the victims resided in Scotland. Piper (D) moved to dismiss for forum non conveniens, contending that Scotland was the proper forum. Reyno (P) opposed the motion on the basis that the Scottish laws were less advantageous to her than American laws. The district court granted the motion, while the court of appeals reversed. The Supreme Court granted certiorari.

ISSUE: May a plaintiff defeat a motion to dismiss for forum non conveniens merely on the basis that the laws of the alternative forum are less advantageous?

HOLDING AND DECISION: (Marshall, J.) No. A plaintiff may not defeat a motion to dismiss for forum non conveniens merely by showing that the substantive law of the alternative forum is less advantageous than that of the present forum. In this case, all the evidence, witnesses, and interests were in Scotland. Thus, the most convenient forum was there. As a result, the motion was properly granted. Reversed.

EDITOR'S ANALYSIS: The Court in this case specifically noted that under some circumstances, the fact that the chosen state's laws are less attractive to the defendant could be used to defeat a motion to dismiss for forum non conveniens. If the state chosen by the plaintiff has the only adequate remedy for the wrong alleged, then the motion may be denied.

QUICKNOTES

FORUM NON CONVENIENS - An equitable doctrine permitting a court to refrain from hearing and determining a case when the matter may be more properly and fairly heard in another forum.

MOTION TO DISMISS - Motion to terminate a trial based on the adequacy of the pleadings.

NOTES:

CHAPTER 3
SUBJECT MATTER JURISDICTION OF THE FEDERAL COURTS

QUICK REFERENCE RULES OF LAW

1. **Federal Question Jurisdiction.** Alleging an anticipated constitutional defense in the complaint does not give a federal court jurisdiction if there is no diversity of citizenship between the litigants. (Louisville & Nashville Railroad v. Mottley)

2. **Diversity Jurisdiction.** For purposes of diversity jurisdiction under 28 U.S.C. §1332(a)(2), the controversy must be between citizens of a state and citizens or subjects of a foreign state, not merely "residents." (Redner v. Sanders)

3. **Diversity Jurisdiction.** Aliens cannot bring suit against each other in federal court due to the requirement of complete diversity. (Saadeh v. Farouki)

4. **Supplemental Jurisdiction.** Complexity of the litigation does not necessarily prevent a court from asserting supplemental subject matter jurisdiction under 28 U.S.C. §1367. (Jin v. Ministry of State Security)

5. **Removal.** A district court's error in failing to remand a case improperly removed does not prevent adjudication if the jurisdictional requirements are satisfied at the time of judgment. (Caterpillar, Inc. v. Lewis)

LOUISVILLE & NASHVILLE R.R. v. MOTTLEY
Railroad company (D) v. Injured passengers (P)
211 U.S. 149 (1908).

NATURE OF CASE: Appeal of a decision overruling a demurrer in an action for specific performance of a contract.

FACT SUMMARY: Mottley (P) was injured on a train owned by Louisville & Nashville Railroad (D), which granted Mottley (P) a lifetime free pass which he sought to enforce.

CONCISE RULE OF LAW: Alleging an anticipated constitutional defense in the complaint does not give a federal court jurisdiction if there is no diversity of citizenship between the litigants.

FACTS: In 1871, Mottley (P) and his wife were injured while riding on the Louisville & Nashville R.R. (D). The Mottleys (P) released their claims for damages against the Louisville & Nashville R.R. (D) upon receiving a contract granting free transportation during the remainder of their lives. In 1907, the Louisville & Nashville R.R. (D) refused to renew the Mottleys' (P) passes relying upon an act of Congress which forbade the giving of free passes or free transportation. The Mottleys (P) filed an action in a Circuit Court of the United States for the Western District of Kentucky. The Mottleys (P) and the Louisville & Nashville R.R. (D) were both citizens of Kentucky. Therefore, the Mottleys (P) attempted to establish federal jurisdiction by claiming that the Louisville & Nashville R.R. (D) would raise a constitutional defense in their answer, thus raising a federal question. The Louisville & Nashville R.R. (D) filed a demurrer to the complaint for failing to state a cause of action. The demurrer was denied. On appeal, the Supreme Court did not look at the issue raised by the litigants, but on their own motion raised the issue of whether the federal courts had jurisdiction to hear the case.

ISSUE: Does an allegation in the complaint that a constitutional defense will be raised in the answer raise a federal question which would give a federal court jurisdiction if no diversity of citizenship is alleged?

HOLDING AND DECISION: (Moody, J.) No. The Supreme Court reversed the lower court's ruling and remitted the case to that court with instructions to dismiss the suit for want of jurisdiction. Neither party to the litigation alleged that the federal court had jurisdiction in this case, and neither party challenged the jurisdiction of the federal court to hear the case. Because the jurisdiction of the circuit court is defined and limited by statute, the Supreme Court stated that it is their duty to see that such jurisdiction is not exceeded. Both parties to the litigation were citizens of Kentucky and so there was no diversity of citizenship. The only way that the federal court could have jurisdiction in this case would be if there were a federal question involved. Mottley (P) did allege in his complaint that the Louisville &

Nashville R.R. (D) based their refusal to renew the free pass on a federal statute. Mottley (P) then attempted to allege information that would defeat the defense of the Louisville & Nashville R.R. (D). This is not sufficient. The plaintiff's complaint must be based upon the federal laws of the Constitution to confer jurisdiction on the federal courts. Mottley's (P) cause of action was not based on any federal laws or constitutional privileges; it was based on a contract. Even though it is evident that a federal question will be brought up at the trial, plaintiff's cause of action must be based on a federal statute or the constitution in order to have a federal question which would grant jurisdiction to the federal courts.

EDITOR'S ANALYSIS: If Mottley (P) could have alleged that he was basing his action on a federal right, it would have been enough to have given the federal court jurisdiction. The federal court would have had to exercise jurisdiction at least long enough to determine whether there actually was such a right. If the federal court ultimately concludes that the claimed federal right does not exist, the complaint would be dismissed for failure to state a claim upon which relief can be granted rather than for lack of jurisdiction. The court has the power to determine the issue of subject matter jurisdiction on its own motion as it did in this case. Subject matter jurisdiction can be challenged at any stage of the proceeding.

QUICKNOTES

DIVERSITY OF CITIZENSHIP - The authority of a federal court to hear and determine cases involving $10,000 or more and in which the parties are citizens of different states, or in which one party is an alien.

FEDERAL QUESTION - The authority of the federal courts to hear and determine in the first instance matters pertaining to the federal Constitution, federal law, or treaties of the United States.

SUBJECT MATTER JURISDICTION - The authority of the court to hear and decide actions involving a particular type of issue or subject.

REDNER v. SANDERS
Parties not identified.
2000 WL 1161080 (S.D.N.Y. 2000).

NATURE OF CASE: Motion to dismiss for lack of diversity jurisdiction.

FACT SUMMARY: When plaintiff claimed he was a "resident" of France, defendants argued that only plaintiff's "citizenship" in France would satisfy federal diversity jurisdictional requirements.

CONCISE RULE OF LAW: For purposes of diversity jurisdiction under 28 U.S.C. § 1332(a)(2), the controversy must be between citizens of a state and citizens or subjects of a foreign state, not merely "residents."

FACTS: Plaintiff filed a complaint in federal court, alleging that he was at all times mentioned "a citizen of the United States residing in France," and that defendants are residents of the State of New York. Defendants moved to dismiss for lack of subject matter jurisdiction, arguing that mere residency in a foreign country does not equate with citizenship of a foreign country as required by 28 U.S.C. § 1332(a)(2).

ISSUE: For purposes of diversity jurisdiction under 28 U.S.C. § 1332(a)(2), must the controversy be between citizens of a state and citizens or subjects of a foreign state, not merely "residents?"

HOLDING AND DECISION: (Griesa, J.) Yes. For purposes of diversity jurisdiction under 28 U.S.C. § 1332(a)(2), the controversy must be between citizens of a state and citizens or subjects of a foreign state, not merely "residents." Here, plaintiff's complaint speaks of his "residing" in France, whereas the statute speaks of *citizenship*. The two are not synonymous. It appears in fact that defendants are citizens of the State of New York. However, for jurisdiction to exist under (a)(2), plaintiff would need to be a citizen of a foreign state, not merely a resident, and the complaint itself actually alleges that plaintiff is a citizen of the United States. Thus, the case does not involve an action between citizens of the United States and a citizen of a foreign state. Accordingly, there is no jurisdiction under § 1332(a)(2). Motion granted and suit dismissed.

EDITOR'S ANALYSIS: In *Redner*, the court noted that plaintiff's affidavit was entirely lacking in details about what his living in France involved. Plaintiff provided no information about exactly where he lived, what kind of a residence he had, whether he had any family in France, or what professional activities he carried out in France.

QUICKNOTES
28 U.S.C. § 1332 – Provides for original jurisdiction in federal district court for all civil actions between citizens of different states.

NOTES:

SAADEH v. FAROUKI
Lender (P) v. Borrower (D)
107 F.3d 52 (D.C. Cir. 1997).

NATURE OF CASE: Appeal from judgment in breach of contract action.

FACT SUMMARY: Saadeh (P), a Greek citizen, sued Farouki (D), a Jordanian citizen with permanent resident status in Maryland.

CONCISE RULE OF LAW: Aliens cannot bring suit against each other in federal court due to the requirement of complete diversity.

FACTS: Saadeh (P), a Greek citizen, loaned money to Farouki (D), an international businessman living as a permanent resident in Maryland. After Farouki (D) defaulted on the loan, Saadeh (P) brought suit in federal district court for breach of contract. The district court granted judgment to Saadeh (P), but on appeal, the Court of Appeals asked the parties to brief the issue of subject matter jurisdiction.

ISSUE: Can aliens bring suit against each other in federal court?

HOLDING AND DECISION: (Rogers, J.) No. Aliens cannot bring suit against each other in federal court due to the requirement of complete diversity. Article III of the Constitution requires only minimal diversity between any two parties on opposite sides of an action. However, Congress has never granted federal district courts the full measure of diversity jurisdiction allowed by the Constitution. Congress has required complete diversity among parties, meaning that a suit could not involve an alien on each side of litigation. In 1988, Congress amended the diversity statute and provided that a permanent resident alien shall be deemed a citizen of the State in which the alien is domiciled. A literal reading of this provision would mean that Congress had abrogated the longstanding rule of complete diversity. But looking at the legislative history of the 1988 amendment reveals that a literal reading would be inappropriate. The amendment was actually made to reduce diversity jurisdiction by eliminating cases in which jurisdiction was proper only a permanent resident remained an alien citizen. There was certainly no intention to allow a suit in federal district court that did not involve a U.S. citizen on either side of the action. Accordingly, subject matter jurisdiction was lacking in Saadeh's (P) suit and dismissal is proper. Reversed.

EDITOR'S ANALYSIS: It should be noted that Farouki (D) became a citizen while the case was already underway. However, it is only a party's status at the time the action is started that is relevant in jurisdictional matters such as this one. Had Saadeh (P) waited until Farouki (P) was a citizen, there may have been jurisdiction.

QUICKNOTES

28 U.S.C. § 1332 - Provides for original jurisdiction in federal district court for all civil actions between citizens of different states.

NOTES:

JIN v. MINISTRY OF STATE SECURITY

Defamed individuals (P) v. Agencies of
Chinese government (D)
254 F.Supp.2d 61 (2003).

NATURE OF CASE: Motion to dismiss for lack of subject matter jurisdiction; motion to dismiss for failure to state a claim.

FACT SUMMARY: When Jin (P) and other Falun Gong practitioners brought suit in federal court, alleging a variety of civil rights and RICO (Racketeer Influenced and Corrupt Organizations Act) violations against the Chinese Ministry of State Security (D) and CTC (Chinese Television) for its extensive campaign within the United States to defame and discredit the Falun Gong practitioners, all defendants moved to dismiss the defamation claim for lack of subject matter jurisdiction.

CONCISE RULE OF LAW: Complexity of the litigation does not necessarily prevent a court from asserting supplemental subject matter jurisdiction under 28 U.S.C. § 1367.

FACTS: Jin (P) and 51 other Falun Gong practitioners brought suit in federal court, alleging a variety of civil rights and RICO violations against the Chinese Ministry of State Security (D) and CTC (Chinese Television) for its extensive campaign within the United States to defame and discredit the Falun Gong practitioners. Falun Gong, a self-improvement practice or discipline similar to Tai Chi, is rooted in ancient Chinese culture. When the Chinese government perceived this practice as a threat to its state security and stability, it undertook a widespread international campaign through mass media to discredit the Falun Gong practitioners, hence Jin's (P) defamation and RICO suit. The Ministry (D) moved to dismiss the defamation claim, arguing that the defamation claim was completely different from and unrelated to the other causes of action asserted in the complaint because it pertained to Falun Gong practitioners as a group while the other claims pertained to individual plaintiffs and that there were complex questions of state law raised by the defamation claim.

ISSUE: Does the complexity of the litigation necessarily prevent a court from asserting supplemental subject matter jurisdiction under 28 U.S.C. § 1367?

HOLDING AND DECISION: (Urbina, Dist. J.) No. Complexity of the litigation does not necessarily prevent a court from asserting supplemental subject matter jurisdiction under 28 U.S.C. § 1367. Here, because Jin's (P) and the other plaintiff's claims include claims under federal civil rights and conspiracy statutes, they have an independent basis for federal jurisdiction. The defamation claims share a common nucleus of operative facts with the other claims. The facts of the claim allege a series of steps, including the production and distribution of video, print, and other communications targeted at the Chinese-American community and public officials in America, taken by Ministry (D) and various other defendants to vilify and defame Jin (P). Whether or not the claim identifies the plaintiffs individually or collectively, the facts supporting the defamation claims are linked to the facts supporting the remaining claims because they form a key part of an alleged overarching campaign to abridge and nullify the rights and liberties of Jin (P) and the other Falun Gong practitioners. Because the defamation claim and the federal claims are related to the point that the plaintiffs would ordinarily be expected to try them all in one proceeding, the claims do derive "from a common nucleus of operative fact." While determining the correct application of the elements may be time-consuming, it does not mean the local law is so unsettled that the court must decline jurisdiction. The defamation claim does not raise complex issues of state law that outweigh the court's interest in promoting judicial economy. Here the interests of judicial economy, convenience, and fairness support the exercise of supplemental jurisdiction. Motion to dismiss for lack of subject matter jurisdiction is denied. However, Ministry's (D) motion to dismiss Jin's (P) defamation claim is granted as being outside the one-year period prescribed by the statute of limitations.

EDITOR'S ANALYSIS: In *Jin*, the court observed that the defense asserted only that the various states differed in their *application* of the elements of defamation, not that the laws themselves were necessarily overly complex.

QUICKNOTES

DEFAMATION - An intentional false publication, communicated publicly in either oral or written form, subjecting a person to scorn, hatred or ridicule, or injuring him or her in relation to his or her occupation or business.

SUPPLEMENTAL JURISDICTION - A doctrine granting authority to a federal court to hear a claim that does not invoke diversity jurisdiction if it arises from the same transaction or occurrence as the primary action.

28 U.S.C. § 1367 - Codifies supplemental jurisdiction and those factors that warrant declining jurisdiction.

CATERPILLAR, INC. v. LEWIS
Manufacturer (D) v. Injured person (P)
519 U.S. 61 (1996).

NATURE OF CASE: Appeal of judgment vacating verdict for the defense in personal injury case.

FACT SUMMARY: A federal district court denied a motion to remand a case to state court even though the case lacked complete diversity and later entered judgment after the nondiverse defendant had settled out of the case.

CONCISE RULE OF LAW: A district court's error in failing to remand a case improperly removed does not prevent adjudication if the jurisdictional requirements are satisfied at the time of judgment.

FACTS: Lewis (P) filed a personal injury claim in state court. The case was removed to federal district court at Caterpillar's (D) request although there was not complete diversity of citizenship among the parties. After the removal, Lewis (P) moved to remand the case to state court for lack of federal jurisdiction. The district court denied the motion. Subsequently, the nondiverse defendant settled out of the case. At trial, Caterpillar (D) prevailed. Lewis (P) appealed, claiming that the district court did not have jurisdiction at the time of removal. The court of appeals agreed and vacated the judgment. Caterpillar (D) appealed.

ISSUE: Does a district court's error in failing to remand a case improperly removed prevent adjudication if the jurisdictional requirements are satisfied at the time of judgment?

HOLDING AND DECISION: (Ginsburg, J.) No. A district court's error in failing to remand a case improperly removed does not prevent adjudication if the jurisdictional requirements are satisfied at the time of judgment. The lack of subject matter jurisdiction at the time of removal is not fatal to later adjudication of the case. The only issue is whether the jurisdictional requirements are met at the time the judgment is entered. In the present case, allowing removal when there was not complete diversity was a mistake by the district court. However, when judgment was entered, complete diversity did exist. Thus, there was sufficient subject matter jurisdiction to adjudicate the case. Reversed.

EDITOR'S ANALYSIS: In the present case, the nondiverse defendant settled out of the litigation prior to judgment. It would present a more difficult question if the nondiverse defendant had not been dismissed from the case by the district court. In such circumstances, the federal court would be acting without any subject matter jurisdiction.

QUICKNOTES

DIVERSITY OF CITIZENSHIP - The authority of a federal court to hear and determine cases involving $10,000 or more and in which the parties are citizens of different states, or in which one party is an alien.

SUBJECT MATTER JURISDICTION - A court's ability to adjudicate a specific category of cases based on the subject matter of the dispute.

NOTES:

CHAPTER 4
THE ERIE PROBLEM

QUICK REFERENCE RULES OF LAW

1. **Constitutionalizing the Issue.** Although the 1789 Rules of Decision Act left federal courts unfettered to apply their own rules of procedure in common law actions brought in federal court, state law governs substantive issues. State law includes not only statutory law, but case law as well. (Erie Railroad v. Tompkins)

2. **Interpreting the Constitutional Command of Erie.** Where a state statute that would completely bar recovery in state court has significant effect on the outcome-determination of the action, even though the suit be brought in equity, the federal court is bound by the state law. (Guaranty Trust Co. v. York)

3. **Interpreting the Constitutional Command of Erie.** The *Erie* doctrine requires that federal courts in diversity cases must respect the definitions of rights and obligations created by state courts, but state laws cannot alter the essential characteristics and functions of the federal courts, and the jury function is such an essential function (provided for in the Seventh Amendment). (Byrd v. Blue Ridge Rural Electric Cooperative)

4. **De-Constitutionalizing Erie.** The *Erie* doctrine mandates that federal courts are to apply state substantive law and federal procedural law, but, where matters fall roughly between the two and are rationally capable of classification as either, the Constitution grants the federal court system the power to regulate their practice and pleading (procedure). (Hanna v. Plumer)

5. **Determining the Scope of Federal Law: Avoiding and Accommodating Erie.** As a matter of federal common law, a state rule of claim preclusion applies to dismissals ordered by either state or federal courts, except where state law is incompatible with federal interests. (Semtek International Inc. v. Lockheed Martin Corporation)

ERIE RAILROAD CO. v. TOMPKINS
Train company (D) v. Pedestrian (P)
304 U.S. 64 (1938).

NATURE OF CASE: Action to recover damages for personal injury allegedly caused by negligent conduct.

FACT SUMMARY: In a personal injury suit, a federal district court trial judge refused to apply applicable state law because such law was "general" (judge-made) and not embodied in any statute.

CONCISE RULE OF LAW: Although the 1789 Rules of Decision Act left federal courts unfettered to apply their own rules of procedure in common law actions brought in federal court, state law governs substantive issues. State law includes not only statutory law, but case law as well.

FACTS: Tompkins (P) was walking in a right of way parallel to some railroad tracks when an Erie Railroad (D) train came by. Tompkins (P) was struck and injured by what he would, at trial, claim to be an open door extending from one of the rail cars. Under Pennsylvania case law (the applicable law since the accident occurred there), state courts would have treated Tompkins (P) as a trespasser in denying him recovery for other than wanton or willful misconduct on Erie's (D) part. Under "general" law, recognized in federal courts, Tompkins (P) would have been regarded as a licensee and would only have been obligated to show ordinary negligence. Because Erie (D) was a New York corporation, Tompkins (P) brought suit in a federal district court in New York, where he won a judgment for $30,000. Upon appeal to a federal circuit court, the decision was affirmed.

ISSUE: Was the trial court in error in refusing to recognize state case law as the proper rule of decision in deciding the substantive issue of liability?

HOLDING AND DECISION: (Brandeis, J.) Yes. The Court's opinion is in four parts: (1) *Swift v. Tyson*, 41 U.S. (16 Pet.) 1 (1842), which held that federal courts exercising jurisdiction on the ground of diversity of citizenship need not, in matters of general jurisprudence, apply the unwritten law of the state as declared by its highest court, is overruled. Section 34 of the Federal Judiciary Act of 1789, c. 20, 28 U.S. § 725 requires that federal courts in all matters except those where some federal law is controlling, apply as their rules of decision the law of the state, unwritten as well as written. Up to this time, federal courts had assumed the power to make "general law" decisions even though Congress was powerless to enact "general law" statutes. (2) *Swift* had numerous political and social defects. The hoped-for uniformity among state courts had not occurred; there was no satisfactory way to distinguish between local and general law. On the other hand, *Swift* introduced grave discrimination by noncitizens against citizens. The privilege of selecting the court

for resolving disputes rested with the noncitizen who could pick the more favorable forum. The resulting far-reaching discrimination was due to the broad province accorded "general law" in which many matters of seemingly local concern were included. Furthermore, local citizens could move out of the state and bring suit in a federal court if they were disposed to do so; corporations, similarly, could simply reincorporate in another state. More than statutory relief is involved here; the unconstitutionality of *Swift* is clear. (3) Except in matters governed by the Federal Constitution or by acts of Congress, the law to be applied in any case is the law of the state. There is no federal common law. The federal courts have no power derived from the Constitution or by Congress to declare substantive rules of common law applicable in a state whether they be "local" or "general" in nature. (4) The federal district court was bound to follow the Pennsylvania case law which would have denied recovery to Tompkins (P).

CONCURRENCE IN PART: (Reed, J.) It is unnecessary to go beyond interpreting the meaning of "laws" in the Rules of Decision Act. Article III, and the Necessary and Proper Clause of Article I of the Constitution, might provide Congress with the power to declare rules of substantive law for federal courts to follow.

EDITOR'S ANALYSIS: *Erie* can fairly be characterized as the most significant and sweeping decision on civil procedure ever handed down by the U.S. Supreme Court. As interpreted in subsequent decisions, *Erie* held that while federal courts may apply their own rules of procedure, issues of substantive law must be decided in accord with the applicable state law—usually the state in which the federal court sits. Note, however, how later Supreme Court decisions have made inroads into the broad doctrine enunciated here.

QUICKNOTES
DIVERSITY OF CITIZENSHIP - The authority of a federal court to hear and determine cases involving $10,000 or more and in which the parties are citizens of different states, or in which one party is an alien.

FEDERAL JURISDICTION - The authority of federal courts to hear and determine cases of a particular nature derived from the United States Constitution and rules promulgated by Congress pursuant thereto.

SUBJECT MATTER JURISDICTION - The authority of the court to hear and decide actions involving a particular type of issue or subject.

GUARANTY TRUST CO. v. YORK
Trustee (D) v. Note holder (P)
326 U.S. 99 (1945).

NATURE OF CASE: Class action alleging fraud and misrepresentation.

FACT SUMMARY: York (P), barred from filing suit in state court because of the state statute of limitations, brought an equity action in federal court based upon diversity of citizenship jurisdiction.

CONCISE RULE OF LAW: Where a state statute that would completely bar recovery in state court has significant effect on the outcome-determination of the action, even though the suit be brought in equity, the federal court is bound by the state law.

FACTS: York (P) sued Guaranty Trust (D) in a federal diversity action. New York substantive law governed. Guaranty Trust (D) asserted the defense of the statute of limitations. York (P) argued that the statute of limitations did not bar the suit because it was on the "equity side" of federal court. The federal court of appeals ruled the suit was not barred, and Guaranty Trust (D) appealed.

ISSUE: Does a state statute of limitations, which would bar a suit in state court, also act as a bar to the same action if the suit is brought in equity in federal court and jurisdiction being based on diversity of citizenship?

HOLDING AND DECISION: (Frankfurter, J.) Yes. A state statute of limitations, which would bar a suit in state court, may also act as a bar to the same action if the suit is brought in equity in federal court and jurisdiction is based on diversity of citizenship. *Erie Railroad Co. v. Tompkins* overruled a particular way of looking at law after its inadequacies had been laid bare. The question is not whether a statute of limitations is deemed a matter of "procedure" in some sense. The question is whether such a statute concerns merely the manner and the means by which a right to recover, as recognized by the state, is enforced, or whether such statutory limitation is a matter of substance in the aspect that alone is relevant to the problem, namely, whether it significantly affects the result of a litigation for a federal court to disregard a law of a state that would be controlling in an action upon the same claim by the same parties in a state court. In essence, the intent of *Erie* was to insure that, in all cases where a federal court is exercising jurisdiction solely because of the diversity of citizenship of the parties, the outcome of the litigation in the federal court should be substantially the same, so far as legal rules determine the outcome of a litigation, as it would be if tried in a state court. Reversed and remanded.

EDITOR'S ANALYSIS: While clarifying *Erie*, the legal foundation supporting *Guaranty Trust* may be undergoing a process of slow erosion by contemporary courts. *Hanna v. Plumer* held that where state law conflicts with the Federal Rules of Civil Procedure, the latter prevails regardless of the effect on outcome of the litigation. And in *Byrd v. Blue Ridge Elec. Cooperative*, the Court suggested that some constitutional doctrines (there, the right to a jury trial in federal court) are so important as to be controlling over state law, regardless of whether application of such constitutional doctrines would result in an outcome different than that which would result under the law of the state in which the federal court sits.

QUICKNOTES

COMITY - A rule pursuant to which courts in one state give deference to the statutes and judicial decisions of another.

DIVERSITY OF CITIZENSHIP - The authority of a federal court to hear and determine cases involving $10,000 or more and in which the parties are citizens of different states, or in which one party is an alien.

BYRD v. BLUE RIDGE ELECTRIC COOPERATIVE
Injured employee (P) v. Electric utility (D)
356 U.S. 525 (1958).

NATURE OF CASE: Negligence action for damages.

FACT SUMMARY: Byrd (P) was injured while connecting power lines for a subcontractor of Blue Ridge Electric Cooperative, Inc. (D).

CONCISE RULE OF LAW: The *Erie* doctrine requires that federal courts in diversity cases must respect the definitions of rights and obligations created by state courts, but state laws cannot alter the essential characteristics and functions of the federal courts, and the jury function is such an essential function (provided for in the Seventh Amendment).

FACTS: Byrd (P) was injured while on a construction job for Blue Ridge (D) and sued Blue Ridge (D) in tort. Although Byrd (P) was employed by an independent contractor, Blue Ridge (D) argued that Byrd (P) was performing the same work as Blue Ridge's (D) regular employees and was therefore a "statutory" employee whose exclusive remedy was under the South Carolina workers' compensation legislation. Blue Ridge (D) contended that despite the *Erie* doctrine, South Carolina law could not be allowed to preclude his right to a jury.

ISSUE: Do *Erie* doctrine considerations require that all state determinations of rights be upheld regardless of their intrusions into federal determinations?

HOLDING AND DECISION: (Brennan, J.) No. The *Erie* doctrine requires that federal courts in diversity cases must respect the definitions of rights and obligations created by state courts, but state laws cannot alter the essential characteristics and functions of the federal courts, and the jury function is such an essential function (provided for in the Seventh Amendment). The South Carolina determination here that immunity is a question of law to be tried by a judge is merely a determination of the form and mode of enforcing immunity. It does not involve any essential relationship or determination of right created by the state. Of course, the *Erie* doctrine will reach even such form and mode determinations where no affirmative countervailing considerations can be found. Here, however, the Seventh Amendment makes the jury function an essential factor in the federal process protected by the Constitution. Reversed and remanded.

EDITOR'S ANALYSIS: This case points up a major retreat by the Court in its interpretation of the *Erie* doctrine. The *Guaranty Trust* case had stated that the *Erie* doctrine required that federal courts not tamper with state remedies for violations of state-created rights. In *Byrd*, the Court retreats, stating that questions of mere "form and mode" of remedy (i.e., trial by jury or judge) is not necessarily the province of the states where essential federal rights (i.e., Seventh Amendment) are involved. Note that the Court does not abandon the *Guaranty Trust* rationale, however (that the outcome of a case should not be affected by the choice of court in which it is filed). The Court expresses doubt that the permitting of trial by jury here will make any difference in the final determination of the case. Note the inconsistency of argument here since the Court first states that trial by jury is an essential right, then states that it is really insignificant after all.

NOTES:

HANNA v. PLUMER

Injured claimant (P) v. Executor of defendant (D)
380 U.S. 460 (1965).

NATURE OF CASE: Appeal of dismissal in federal diversity tort action.

FACT SUMMARY: Hanna (P) filed tort action in federal court in Massachusetts, where Plumer (D) resided, for an auto accident that occurred in South Carolina.

CONCISE RULE OF LAW: The *Erie* doctrine mandates that federal courts are to apply state substantive law and federal procedural law, but, where matters fall roughly between the two and are rationally capable of classification as either, the Constitution grants the federal court system the power to regulate their practice and pleading (procedure).

FACTS: In this diversity suit for personal injuries, Plumer (D) represented the estate of one of the drivers involved. Massachusetts law provided that suits required personal service of process on the estate's executor. Process was instead served under Fed. R. Civ. P. 4(d)(1), which allowed for the summons and complaint to be left with a competent adult at the defendant's residence. The federal circuit court agreed with the federal district court that the claim should be dismissed because of Hanna's (P) failure to comply with the state's method of serving process within the applicable limitations period. Hanna (P) appealed.

ISSUE: Does the *Erie* doctrine classification of "substantive law questions" extend to embrace questions involving both substantive and procedural considerations merely because such a question might have an effect on the determination of the substantive outcome of the case?

HOLDING AND DECISION: (Warren, C.J.) No. The *Erie* doctrine mandates that federal courts are to apply state substantive law and federal procedural law, and, where matters fall roughly between the two and are rationally capable of classification as either, the Constitution grants the federal court system the power to regulate their practice and pleading (procedure). It is well settled that the Enabling Act for the Federal Rules of Civil Procedure requires that a procedural effect of any rule on the outcome of a case be shown to actually "abridge, enlarge, or modify" the substantive law in a case for the *Erie* doctrine to come into play. Where, as here, the question only goes to procedural requirements (i.e., service of summons, a dismissal for improper service here would not alter the substantive right of Hanna [P] to serve Plumer [D] personally and refile or effect the substantive law of negligence in the case), Article III and the Necessary and Proper Clause provide that the Congress has a right to provide rules for the federal court system such as Fed. R. Civ. P. 4(d)(1). "Outcome determination analysis was never intended to serve as

a talisman" for the *Erie* doctrine. The judgment of the appellate court must be reversed.

CONCURRENCE: (Harlan, J.) I agree with the result of the Court and its rejection of the outcome determination test. However, the Court was wrong in stating that anything arguably procedural is constitutionally placed within the province of the federal government to regulate. The test for "substantive" would be whether "the choice of rule would substantially affect those primary decisions respecting human conduct which our constitutional system leaves to state regulation."

EDITOR'S ANALYSIS: This case points up a return to the basic rationales of *Erie R. Co. v. Tompkins*, 304 U.S. 64 (1938). First, the Court asserts that one important consideration in determining how a particular question should be classified (substantive or procedural) is the avoidance of "forum shopping" (the practice of choosing one forum such as federal, to file in, in order to gain the advantages of one), which permits jurisdictions to infringe on the substantive law-defining powers of each other. Second, the Court seeks to avoid inequitable administration of the laws which would result from allowing jurisdictional considerations to determine substantive rights. Justice Warren here, in rejecting the "outcome determination" test, asserts that any rule must be measured ultimately against the Federal Rules Enabling Act and the Constitution.

QUICKNOTES

PROCEDURAL LAW - Law relating to the process of carrying out a lawsuit and not to the substantive rights asserted by the parties.

SUBSTANTIVE LAW - Law that pertains to the rights and interests of the parties and upon which a cause of action may be based.

SEMTEK INTL., INC. v. LOCKHEED MARTIN CORPORATION
Injured party (P) v. Alleged wrongdoer (D)
531 U.S. 497 (2001).

NATURE OF CASE: Appeal from affirmance of dismissal of state action on res judicata grounds, giving effect to dismissal by federal court sitting in diversity jurisdiction.

FACT SUMMARY: When Semtek International, Inc.'s (Semtek's) (P) breach of contract and tort claims against Lockheed Martin Corp. (Lockheed) (D) were barred by California's two-year statute of limitations, Semtek (P) filed the same claims in state court in Maryland, which had a three-year statute of limitations.

CONCISE RULE OF LAW: As a matter of federal common law, a state rule of claim preclusion applies to dismissals ordered by either state or federal courts, except where state law is incompatible with federal interests.

FACTS: Semtek International, Inc. (Semtek) (P) sued Lockheed Martin Corp. (Lockheed) (D) for breach of contract and tort claims. After removal to federal court in California, the action was dismissed because it was were barred by California's two-year statute of limitations. Semtek (P) filed the same claims in state court in Maryland, which had a three-year statute of limitations. The Maryland court dismissed the case on the ground of res judicata. In affirming, the Maryland Court of Special Appeals held that, regardless of whether California state law would have accorded claim preclusive effect to a statute-of-limitations dismissal by one of its own courts, the California federal court's dismissal barred the Maryland complaint because the res judicata effect of federal diversity judgments is prescribed by federal law, under which the earlier dismissal was on the merits and claim preclusive.

ISSUE: As a matter of federal common law, does a state rule of claim preclusion apply to dismissals ordered by either state or federal courts, except where state law is incompatible with federal interests?

HOLDING AND DECISION: (Scalia, J.) Yes. As a matter of federal common law, a state rule of claim preclusion applies to dismissals ordered by either state or federal courts, except where state law is incompatible with federal interests. Semtek (P) asserts that *Dupasseur v. Rochereau,* 21 Wall. 130 (1875), which held that the res judicata effect of a federal diversity judgment "is such as would belong to judgments of the State courts rendered under similar circumstances," governs here. That case is not dispositive, however, because it was decided under the Conformity Act of 1872, which required federal courts to apply the procedural law of the forum state in nonequity cases. However,

claim-preclusive effect is not, as Lockheed (D) asserts, required by Fed. R. Civ. P. § 41(b)—which provides that, unless the court "otherwise specifies," an involuntary dismissal, other than a dismissal for lack of jurisdiction, improper venue, or failure to join a party under Rule 19, "operates as an adjudication upon the merits." Although the original connotation of a judgment "on the merits" was one that passes directly on the substance of a claim (which would be claim-preclusive), the meaning of the term has changed, and does not necessarily designate a judgment effecting claim preclusion. There are a number of reasons that support this conclusion. First, it would be peculiar to announce a federally prescribed rule on claim preclusion in a default rule for determining a dismissal's import, or to find a rule governing the effect to be accorded federal judgments by other courts ensconced in rules governing the internal procedures of the rendering court itself. Moreover, if the rule were interpreted as Lockheed (D) suggests, it would in many cases violate the federalism principle of *Erie R. Co. v. Tompkins,* 304 U.S. 64 (1938), by engendering substantial variations in outcomes between state and federal litigation which would likely influence forum choice. Finally, the Court itself has never relied upon Rule 41(b) when recognizing the claim-preclusive effect of federal judgments in federal-question cases. Rule 41(a) makes clear that "an adjudication upon the merits" in Rule 41(b) is the opposite of a dismissal without prejudice—which means that it prevents refiling of the claim in the same court. That is undoubtedly a necessary condition, but not a sufficient one, for claim-preclusive effect in other courts. Given that neither Semtek's (P) approach, nor Lockheed's (D) approach is satisfactory, what does govern the claim-preclusive effect of the California federal diversity judgment in Maryland state court? The answer is that federal common law governs the claim-preclusive effect of a dismissal by a federal court sitting in diversity, and that it is up to this Court to determine the appropriate federal rule. Since in diversity cases state, rather than federal, substantive law is at issue, there is no need for a uniform federal rule; and nationwide uniformity is better served by having the same claim-preclusive rule (the state rule) apply whether the dismissal has been ordered by a state or a federal court. Any other rule would produce the sort of forum shopping and inequitable administration of the laws that *Erie* seeks to avoid. While the federal reference to state law will not be workable in situations in which the state law is incompatible with federal interests, no such conflict exists here. Reversed and remanded.

EDITOR'S ANALYSIS: An example of where federal reference to state law will not work is where state law has not given claim-preclusive effect to dismissals for willful violation of discovery orders. In such a case, the federal courts' interest in the integrity of their own processes might justify a federal rule of claim preclusion that does not reflect state law. Of course, that kind of exceptional case was not before the court.

CHAPTER 5
INCENTIVES TO LITIGATE

QUICK REFERENCE RULES OF LAW

1. **Liquidated, Statutory, and Punitive Damages**. Punitive damages may be awarded only when they are reasonable and proportionate to the wrong committed. (State Farm Mutual Automobile Insurance Co. v. Campbell)

2. **Is There a Remedial Hierarchy?** The main prerequisite to obtaining injunctive relief is a finding that plaintiff is being threatened by some injury for which he has no adequate legal remedy. (Sigma Chemical Co. v. Harris)

3. **From Fee Spreading to Fee Shifting.** A court may in its discretion accept a settlement that denies statutorily authorized fees. (Evans v. Jeff D.)

4. **From Fee Spreading to Fee Shifting.** An award of attorney's fees and costs to a "prevailing party" under federal statutes, may be awarded only to a party who has secured a judgment on the merits or a court-ordered consent decree. (Buckhannon Board and Care Home, Inc. v. West Virginia Department of Health and Human Resources)

5. **Preliminary Injunctions and Temporary Restraining Orders: The Basic Problem.** A preliminary injunction should be granted if the moving party demonstrates either a combination of probable success and the possibility of irreparable harm, or that serious questions are raised and the balance of hardship tips sharply in his favor. (William Inglis & Sons Baking Co. v. ITT Continental Baking Co.)

6. **Provisional Remedies and Due Process.** Procedural due process requires that parties whose rights are to be affected are entitled to be heard at a meaningful time; and in order that they may enjoy that right they must be notified. (Fuentes v. Shevin)

STATE FARM MUTUAL AUTOMOBILE INSURANCE CO. v. CAMPBELL

Insurance company (D) v. Insured motorist (P)
538 U.S. 408 (2003).

NATURE OF CASE: Appeal from a punitive damages award.

FACT SUMMARY: When Campbell (P) received a jury award of $1 million in compensatory damages and $145 million in punitive damages, State Farm (D) appealed, arguing that such a disproportionate award of punitive damages violated due process.

CONCISE RULE OF LAW: Punitive damages may be awarded only when they are reasonable and proportionate to the wrong committed.

FACTS: Campbell (P), driving on the wrong side of a two-lane highway, caused an oncoming vehicle to swerve and crash, killing its driver and permanently disabling another driver. In the ensuing wrongful death suit and tort action against him, Campbell (P) insisted he was not at fault. Campbell's insurer, State Farm (D), against the advice of its own investigators, contested Campbell's (P) liability and refused to settle with the families of the deceased and injured. Instead, State Farm (D) took the case to trial where a jury determined that Campbell (P) was 100 percent at fault and returned a judgment of $185,849 against Campbell (P), far more than the amount offered in settlement. After State Farm (D) refused to cover Campbell's (P) excess liability, the injured parties and Campbell (P) reached an agreement by which the estate would not seek satisfaction of their claim against Campbell (P) in exchange for which Campbell (P) would pursue a bad faith action against State Farm (D) and would give most of the recovery, if any, to the injured parties. Campbell filed the suit and went to trial, resulting in a jury award of $2.6 million (later reduced to $1 million) in compensatory damages and $145 million in punitive damages. State Farm (D) appealed.

ISSUE: May punitive damages be awarded only when they are reasonable and proportionate to the wrong committed?

HOLDING AND DECISION: (Kennedy, J.) Yes. Punitive damages may be awarded only when they are reasonable and proportionate to the wrong committed. This case is neither close nor difficult. It was error to reinstate the jury's $145 million punitive damages award. While State Farm's (D) handling of Campbell's (P) claim merits no praise, a more moderate punishment for its reprehensible conduct could have satisfied the state's legitimate objectives, and the state courts should have gone no further. This case, instead, was wrongfully used as a platform to expose, and punish, the perceived deficiencies of State Farm's (D) operations throughout the country. Furthermore, the Utah courts erred in relying upon evidence of State Farm's (D) other state's practices and conduct that bore no relation to Campbell's (P) harm. Due process does not permit courts, in the calculation of punitive damages, to adjudicate the merits of other parties' hypothetical claims against a defendant under the guise of the reprehensibility analysis. Single-digit multipliers are more likely to comport with due process, while still achieving the state's goals of deterrence and retribution, than awards with ratios of 500 to 1 or, as here, 145 to 1. Finally, the wealth of a defendant cannot justify an otherwise unconstitutional punitive damages award. Reversed and remanded.

DISSENT: (Ginsburg, J.) The Supreme Court has no warrant to reform state law governing awards of punitive damages.

EDITOR'S ANALYSIS: In *State Farm*, the Court noted that although punitive damages awards serve the same purposes as criminal penalties, defendants subjected to punitive damages in civil cases have not been accorded the protections applicable in a criminal proceeding. This fact, said the Court, increases the Court's concern over the imprecise manner in which punitive damages systems are administered.

QUICKNOTES

PUNITIVE DAMAGES - Damages exceeding the actual injury suffered for the purposes of punishment, deterrence and comfort to plaintiff.

NOTES:

SIGMA CHEMICAL CO. v. HARRIS
Chemical company employer (P) v. Purchasing agent (D)
605 F. Supp. 1253 (E.D. Mo. 1985).

NATURE OF CASE: Action for permanent injunction and determination of the validity of a restrictive covenant.

FACT SUMMARY: In Sigma Chemical's (P) action against Harris (D) for breach of a restrictive covenant, Sigma (P) contended that a permanent injunction should be entered against Harris (D) for violating the terms of the employment contract because he was aware of the restrictions imposed upon him by the contract, and that he took a voluntary risk by deciding to violate the contract.

CONCISE RULE OF LAW: The main prerequisite to obtaining injunctive relief is a finding that plaintiff is being threatened by some injury for which he has no adequate legal remedy.

FACTS: Sigma Chemical (P) employed Harris (D) as a purchasing agent whose job consisted of matching the right chemical supplier with a chemical product sold by Sigma (P). Harris (D) signed an agreement, when he went to work for Sigma (P), that he would not work for a competitor for two years after leaving Sigma (P), and even after that period would not disclose any confidential information acquired from Sigma (P). Harris (D) became dissatisfied with Sigma (P), began looking for another job and, after finding one with a competitor of Sigma's (P), quit his Sigma (P) job. At the new job, Harris (D) used information acquired during his employment at Sigma (P) which helped his new employer find new sources of various chemicals. Sigma (P) then sued Harris(D) for breach of his employment contract, contending that a permanent injunction should be entered against Harris (D) for violating the terms of the contract because Harris (D) was aware of the restrictions imposed upon him by that contract, and that he took a voluntary risk by deciding to violate the contract.

ISSUE: Is the main prerequisite to obtaining injunctive relief a finding that plaintiff is being threatened by some injury for which he has no adequate legal remedy?

HOLDING AND DECISION: (Nangle, C.J.) Yes. The main prerequisite to obtaining injunctive relief is a finding that plaintiff is being threatened by some injury for which he has no adequate legal remedy. Also, a determination whether to issue an injunction involves a balancing of the interests of the parties who might be affected by the court's decision—the hardship on plaintiff if relief is denied as opposed to the hardship to defendant if it is granted. Here, it is clear that Harris (D) is violating the restrictive covenant by working for Sigma's (P) competitor. Under these circumstances, there is a strong threat of irreparable injury to Sigma (P). The harm that would occur to Harris (D) if the injunction should be granted is not insubstantial, but the threat of harm to Sigma (P) greatly outweighs the threat of harm to Harris (D).

EDITOR'S ANALYSIS: Courts consider two factors in discussing the propriety of issuing an injunction. These are: the inadequacy of legal remedy and the balance of hardships to the two parties. Injunctions are by far the most prevalent form of equitable relief and with an injunction, courts will order parties to do things or to refrain from doing them.

QUICKNOTES
EQUITABLE RELIEF - A remedy that is based upon principles of fairness as opposed to rules of law.

INJUNCTION - A remedy imposed by the court ordering a party to cease the conduct of a specific activity.

RESTRICTIVE COVENANT - A promise contained in a deed to limit the uses to which the property will be made.

NOTES:

EVANS v. JEFF D.
Mentally disabled children (P) v. State (D)
475 U.S. 717 (1986).

NATURE OF CASE: Review of settlement approved by court in class action for injunctive relief.

FACT SUMMARY: The legal aid attorney representing a class of handicapped children (P) accepted settlement offer that denied attorney fees.

CONCISE RULE OF LAW: A court may in its discretion accept a settlement that denies statutorily authorized fees.

FACTS: Johnson, an Idaho Legal Aid Society attorney, represented a class of emotionally and mentally disturbed children (P) seeking injunctive relief from the State of Idaho (D) to improve their treatment. Johnson accepted a settlement offer which granted the plaintiff class generous injunctive relief, but denied Johnson his statutorily authorized fees. Legal Aid contended that the court abused its discretion in accepting a settlement conditioned on the denial of attorney fees and sought appellate review. Legal Aid argued that Johnson was forced to accept the settlement to obtain the most favorable relief for his clients because of his ethical obligation to his clients, and, therefore, the court had a duty to reject the settlement. The appellate court found an abuse of discretion. The State (D) appealed.

ISSUE: May a court in its discretion accept a settlement that denies statutorily authorized fees?

HOLDING AND DECISION: (Stevens, J.) Yes. A court may in its discretion accept a settlement which denies statutorily authorized fees. The Fees Act and its legislative history do not indicate that Congress intended to ban fee waivers conditioned on favorable settlement terms. Courts may appraise the reasonableness of settlement offers that deny fees on a case-by-case basis until Congress commands that fees be paid. Reversed.

EDITOR'S ANALYSIS: Ethical issues abound in the area of attorney fees. It is good practice to discuss the issue of fees with clients early on in representation. Many states have statutes that require the attorney fee agreement to be in writing if the fees are likely to exceed a set amount. If Johnson had a written fee agreement with his clients, this might have provided him with some leverage. If Johnson had disclosed the fact that he had a written fee agreement and the State (D) had continued to push for a settlement without fees, this might be construed as tortious interference with contract.

QUICKNOTES

INJUNCTIVE RELIEF - A count order issued as a remedy, requiring a person to do, or prohibiting that person from doing, a specific act.

SETTLEMENT OFFER - An offer made by one party to a lawsuit to the other agreeing upon the determination of rights and issues between them, thus disposing of the need for judicial determination.

NOTES:

BUCKHANNON BOARD AND CARE HOME, INC. v. WEST VIRGINIA DEPARTMENT OF HEALTH AND HUMAN RESOURCES

Declaratory relief complainant (P) v. State (D)
532 U.S. 598 (2001).

NATURE OF CASE: Appeal of denial of attorney's fees award.

FACT SUMMARY: Buckhannon Board and Care Home, Inc. (P) brought suit to declare provisions of a state statute invalid as violating a federal statute. When the state statute was amended to delete the attacked provisions, Buckhannon (P) sought attorney's fees under the federal statute even though its federal court suit was dismissed as moot.

CONCISE RULE OF LAW: An award of attorney's fees and costs to a "prevailing party" under federal statutes, may be awarded only to a party who has secured a judgment on the merits or a court-ordered consent decree.

FACTS: Buckhannon Board and Care Home, Inc. (P), which operated care homes and assisted living facilities, ran afoul of a state regulation that required residents to be sufficiently ambulatory to get out of a burning building. After receiving a cease and desist order from the West Virginia Department of Health and Human Resources (D) requiring closure of its residential care facilities, Buckhannon (P) brought suit against the latter, seeking declaratory and injunctive relief that the self-preservation requirement violated the Fair Housing Amendments Act of 1990. The West Virginia Legislature subsequently enacted legislation eliminating the self-preservation requirement, and the federal district court dismissed Buckhannon's (P) suit as moot. Buckhannon (P) thereupon requested attorney's fees as the "prevailing party" under the Fair Housing Amendments Act. The court denied the motion, the court of appeals affirmed, and Buckhannon (P) appealed.

ISSUE: May an award of attorney's fees and costs to a "prevailing party" under federal statutes, be awarded only to a party who has secured a judgment on the merits or a court-ordered consent decree?

HOLDING AND DECISION: (Rehnquist, C.J.) Yes. An award of attorney's fees and costs to a "prevailing party" under federal statutes, may be awarded only to a party who has secured a judgment on the merits or a court-ordered consent decree. In designating those parties eligible for an award of litigation costs, Congress employed the term "prevailing party," a legal term of art which indicates one who has been awarded some relief by the court. Enforceable judgments on the merits and court-ordered consent decrees create the "material alteration of the legal relationship of the parties" necessary to permit an award of attorney's fees. However, the "catalyst theory," which would allow

an award where there is no judicially sanctioned change in the relationship of the parties, should not give rise to an attorney fees award. A defendant's voluntary change in conduct, although perhaps accomplishing what the plaintiff sought to achieve by the lawsuit, lacks the necessary judicial *imprimatur* on the change. The legislative history on the issue is at best ambiguous as to the availability of the "catalyst" theory for awarding attorney's fees. Particularly in view of the "American Rule" that attorney's fees will not be awarded absent *explicit* statutory authority, such legislative history is clearly insufficient to alter the accepted meaning of the statutory term. Affirmed.

DISSENT: (Ginsburg, J.) To "prevail" so as to receive attorney's fees, it should not be a requirement that the court enter a judgment on the merits. Nor should there necessarily be any finding of wrongdoing. A court-approved settlement will do. The catalyst rule, as applied by the clear majority of Federal Circuits, is a key component of the fee-shifting statutes Congress adopted to advance enforcement of civil rights.

EDITOR'S ANALYSIS: In *Buckhannon*, the U.S. Supreme Court noted that, in addition to judgments on the merits, settlement agreements enforced through a consent decree may serve as the basis for an award of attorney's fees.

NOTES:

WILLIAM INGLIS & SONS BAKING CO. v. ITT CONTINENTAL BAKING CO.

Baker (P) v. Baking company (D)

526 F.2d 86 (9th Cir. 1976).

NATURE OF CASE: Appeal from denial of preliminary injunction.

FACT SUMMARY: Inglis (P) brought this suit for a preliminary injunction against ITT (D) for violations of antitrust provisions, and the district court denied the injunction on the ground of the lack of probability that Inglis (P) would succeed on the merits.

CONCISE RULE OF LAW: A preliminary injunction should be granted if the moving party demonstrates either a combination of probable success and the possibility of irreparable harm, or that serious questions are raised and the balance of hardship tips sharply in his favor.

FACTS: Inglis (P) brought suit for a preliminary injunction against ITT (D) and other bakers for alleged violations of the Sherman Act, the Robinson-Patman Act, and applicable California laws. The district court applied only the probable success-irreparable injury test and denied the injunction on the ground that the court was not convinced of the probability that Inglis (P) would succeed on the merits. Inglis (P) appealed.

ISSUE: Should a preliminary injunction be granted if the moving party demonstrates either a combination of probable success and the possibility of irreparable harm, or that serious questions are raised and the balance of hardship tips sharply in his favor?

HOLDING AND DECISION: (Skopil, J.) Yes. A grant or denial of a preliminary injunction is subject to reversal only if the lower court based its decision upon an erroneous legal premise or abused its discretion. The district court in this case did not abuse its discretion. However, it did fail to apply an alternative test as to whether a moving party is entitled to a preliminary injunction. A preliminary injunction should be granted if the moving party demonstrates either a combination of probable success and the possibility of irreparable harm, or that serious questions are raised and the balance of hardship tips sharply in his favor. The district court applied only the first part of the test. Reversed and remanded.

EDITOR'S ANALYSIS: This decision does not ensure Inglis (P) that it will obtain the preliminary injunction sought. It means only that the district court upon remand must consider whether there has been a raising of a serious question and a sharp tip of the balance of hardship. A court has wide latitude in this sort of equitable decision.

QUICKNOTES

JUDGMENT ON THE MERITS - A determination of the rights of the parties to litigation based on the presentation evidence, barring the party from initiating the same suit again.

PRELIMINARY INJUNCTION - An order issued by the court at the commencement of an action, requiring a party to refrain from conducting a specified activity that is the subject of the controversy, until the matter is determined.

NOTES:

FUENTES v. SHEVIN
Owner of chattels (P) v. Court (D)
407 U.S. 67 (1972).

NATURE OF CASE: Constitutional challenge to Florida's prejudgment replevin procedure on due process grounds.

FACT SUMMARY: Fuentes (P) had her stove and stereo picked up by the sheriff prior to the adjudication of a suit filed by Firestone for nonpayment of the installment sales contract.

CONCISE RULE OF LAW: Procedural due process requires that parties whose rights are to be affected are entitled to be heard at a meaningful time; and in order that they may enjoy that right they must be notified.

FACTS: Margarita Fuentes (P) purchased a gas stove and service policy, and later a stereo from Firestone Tire and Rubber Co. After a year, there arose a dispute between Fuentes (P) and Firestone over the servicing of the stove. Firestone filed an action for replevin of both the stove and the stereo, claiming Fuentes (P) had defaulted on her installment payments. Before she was served with the complaint, Firestone obtained a writ of replevin and the sheriff seized the stove and stereo. The prejudgment replevin statutes did not require a convincing showing that the goods were wrongfully detained before seizure. A person could merely file a complaint, post a bond, and request a writ. To obtain a hearing, the person whose property was seized had to initiate a suit for a hearing. Fuentes (P) attacked the prejudgment replevin statute as violative of due process. The state court upheld the legislation, and Fuentes (P) appealed.

ISSUE: Are these state statutes constitutionally defective in that they fail to provide for a hearing at a meaningful time?

HOLDING AND DECISION: (Stewart, J.) Yes. Procedural due process requires that a party whose rights are being affected be given a meaningful opportunity to be heard; and in order that they may enjoy that right they must be notified. The constitutional right to be heard is a basic aspect of the duty of government to follow a fair process of decision-making when it acts to deprive a person of his possessions. This right to be heard minimizes substantively unfair or mistaken deprivations of property, a danger that is especially great when the state seizes goods simply upon the application of and for the benefit of a private party. Without due process of law, there would be no safeguards to protect a person's property from governmental interference. The right to speak out in one's own defense before an impartial arbitrator is a fundamental right which must be protected. If the right to notice and a hearing is to serve its full purpose, then it is clear that it must be granted at a time when the deprivation can still be prevented. While return of possession and damages can be granted at a later hearing, nothing can undo the fact that a person's property was

arbitrarily taken from him without procedural due process of law. That the hearing required by due process is subject to waiver, and is not fixed in form, does not affect its root requirement that an individual be given an opportunity for a hearing before he is deprived of any significant property interest, except for extraordinary situations where some valid governmental interest is at stake that justifies postponing the hearing until after the event. The statute's requirements of requesting a writ, posting bond, and stating in a conclusory fashion that the property is wrongfully held merely tests the applicant's own belief in his rights. Since his private gain is at stake, the danger is all too great that his confidence in his cause will be misplaced. While possession may be reinstated by the posting of a counter-bond, it is well settled that a temporary, nonfinal deprivation of property is nonetheless violative of the Due Process Clause of the Fourteenth Amendment. Moreover, the Due Process Clause encompasses both the possessory rights to property and situations where the title is in dispute. Situations requiring a postponement of notice and hearing are truly unusual. They require an important governmental purpose, a special need for prompt action, and are initiated by and for the benefit of the government as opposed to a private individual (*e.g.*, war effort, economic disaster, *etc.*). The contention that the parties waived their constitutional rights is also without merit, since waiver requires clear and explicit language indicating exactly the rights to be waived. For the above-mentioned reasons, both Florida's and Pennsylvania's prejudgment replevin statutes violate the Due Process Clause of the Fourteenth Amendment.

EDITOR'S ANALYSIS: In California, Michigan, and a large number of other states, the writ of replevin is now referred to as claim and delivery. In California, this action is contained in § 511.010, et seq. of the Code of Civil Procedure. A hearing is required for the granting of a writ of possession (comparable to the prior writ of replevin) under the guidelines set out in § 512.010. Exceptions are made for property feloniously taken, credit cards and property acquired in the normal course of trade or business for commercial use. It must be alleged that the property is not necessary for the support of the defendant or his family and that there is a danger that the property will become unavailable to levy, its value will be substantially impaired, and it is necessary to protect the property (§ 512.020). At the hearing, the court will make its determination based on affidavits, pleadings, and other evidence on record. Upon showing of good cause, the court may admit additional evidence or continue the hearing until the new evidence can be obtained (§ 512.050). Finally, with regard to

Continued on next page.

waiver of a hearing requirement, it appears that it is permissible if the parties are acting at arm's length and have equal bargaining power, *D. H. Overmeyer Co. v. Frick Co.*, 405 U.S. 174 (1972); however, if the consumer has no option but to buy on credit, the parties are not equal in bargaining power and the clause is unconscionable, *Kosches v. Nichols*, 327 N.Y.S. 2d 968 (1971). This is but another example of consumer protection. The businessman can waive his constitutional rights, but the consumer cannot.

NOTES:

QUICKNOTES

GARNISHMENT - Satisfaction of a debt by deducting payments directly from the debtor's wages before they are paid to him by his employer; due process requires that the debtor be first given notice and an opportunity to be heard.

PROCEDURAL DUE PROCESS - The constitutional mandate that if the state or federal government acts so as to deny a citizen of a life, liberty or property interest the individual is first entitled to notice and the right to be heard.

REPLEVIN - An action to recover personal property wrongfully taken.

6

CHAPTER 6
PLEADING

QUICK REFERENCE RULES OF LAW

1. **The Functions of Pleading.** A Civil Rights Act §1985(2) claim requires that the plaintiff suffer actual injury and discharge from at-will employment does not constitute actual injury. (Haddle v. Garrison (I))

2. **The Functions of Pleading.** A Civil Rights Act claim under §1985(2) does not require an injury to a constitutionally protected property interest. (Haddle v. Garrison (II))

3. **Ethical Limitations.** Rule 11 sanctions may be appropriate for an attorney's filing of a clearly defective complaint and taking no steps to amend or dismiss it. (Walker v. Norwest Corp.)

4. **Ethical Limitations.** Rule 11 sanctions are limited to papers signed in violation of the rule, not to other conduct. (Christian v. Mattell, Inc.)

5. **Special Claims: Requiring and Forbidding Specificity in Pleading.** Under Federal Rule of Civil Procedure 9(b), the time, place, and nature of alleged misrepresentations must be disclosed to a party accused of fraud. (Stradford v. Zurich Insurance Co.)

6. **Allocating the Elements.** In an action to redress the deprivation of rights secured by the U.S. Constitution and laws under 42 U.S.C. § 1983, the complaint need not allege the defendant's bad faith in order to state a claim for relief. (Gomez v. Toledo)

7. **Responding to the Complaint: Answer — Denials.** In the federal courts, a defendant who knowingly makes inaccurate statements may be estopped from denying those inaccurate statements at the trial. (Zielinski v. Philadelphia Piers, Inc.)

8. **Responding to the Complaint: Answer — Affirmative Defenses.** It is the obligation of a defendant in an action for trespass to affirmatively plead and prove matters in justification. (Layman v. Southwestern Bell Telephone Co.)

9. **Amendments — The Basic Problem: Prejudice.** The opponent of a motion for leave to amend must show he will be prejudiced by the grant of leave under Federal Rule of Civil Procedure 15(a). (Beeck v. Aquaslide 'N' Drive Corp.)

10. **Amendments — Statutes of Limitations and Relation Back.** A claim that does not arise out of the same conduct, transaction, or occurrence as the original claim does not relate back to the original pleading. (Moore v. Baker)

11. **Amendments — Statutes of Limitations and Relation Back.** When allegations in an amended complaint and the original complaint derive from the same nucleus of operative facts, the amended complaint relates back to the date of the original complaint. (Bonerb v. Richard J. Caron Foundation)

HADDLE v. GARRISON (I)
Employee (P) v. Employer (D)
Unpublished Opinion (S.D. Ga. 1996).

NATURE OF CASE: Motion to dismiss for failure to state a claim.

FACT SUMMARY: Haddle (P) sued his employer for allegedly conspiring to fire him to deter from testifying at a federal criminal trial.

CONCISE RULE OF LAW: A Civil Rights Act §1985(2) claim requires that the plaintiff suffer actual injury and discharge from at-will employment does not constitute actual injury.

FACTS: Haddle (P), an employee at Healthmaster (D), alleged that he was terminated in an attempt to deter his participation as a witness at a federal criminal trial. Haddle (P) filed suit in district court for violation of §1985(2) of the Civil Rights Act. Healthmaster (D) and their officers (D) moved to dismiss for failure to state a claim upon which relief can be granted. They argued that because Haddle (P) was an at-will employee, there was no actual injury as required by §1985(2).

ISSUE: Does discharge from at-will employment constitute actual injury for purposes of Civil Rights Act §1985(2)?

HOLDING AND DECISION: (Alaimo, J.) No. A Civil Rights Act §1985(2) claim requires that the plaintiff suffer actual injury and discharge from at-will employment does not constitute actual injury. Section 1985(2) provides that one or more persons may not engage in a conspiracy to deter, intimidate or threaten another from attending and testifying at a federal court proceeding and cause an injury. FED. R. CIV. P. 12(b)(6) permits a defendant to move to dismiss a complaint where the plaintiff has failed to state a claim upon which relief can be granted. This motion attacks the legal sufficiency of the complaint. Consequently, a court must assume that all of the factual allegations of the complaint are true in deciding the motion. In the present case, the Eleventh Circuit has already ruled that at-will employees have no constitutionally protected property interest in continued employment and thus suffer no actual injury under §1985(2) when discharged. Accordingly, Haddle (P) has failed to state a federal claim, even if his allegations about the conspiracy to deter him from testifying are true. The motion to dismiss is granted.

EDITOR'S ANALYSIS: On appeal, the Eleventh Circuit affirmed this decision in per curiam decision. However, the U.S. Supreme Court eventually took up the case because it conflicted with the decisions in two other circuits. In the end, Haddle's (P) appeal was upheld and the dismissal reversed.

QUICKNOTES

FED. R. CIV. P. 12 - Allows for successive motions to dismiss for failure to state a claim.

HADDLE v. GARRISON (II)
Employee (P) v. Employer (D)
525 U.S. 121 (1998).

NATURE OF CASE: Appeal from dismissal of Civil Rights Act action.

FACT SUMMARY: Haddle (P) sued his employer for allegedly conspiring to fire him to deter from testifying at a federal criminal trial.

CONCISE RULE OF LAW: A Civil Rights Act claim under §1985(2) does not require an injury to a constitutionally protected property interest.

FACTS: Healthmaster (D), and officers Garrison (D) and Kelly (D), were indicted by a federal grand jury in 1995. Haddle (P), an employee, had cooperated with the investigation and was expected to appear as a witness at the resulting criminal trial. Garrison (D) and Kelly (D) allegedly conspired with the other officers at Healthmaster (D) to terminate Haddle (P) in retaliation. Haddle (P) filed suit in district court for violation of §1985 of the Civil Rights Act. Healthmaster (D) and the officers (D) moved to dismiss for failure to state a claim upon which relief can be granted. The district court ruled that because Haddle (P) was an at-will employee, there was no actual injury as required by §1985. The dismissal motion was granted and the court of appeals affirmed. Since the Eleventh Circuit's decision conflicted with the holdings in two other circuits, the U.S. Supreme Court granted certiorari.

ISSUE: Does a Civil Rights Act claim under §1985(2) require an injury to a constitutionally protected property interest?

HOLDING AND DECISION: (Rehnquist, J.) No. A Civil Rights Act claim under §1985(2) does not require an injury to a constitutionally protected property interest. Section 1985(2) provides that one or more persons may not engage in a conspiracy to deter, intimidate or threaten another from attending and testifying at a federal court proceeding. The Eleventh Circuit held that there was no injury to Haddle (P) because he had no property interest in at-will employment that could give rise to damages. However, nothing in the language of §1985(2) or the remedial provisions establishes this requirement. The section is directed against intimidation or retaliation against witnesses, not the deprivation of property. The fact that employment at will is not property, does not mean that the loss of this employment does not cause injury. Such harm has long been a compensable injury under tort law and is similar to intentional interference with contractual relations. Dismissal of Haddle's (P) complaint for failure to state a claim was in error. Reversed and remanded.

EDITOR'S ANALYSIS: Haddle (P) claims that the district court had declined to exercise supplemental jurisdiction over. Given the reversal, those claims would probably be joined on remand.

WALKER v. NORWEST CORP.
Minor (P) v. Fiduciary (D)
108 F.3d 158 (8th Cir. 1996).

NATURE OF CASE: Appeal of an award of Rule 11 sanctions.

FACT SUMMARY: Jimmy Lee Walker, III (P), his guardian, Cynthia Walker (P), and their attorney, Massey, appealed Rule 11 sanctions imposed against Massey when Massey failed to amend or dismiss a clearly defective complaint he had filed.

CONCISE RULE OF LAW: Rule 11 sanctions may be appropriate for an attorney's filing of a clearly defective complaint and taking no steps to amend or dismiss it.

FACTS: Jimmy Walker (P), a minor, through his attorney, Massey, filed a complaint in federal court against Norwest (D), in which the attorney failed to plead complete diversity of citizenship, and indeed, pleaded facts which tended to show there was not complete diversity. Upon receiving the complaint, Norwest (D) wrote to Massey informing him that the complaint showed on its face that there was no diversity jurisdiction. The letter asked Massey to dismiss the complaint and warned that if he did not, Norwest (D) would seek sanctions, including attorney's fees. Massey acknowledged Norwest's (D) correspondence, but made no substantive response to the deficiency which Norwest's (D) counsel had pointed out. The federal district court granted Norwest's (D) motion to dismiss and for Rule 11 sanctions against Walker and Massey, and Walker and Massey appealed.

ISSUE: May Rule 11 sanctions be appropriate for an attorney's filing of a clearly defective complaint and taking no steps to amend or dismiss it?

HOLDING AND DECISION: (Gibson, Cir.J.) Yes. Rule 11 sanctions may be appropriate for an attorney's filing of a clearly defective complaint and taking no steps to amend or dismiss it. Even though it was the Walkers' (P) burden to plead, and if necessary, prove diversity, they did not allege that all of the defendants were domiciled in a state other than South Dakota. Instead, they argued that finding out the defendants' (D) citizenship would be more trouble than they should be expected to take. However, this is a burden that plaintiffs desiring to invoke diversity jurisdiction have assumed since the days of Chief Justice Marshall. As to Massey's contention that the court should have inquired into his financial circumstances before imposing the monetary sanction, not only did Massey fail to argue this point to the district court, but there was no evidence in the record to support such an argument. Finally, Massey never did allege citizenship for many of the defendants and never identified which defendants should be dismissed to create diversity jurisdiction. Affirmed.

EDITOR'S ANALYSIS: In *Walker*, the court made clear that a district court is not obliged to do a party's research for them.

QUICKNOTES
DIVERSITY OF CITIZENSHIP - The authority of a federal court to hear and determine cases involving $10,000 or more and in which the parties are citizens of different states, or in which one party is an alien.

DIVERSITY JURISDICTION - The authority of a federal court to hear and determine cases involving $10,000 or more and in which the parties are citizens of different states, or in which one party is an alien.

FED. R. CIV. P. 11 - Sets forth the requirement that every pleading or written paper be signed by at least one attorney of record; the representations made by the attorney to the court upon the signing of such document; and the sanctions for violation of the provision.

NOTES:

CHRISTIAN v. MATTELL, INC.
Alleged infringed toymaker (P) v. Alleged infringing toymaker (D)
286 F.3d 1118 (9th Cir. 2003).

NATURE OF CASE: Appeal of an award of Rule 11 sanctions.

FACT SUMMARY: When the court awarded Rule 11 sanctions against Claudene Christian (P) and her attorney, Hicks, for a combination of frivolous pleading and improper discovery tactics, Christian (P) and Hicks argued that Rule 11 sanctions must be limited to papers signed in violation of the rule, not to other conduct.

CONCISE RULE OF LAW: Rule 11 sanctions are limited to papers signed in violation of the rule, not to other conduct.

FACTS: Claudene Christian (P), who created and marketed a cheerleader doll, filed a complaint alleging that the toymaker Mattell (D) infringed the copyright on her doll. Mattell (D) proferred evidence that its copyright predated Christian's (P) doll, however Christian (P), through her attorney Hicks, refused voluntarily to dismiss the suit. The federal district court granted Mattell's (D) motion for summary judgment and for Rule 11 sanctions, finding that Christian's (P) attorney, Hicks, had filed a meritless claim and that Hicks had demonstrated that his conduct fell far below the proper standards of attorneys, including, among other things, unprofessional behavior during discovery proceedings and misrepresentations to the court during oral arguments. The court awarded Mattell (D) $501,565 in attorneys' fees. Christian (P) and Hicks appealed.

ISSUE: Are Rule 11 sanctions limited to papers signed in violation of the rule, not to other conduct?

HOLDING AND DECISION: (McKeown, Cir.J.) Yes. Rule 11 sanctions are limited to papers signed in violation of the rule, not to other conduct. While the laundry list of Hicks' outlandish conduct is a long one and raises questions as to his respect for the judicial process, nonetheless Rule 11 sanctions are limited to papers signed. Conduct in depositions, discovery meetings of counsel, oral representations at hearings, and behavior in prior proceedings do *not* fall within the ambit of Rule 11. Here, the orders clearly demonstrate that the district court decided, at least in part, to sanction Hicks because he signed and filed a factually and legally meritless complaint and *also* strongly suggest that the court considered "extra-pleadings conduct" as a basis for the Rule 11 sanctions. Because it cannot from the record be determined for certain whether the district court granted Mattell's (P) Rule 11 motion as a result of an impermissible intertwining of its conclusion about the complaint's frivolity and Hicks' extrinsic misconduct, the district court Rule 11 order is vacated and the matter remanded to delineate the factual and legal basis for its sanctions orders.

EDITOR'S ANALYSIS: In *Christian*, the court emphasized that Rule 11 does not authorize sanctions for "extra-pleadings conduct" such as, for example, discovery abuses or misstatements made to the court during an oral presentation.

QUICKNOTES

FED. R. CIV. P. 11 - Sets forth the requirement that every pleading or written paper be signed by at least one attorney of record; the representations made by the attorney to the court upon the signing of such document; and the sanctions for violation of the provision.

NOTES:

STRADFORD v. ZURICH INSURANCE CO.

Insured (P) v. Insurer (D)

2002 WL 31027517 (S.D.N.Y. 2002).

NATURE OF CASE: Motion to dismiss counterclaim.

FACT SUMMARY: When Dr. Stradford (P) sued his insurer, Zurich Insurance Company (Northern) (D), for property damage, Northern (P) counterclaimed for fraud, contending that Stradford (P) was fully aware the damage had occurred during a period in which the policy had lapsed for nonpayment of premiums. Stradford (P) moved to dismiss the fraud claim.

CONCISE RULE OF LAW: Under Federal Rule of Civil Procedure 9(b), the time, place, and nature of alleged misrepresentations must be disclosed to a party accused of fraud.

FACTS: Dr. Stradford (P), a dentist, brought suit against his insurer, Zurich Insurance Company (Northern) (D) for water damage allegedly occuring to his property during a period which Northern (D) claimed was an interim period when the insurance had lapsed because of Stradford's (P) failure to make premium payments. Northern (D), accordingly, counterclaimed against Stradford (P), contending that Stradford (P), by making the claim and filing the suit, knowingly had devised a scheme and artifice to defraud the insurer and obtain money by false pretenses and representations. Stradford (P) moved to dismiss the counterclaim that was based in fraud for failure to state the fraud claim with sufficient particularity.

ISSUE: Under Federal Rule of Civil Procedure 9(b), must the time, place, and nature of alleged misrepresentations be disclosed to a party accused of fraud?

HOLDING AND DECISION: (Buchwald, J.) Yes. Under Federal Rule of Civil Procedure 9(b), the time, place, and nature of alleged misrepresentations must be disclosed to a party accused of fraud. Here, Northern's (D) counterclaims simply failed to identify the statement made by Stradford (P) that they claimed to be false. Thus, it is unclear from the face of the counterclaims whether Northern (D) was asserting that Stradford's (P) claimed losses were improperly inflated, that Stradford's (P) office never even flooded, or that the offices flooded, but not during the term of the insurance policy. In essence, Northern (D) claimed that Stradford (P) lied, but failed to identify the lie. The primary purpose of Rule 9(b) is to afford a litigant accused of fraud fair notice of the claim and the factual ground upon which it is based. Here, Northern's (D) counterclaims failed to provide Stradford (P) with fair notice of precisely which statement, or which aspect of his claim, Northern (D) alleged to be false. The counterclaims were therefore insufficient under Rule 9(b) and must be dismissed. However, in accordance with the practice of the Second Circuit, Northern (D) is permitted to file an amended pleading, which it has done, which cures the defects found in the counterclaims by making it clear that it was alleging that Stradford's (P) office was flooded at a time when he had permitted the insurance policy to lapse, yet that he misrepresented the date of the loss to try to bring the loss within the coverage period. Defendant's request for permission to move for summary judgment is granted.

EDITOR'S ANALYSIS: Fed. R. Civ. P. 9(b) provides that in all averments of fraud or mistake, the circumstances constituting fraud or mistake shall be stated with particularity. Malice, intent, knowledge, and other condition of mind of a person may be averred generally.

QUICKNOTES

FED. R. CIV. P. 9(b) - Sets forth the requirements for pleading fraud or mistake and requires the circumstances constituting fraud or mistake to be plead with particularity; malice, intent, knowledge and other conditions of the mind of a person may be plead generally.

NOTES:

GOMEZ v. TOLEDO
Police agent (P) v. Police superintendent (D)
446 U.S. 635 (1980).

NATURE OF CASE: Appeal from dismissal for failure to allege bad faith.

FACT SUMMARY: Gomez (P) brought this action against Toledo (D), Superintendent of the Police in Puerto Rico, for discharging him after he had reported the falsification of evidence by colleagues, but Gomez' (P) complaint did not allege that Toledo (D) had acted in bad faith.

CONCISE RULE OF LAW: In an action to redress the deprivation of rights secured by the U.S. Constitution and laws under 42 U.S.C. § 1983, the complaint need not allege the defendant's bad faith in order to state a claim for relief.

FACTS: Gomez (P) was an agent of the Puerto Rican police. In 1975, he submitted a sworn statement to his superior that certain co-agents had falsified evidence with respect to a criminal investigation. He later testified in the trial arising out of that investigation as a defense witness and swore there that the co-agents had falsified the evidence in question. Thereafter, criminal charges were brought against Gomez (P) for wiretapping the other agents' telephones, but the charges were dismissed upon a finding of no probable cause to believe the allegations to be true. In the meantime, Gomez (P) had been transferred out of the investigative branches and into Police Headquarters and then to the Police Academy. Gomez (P) was reinstated by court order and granted back pay, but sought damages for the violation of his procedural due process rights under 42 U.S.C. § 1983. His complaint did not allege bad faith on the part of Toledo (D), who contended that his qualified immunity required such an allegation.

ISSUE: In an action to redress the deprivation of rights secured by the U.S. Constitution and laws under 42 U.S.C. § 1983, must the complaint allege the defendant's bad faith in order to state a claim for relief?

HOLDING AND DECISION: (Marshall, J.) No. The purpose of § 1983 is to provide a damages remedy against an offending party who has deprived a plaintiff of constitutional guarantees and guarantees of federal laws. Though a defendant has a qualified immunity as a public official if he acted in good faith, no allegation of bad faith is required in a complaint that alleges a deprivation in violation of the law. The immunity of a defendant is a defense which he must plead, not the plaintiff. Nothing in the legislative history of § 1983 suggests that bad faith allegation is required in a complaint of this type. In an action to redress the deprivation of rights secured by the U.S. Constitution and laws under 42 U.S.C. § 1983, the complaint need not allege the defendant's bad faith in order to state a claim for relief. Reversed.

EDITOR'S ANALYSIS: If a right secured by the U.S. Constitution or laws is taken away from a plaintiff, it is not easy to envision any state of mind on the part of the offender other than bad faith, unless the "right" is abrogated legally. In any case, it is up to the defendant to show that he acted in good faith or that the plaintiff did not have a right secured by federal law.

QUICKNOTES

42 U.S.C. § 1983 - Provides that every person, who under color of state law subjects or causes to be subjected any citizen of the United States or person within its jurisdiction to be deprived of rights, privileges and immunities guaranteed by the federal constitution and laws, is liable to the injured party at law or in equity.

PUBLIC OFFICIAL - An individual who is either elected or appointed to a position which is authorized to exercise the government's sovereign powers.

QUALIFIED IMMUNITY - An affirmative defense relieving officials from civil liability for the performance of activities within their discretion so long as such conduct is not in violation of an individual's rights pursuant to law as determined by a reasonable person standard.

NOTES:

ZIELINSKI v. PHILADELPHIA PIERS, INC.
Injured forklift operator (P) v. Rival forklift company (D)
139 F. Supp. 408 (E.D. Pa. 1956).

NATURE OF CASE: Action in torts to recover damages for personal injuries.

FACT SUMMARY: Philadelphia Piers, Inc. (D) was estopped to deny ownership of a forklift and the agency of the operator.

CONCISE RULE OF LAW: In the federal courts, a defendant who knowingly makes inaccurate statements may be estopped from denying those inaccurate statements at the trial.

FACTS: Zielinski (P) was injured on February 9, 1953, while operating a forklift on Pier 96 for J.A. McCarthy. Zielinski (P) alleged in his complaint that Sandy Johnson was operating a forklift owned by Philadelphia Piers, Inc. (D) and was their agent as well. Because of the negligent manner in which Sandy Johnson operated the forklift, Zielinski (P) was injured. A complaint was served on Philadelphia Piers, Inc. (D). Actually, Sandy Johnson worked for Carload Contractors, Inc., who had leased the forklift from Philadelphia Piers (D). Sandy Johnson had worked for Philadelphia Piers (D) for the previous 15 years and wasn't aware that he was now working for Carload Contractors, Inc. Sandy Johnson testified at a deposition taken August 18, 1953, that he had worked for Philadelphia Piers (D). As soon as Carload Contractors, Inc. found out about the accident, they made a report to their insurance company. When Philadelphia Piers (D) received the complaint, they forwarded it on to their insurance company, which was the same insurance company of Carload Contractors, Inc., telling them of the mistake and asking them to take care of it. Philadelphia Piers (D) was at the deposition when Sandy Johnson testified that he worked for Philadelphia Piers (D), and by receiving the complaint and the letter they sent to their insurance company, it was clear that they knew of Zielinski's (P) mistake. Zielinski (P) didn't find out that he was suing the wrong party until the pretrial conference held on September 27, 1955. Zielinski (P) requested a ruling that for the purposes of this case the forklift operated by Sandy Johnson was owned by Philadelphia Piers (D), and that Sandy Johnson was its agent acting in the course of his employment. In other words, Philadelphia (D) would be estopped to deny the facts they allowed Zielinski (P) to believe.

ISSUE: If a defendant makes an ineffective denial of part of the complaint and knowingly allows the plaintiff to continue to rely on the facts as stated in the complaint, may the defendant be estopped to deny the facts as they are contained in the complaint?

HOLDING AND DECISION: (Van Dusen, J.) Yes. Philadelphia Piers (D) made a general denial of the paragraph in the complaint that alleged that Sandy Johnson was an agent of Philadelphia Piers (D) and was driving their forklift. It was clear from interrogatories that they were aware of the accident and the facts involved because they made an investigation and forwarded their report to their insurance company. Philadelphia Piers (D) should have made a specific denial of parts of the complaint they believed and knew to be false and admitted the parts which were true. This would have warned Zielinski (P) that he was suing the wrong party. This case was being tried in the district court sitting in Pennsylvania and there were no federal court decisions on this point, so the Pennsylvania law was used. The Pennsylvania rule is that where an improper and ineffective answer has been filed, an allegation of agency in the complaint requires a statement to the jury that agency is admitted if the time allowed to amend an answer has already passed. Philadelphia Piers (D) was under no duty to advise Zielinski (P) of his error other than by appropriate pleadings, but neither did they have a right, knowing of the mistake, to foster it by its acts of omission. Therefore, Philadelphia Piers (D) will be estopped to deny Sandy Johnson's agency and their ownership of the forklift and the jury will be instructed as Zielinski (P) requested. Philadelphia Piers (D) will not be prejudiced by having to defend this action, cause it will be their insurance company who will have to do it and they are the insurance company for the proper defendants.

EDITOR'S ANALYSIS: Rule 8(b) of the Fed. R. Civ. P. requires that denials fairly meet the substance of the averments denied. This requirement, together with the basic requirement of good faith in pleading contained in Rule 11, probably would provide adequate grounds for the decision in this case. Rule 8(b) also requires that the party shall state in short and plain terms his defenses to each claim asserted against him. If Philadelphia Piers (D) had stated that their defense to the complaint was that they were not the employers or owners of the personnel or machinery involved, Zielinski (P) would have been able to bring this action against the proper party. Philadelphia Piers (D) seemed to lack the good faith that the federal rules require because they waited until the time of trial to raise their defense that Zielinski had sued the wrong party.

QUICKNOTES

COMPLAINT - The initial pleading commencing litigation which sets forth a claim for relief.

FED. R. CIV. P. 8 - Sets forth the general rules of pleading a claim for relief.

GENERAL DENIAL - Type of pleading contradicting all the assertions of a former pleading.

LAYMAN v. SOUTHWESTERN BELL TELEPHONE CO.

Real estate owner (P) v. Telephone company (D)

Mo. Ct. App., 554 S.W.2d 477 (1977).

NATURE OF CASE: Appeal from denial of damages for trespass.

FACT SUMMARY: In Layman's (P) suit against Southwestern Bell (D) for trespass, Layman (P) contended that Bell (D) had entered her land and had installed underground telephone wires and cables without her consent and, in doing so, had depreciated the value of her land.

CONCISE RULE OF LAW: It is the obligation of a defendant in an action for trespass to affirmatively plead and prove matters in justification.

FACTS: Layman (P) owned real estate in Jefferson County, Missouri. Layman (P) brought suit for trespass against Southwestern Bell (D), contending that Bell (D) had entered her land and had installed underground telephone wires and cables without her consent and, in doing so, had depreciated the value of her land. After hearing the evidence, the court rendered judgment in Bell's (D) favor, stating that there was "insufficient evidence to establish the trespass pleaded and sought to be proved." Layman (P) appealed.

ISSUE: Is it the obligation of a defendant in an action for trespass to affirmatively plead and prove matters in justification?

HOLDING AND DECISION: (Weier, J.) Yes. It is the obligation of a defendant in an action for trespass to affirmatively plead and prove matters in justification. Here, Layman (P) contends that the trial court erred when it permitted Bell (D) to introduce evidence that it had received an assignment of an easement originally executed by owners of the land previous to Layman (P). Layman (P) argued that Bell (D) had pleaded only as general denial and not an affirmative defense of easement to Layman's (P) claim of trespass. Layman (P) further argued that affirmative defenses, such as easement in a trespass case, must be affirmatively pleaded as a condition to the admissibility of such evidence at the trial, and that because Bell (D) did not do so, such evidence should not be admissible. It seems clear that the right of Bell (D) to enter upon Layman's (P) land would have to be proven by some competent evidence which would give that right to Bell (D). If Bell (D) avers that Layman's (P) theory of liability does not apply because of additional facts which placed Bell (D) in a position to avoid any legal responsibility for its action, that defense, rather than a general denial, must be set forth in its answer. Bell (D) did not do this, and, thus, Layman's (P) objection to introduction of the easement evidence when it was not pleaded in justification of the trespass should have been sustained. Reversed.

EDITOR'S ANALYSIS: In some situations, a plaintiff must allege a certain matter and a defendant must allege the opposite in the form of an affirmative defense, rather than just denying plaintiff's allegations. For example, the plaintiff in a defamation suit must allege the falsity of the statement, but the truth of the statement is an affirmative defense that must be pleaded. The rationale for this rule seems to be that the facts in question are such an integral part of the claim that plaintiff must make the initial allegation, but that the responsibility for pleading and proving such matters will be placed on the defendant.

QUICKNOTES

AFFIRMATIVE DEFENSE - A manner of defending oneself against a claim not by denying the truth of the charge but by the introduction of some evidence challenging the plaintiff's right to bring the claim.

GENERAL DENIAL - Type of pleading contradicting all the assertions of a former pleading.

NOTES:

BEECK v. AQUASLIDE 'N' DIVE CORP.

Injured slide user (P) v. Slide manufacturer (D)

562 F.2d 537 (8th Cir. 1977).

NATURE OF CASE: Appeal from grant of leave to amend.

FACT SUMMARY: Beeck (P) was injured on a pool slide alleged to have been manufactured by Aquaslide (D), and after Aquaslide (D) admitted manufacture in its answer, the district court granted it leave to amend to deny manufacture over Beeck's (P) objection.

CONCISE RULE OF LAW: The opponent of a motion for leave to amend must show he will be prejudiced by the grant of leave under Federal Rule of Civil Procedure 15(a).

FACTS: Beeck (P) was injured while using the slide at a social gathering at Kimberly Village, Davenport, Iowa. Beeck (P) then brought this action in district court under diversity jurisdiction alleging that Aquaslide (D) was liable under theories of negligence, strict liability, and breach of implied warranty. Aquaslide (D) answered the complaint, admitting that it manufactured the slide in question in reliance upon the opinions of insurance investigators. The district court then granted Aquaslide (D) leave to amend the answer to deny this fact and permitted a separate trial on the question of manufacture over the objection of Beeck (P). The jury found for Aquaslide (D) and the court entered summary judgment against Beeck (P). By the time of the amendment, the statute of limitations for Beeck's (P) cause of action had run, and Beeck (P) appealed.

ISSUE: Must an opponent of a motion for leave to amend show he will be prejudiced by the grant of leave under Fed. R. Civ. P. 15(a)?

HOLDING AND DECISION: (Benson, J.) Yes. Fed. R. Civ. P. 15(a) provides that "leave shall be freely given when justice so requires." The grant or denial of such leave to amend is within the sound discretion of the trial judge. The party opposing the motion for leave must show he will be prejudiced by the grant of leave under Fed. R. Civ. P. 15(a). In this case, Aquaslide (D) relied upon the conclusions of three separate insurance companies and their investigators and were thus not negligent in determining the facts in question, and it was not an abuse of discretion to give Aquaslide (D) a chance to correct a fact disputed. Beeck (P) alleged that he was prejudiced because his action was foreclosed by the running of the statute of limitations. This argument required the trial judge to assume that Aquaslide (D) would prevail on the manufacturing issue, and the judge properly refused to so presume. Neither was the grant of separate trials improper. A substantial issue of material fact was raised which would exonerate Aquaslide (D) if resolved in its favor. There was thus no abuse of discretion. Affirmed.

EDITOR'S ANALYSIS: Because of the running of the statute of limitations, it would be unlikely, if not impossible, that Beeck (P) would be able to move against any other party. The court had to counterbalance this injustice against that of precluding Aquaslide (D) from proving that it did not manufacture the slide which caused the injury. Since the amendment and the separate trial gave Beeck (P) a chance to disprove Aquaslide's (D) argument, and since the Fed. R. Civ. P. technically permitted the amendment and severance, the balance was struck in Aquaslide's (D) favor.

QUICKNOTES

AMENDMENT TO PLEADING - The modification of a pleading either as a matter of course upon motion to the court or by consent of both parties; a party is entitled to change its pleading once as a matter of course before a responsive pleading has been served.

FED. R. CIV. P. 15(a) - Sets forth the rule that a party may amend its pleading once as a matter of course at any time before a responsive pleading is served, or within 20 days if no responsive pleading is permitted and the action has not been placed on the trial calendar; otherwise a party may amend its pleading only by leave of court or written consent of the opposing party; a party is required to plead in response to an amended pleading within the time remaining for response to the original pleading or within ten days of service of the amended pleading, whichever is longer, unless otherwise stated by court order.

ISSUE OF MATERIAL FACT - A fact that is disputed between two or more parties to litigation that is essential to proving an element of the cause of action or a defense asserted or would otherwise affect the outcome of the proceeding.

NOTES:

MOORE v. BAKER
Patient (P) v. Physician (D)
989 F.2d 1129 (11th Cir. 1993).

NATURE OF CASE: Appeal of denial of motion to amend pleading in non-consent action.

FACT SUMMARY: Moore (P) initially alleged that Dr. Baker (D) violated the informed consent law, but then sought to include a claim for medical malpractice.

CONCISE RULE OF LAW: A claim that does not arise out of the same conduct, transaction, or occurrence as the original claim does not relate back to the original pleading.

FACTS: Moore (P) consulted Dr. Baker (D) to correct a blockage of her carotid artery. Baker (D) recommended surgery and warned Moore (P) of the risks. The operation left Moore (P) permanently disabled. Moore's (P) initial complaint alleged only a violation of Georgia's informed consent law. The trial court granted Baker's (D) motion for summary judgment. The statute of limitations ran the day after Moore (P) filed the original complaint. Moore (P) then sought to amend the complaint to include a claim for negligence, asserting that the new claim should relate back to the date of the original complaint. The trial court denied Moore's (P) motion, and Moore (P) appealed.

ISSUE: May a claim that does not arise out of the same conduct, transaction, or occurrence as the original claim relate back to the original pleading?

HOLDING AND DECISION: (Morgan, Sr.Cir.J.) No. A claim that does not arise out of the same conduct, transaction, or occurrence as the original claim may not relate back to the original pleading. In this case, the new claim arises out of alleged actions which are distinct in time and involve separate and distinct conduct. The failure-to-warn claim focused on actions prior to surgery, while the negligence claim focuses on actions during and post-surgery. Motion to amend denied.

EDITOR'S ANALYSIS: Whether the conduct, transaction, or occurrence in the amended complaint relates back to the original complaint to avoid the bar of a statute of limitations is a subjective test open to argument and interpretation. The role of the appellate court is to decide whether the trial court abused its discretion in applying this test to the facts of the case.

QUICKNOTES

AMENDMENT TO PLEADING - The modification of a pleading either as a matter of course upon motion to the court or by consent of both parties; a party is entitled to change its pleading once as a matter of course before a responsive pleading has been served.

RELATION BACK DOCTRINE - Doctrine which holds that a party may not amend its pleading to set forth a new or different claim or defense unless it involves the subject matter of the original pleading; under FED. R. CIV. P. 15, if a party amends its pleading as a matter of course before a responsive pleading is served, such amendment is said to relate back to the original pleading if it involves the subject matter of the original pleading.

NOTES:

BONERB v. RICHARD J. CARON FOUNDATION
Injured basketball player (P) v. Foundation (D)
159 F.R.D. 16 (W.D.N.Y. 1994).

NATURE OF CASE: Motion to amend complaint in personal injury action.

FACT SUMMARY: After Bonerb (P) filed suit for injuries received on a basketball court while he was being treated at the Richard J. Caron Foundation (D), he sought to amend his complaint to add a cause of action for "counseling malpractice."

CONCISE RULE OF LAW: When allegations in an amended complaint and the original complaint derive from the same nucleus of operative facts, the amended complaint relates back to the date of the original complaint.

FACTS: Bonerb (P) slipped and fell while playing basketball at the Richard J. Caron Foundation (D) while participating in the Foundation's (D) mandatory exercise program. Bonerb's (P) original complaint alleged the Foundation's (D) basketball court was negligently maintained. Bonerb (P) sought to amend the complaint to include a new claim for counseling malpractice. Bonerb (P) sought to relate back the malpractice claim to the date of the original complaint since the statute of limitations had expired for asserting a malpractice claim.

ISSUE: May allegations in an amended complaint relate back to the date of the original complaint when the new claim derives from the same nucleus of operative facts as the original complaint?

HOLDING AND DECISION: (Heckman, Mag.J.) Yes. Allegations in an amended complaint may relate back to the date of the original complaint when the new claim derives from the same nucleus of operative facts as the original complaint. The determining factor is whether the facts stated in the original complaint put the defendant on notice of the claim which plaintiff later seeks to add. Here, Bonerb (P) is using the same factual allegations in the amended complaint as in the original complaint. Bonerb (P) has merely changed the legal theory upon which the claim is based. Motion to amend is granted.

EDITOR'S ANALYSIS: Amendment to a pleading may occur in an answer as well as a complaint. Fed. R. Civ. P. 15(a) allows relation back for claims and defenses asserted in the original pleading or attempted to be set forth in the original pleading which arose from the conduct, transaction, or occurrence of the original pleading.

QUICKNOTES

FED. R. CIV. P. 15(a) - Sets forth the rule that a party may amend its pleading once as a matter of course at any time before a responsive pleading is served, or within 20 days if no responsive pleading is permitted and the action has not been placed on the trial calendar; otherwise a party may amend its pleading only by leave of court or written consent of the opposing party; a party is required to plead in response to an amended pleading within the time remaining for response to the original pleading or within ten days of service of the amended pleading, whichever is longer, unless otherwise stated by court order.

NUCLEUS OF OPERATIVE FACTS - An underlying fact situation common to those pleadings asserting it.

RELATION BACK DOCTRINE - Doctrine which holds that a party may not amend its pleading to set forth a new or different claim or defense unless it involves the subject matter of the original pleading; under FED. R. CIV. P. 15, if a party amends its pleading as a matter of course before a responsive pleading is served, such amendment is said to relate back to the original pleading if it involves the subject matter of the original pleading.

NOTES:

CHAPTER 7
DISCOVERY

QUICK REFERENCE RULES OF LAW

1. **Relevance.** Discovery requests which are narrowly tailored to the specific claims of the case are proper. (Davis v. Precoat Metals)

2. **Relevance.** Only evidence which is relevant to the issue being litigated may be discovered. (Steffan v. Cheney)

3. **The General Problem of Privacy.** Protective orders are appropriate to preclude discovery of irrelevant and private information. (Stalnaker v. Kmart Corp.)

4. **A Special Instance: Physical and Mental Examinations.** Under Federal Rule of Civil Procedure 35: (1) the rule which provides for physical and mental examinations of parties is applicable to defendants as well as plaintiffs; (2) though the person to be examined under the rule must be a party to the action, he need not be an opposing party vis-a-vis the movant; and (3) a person who moves for a mental or physical examination of a party who has not asserted her mental or physical condition either in support of or in defense of a claim must affirmatively show that the condition sought to be examined is really in controversy and that good cause exists for the particular examination requested. (Schlagenhauf v. Holder)

5. **Privilege and Trial Preparation Material.** Material obtained by counsel in preparation for litigation is the work product of the lawyer, and while such material is not protected by the attorney-client privilege, it is not discoverable on mere demand without a showing of necessity or justification. (Hickman v. Taylor)

6. **Expert Information.** Under exceptional circumstances, if it is impractical for the party seeking discovery to obtain facts or opinions on the same subject by other means; a party may, by interrogatories or by deposition, discover information by an expert who has been retained or specially employed by another party in anticipation of litigation and who is not to be called as a witness. (Thompson v. The Haskell Co.)

7. **Expert Information.** A nontestifying expert is immune from discovery unless exceptional circumstances apply. (Chiquita International Ltd. v. M/V Bolero Reefer)

8. **Remedies: Management & Sanctions.** When confronted with a difficult scope of discovery dispute, the parties themselves should confer in an effort to reach an acceptable compromise or narrow the scope of their disagreement. (Thompson v. Department of Housing & Urban Development)

9. **Remedies: Management & Sanctions.** A federal court has the latitude to fashion an "appropriate sanction," in addition to an award of expenses, for discovery abuse. (Poole v. Textron, Inc.)

DAVIS v. PRECOAT METALS

Employee (P) v. Employer (D)

2002 WL 1759828 (N.D. Ill. 2002).

NATURE OF CASE: Motion to compel discovery.

FACT SUMMARY: When Davis (P), a minority employee of Precoat Metals (D), and others sued Precoat (D) for discrimination under federal civil rights legislation and requested discovery regarding similar complaints of other employees, Precoat (D) argued that such information was not a proper subject for a discovery request.

CONCISE RULE OF LAW: Discovery requests which are narrowly tailored to the specific claims of the case are proper.

FACTS: Davis (P) and other African-American and Latino employees, working at Precoat's (D) Chicago plant, brought suit against their employer, Precoat Metals (D), alleging race and national origin discrimination and retaliation in violation of Title VII of the Civil Rights Act of 1964. They alleged a hostile working environment, including being subjected to racially insulting and derogatory comments by management-level employees of Precoat (D). Davis (P) sought discovery regarding other employees' complaints made against Precoat (D) by non-clerical/ non-administrative employees who worked at the same plant as Davis (P), namely, the Chicago plant. Precoat (D) argued that such information was nondiscoverable.

ISSUE: Are discovery requests which are narrowly tailored to the specific claims of the case proper?

HOLDING AND DECISION: (Nolan, Mag.J.) Yes. Discovery requests which are narrowly tailored to the specific claims of the case are proper. In their discovery motion, plaintiffs have limited their request to: (1) the time period of the alleged discrimination; (2) complaints by employees who worked at the same Chicago plant where the plaintiffs worked; and (3) complaints of race and national original discrimination, the same types of discrimination alleged in plaintiffs' complaint. Here, such request for information is properly discoverable and is narrowly tailored to this specific lawsuit. Davis (P) is correct in his argument that other employees' complaints of discrimination may be relevant to establish pretext since an employer's general policy and practice with respect to minority employment may certainly be relevant to a discrimination issue. Here, Davis (P) does not seek discovery related to *all* alleged unequal employment practices by Precoat Metals (D), nor does Davis (P) seek complaints by employees who did not work at the Chicago plant. Rather, plaintiffs have limited their discovery requests to complaints alleging race and national origin discrimination filed by other employees who worked at the same plant as the plaintiffs. The motion of Davis (P) to compel discovery is granted.

EDITOR'S ANALYSIS: Federal Rule of Civil Procedure 26(b)(1) permits discovery into any matter, not privileged, that is relevant to the claim or defense of any party. Discoverable information is not limited to that which would be admissible at trial. Information is relevant for purposes of Rule 26 if the discovery appears reasonably calculated to lead to the discovery of admissible evidence.

QUICKNOTES

FED. R. CIV. P. 26 - Protects work product revealing an attorney's mental processes absent a strong showing of necessity and unavailability.

NOTES:

STEFFAN v. CHENEY

Homosexual naval candidate (P) v. Secretary of Defense (D)
920 F.2d 74 (D.C. Cir. 1990).

NATURE OF CASE: Appeal from dismissal of action for wrongful discharge from U.S. Naval Academy.

FACT SUMMARY: Steffan (P), who was discharged from the U.S. Naval Academy after he truthfully responded in the affirmative to a superior's inquiry as to whether he was homosexual, argued that his wrongful discharge action should not have been dismissed because the district court erroneously allowed irrelevant questions as to whether he had engaged in homosexual activities during or after his tenure as a midshipman.

CONCISE RULE OF LAW: Only evidence which is relevant to the issue being litigated may be discovered.

FACTS: Steffan (P), while he was a midshipman at the U.S. Naval Academy, responded truthfully to a superior who asked him if he was a homosexual. Steffan (P) resigned from the Academy after an administrative board, shortly before he was to graduate at the head of his class, recommended that Steffan (P) be discharged, based solely on his statement. Steffan (P) brought suit against Secretary of Defense Cheney (D), alleging that he was constructively discharged from the service and challenging the constitutionality of the regulation that provided for discharge of homosexuals. During discovery, Steffan (P), invoking his Fifth Amendment privilege against self-incrimination, refused to answer questions as to whether he had ever engaged in homosexual activities during the time he was a midshipman or after his discharge. Additionally, he objected that the questions were not relevant to the legality of his separation. After giving a warning, the district court dismissed Steffan's (P) action for failure to comply with discovery orders, but the court acknowledged that Steffan (P) was discharged for his statement, not for acts. The court held, however, that the questions were relevant because the Navy could "refuse reinstatement on the grounds an individual has engaged in homosexual acts." Steffan (P) appealed.

ISSUE: May evidence which is irrelevant to the issue being litigated be discovered?

HOLDING AND DECISION: (Per curiam) No. Only evidence which is relevant to the issue being litigated may be discovered. The law is quite clear on this issue. Further, judicial review must be confined to the grounds upon which the action was based. Here, the action was brought for invalid separation from the Naval Academy. If the basis for separation from the Academy was homosexual conduct, then the questions may have been relevant and the information discoverable. However, in the instant case, the basis for separation was a statement made by Steffan (P) in response to an inquiry by Academy supervisors. This does not put

into question whether he engaged in the potentially disqualifying activity. Therefore, this area was not discoverable, unless the court could find another ground to assert relevance. Reversed and remanded.

EDITOR'S ANALYSIS: Discovery is allowed on issues which are admissible or will lead to admissible evidence. However, discovery may be denied even when the issue is relevant if it invades the right of privacy of the individual. In these instances, the court must weigh the judicial concept of fair play requiring disclosure of evidence relevant to a claim against the constitutional rights of the individual. Clearly, if the right being invaded is a fundamental right, then discovery will be denied, unless the government can demonstrate a compelling need.

QUICKNOTES

DISCOVERY - Pretrial procedure during which one party makes certain information available to the other.

FUNDAMENTAL RIGHT - A liberty that is either expressly or impliedly provided for in the United States Constitution, the deprivation or burdening of which is subject to a heightened standard of review.

RELEVANT EVIDENCE - Evidence having any tendency to prove or disprove a disputed fact.

NOTES:

STALNAKER v. KMART CORP.
Employee (P) v. Employer (D)
71 Fair Empl. Prac. Cas. BNA 705 (D. Kan. 1996).

NATURE OF CASE: Motion for protective order in sexual harassment action.

FACT SUMMARY: Stalnaker (P) sought to discover information about her co-workers' voluntary romantic conduct for use in her sexual harassment suit.

CONCISE RULE OF LAW: Protective orders are appropriate to preclude discovery of irrelevant and private information.

FACTS: Stalnaker (P) brought a sexual harassment suit against her employer, Kmart (D) and another employee, Graves (D). Stalnaker (P) alleged that Graves (D) created a hostile working environment and inappropriately touched her. As part of discovery, Stalnaker (P) sought to discover information concerning the voluntary romantic conduct of four other employees who were not parties to the action. Kmart (D) moved for a protective order against this discovery.

ISSUE: Are protective orders appropriate to preclude discovery of irrelevant and private information?

HOLDING AND DECISION: (Rushfelt, Mag.J.) Yes. Protective orders are appropriate to preclude discovery of irrelevant and private information. Fed. R. Civ. P. 26 provides for broad and liberal discovery, including information that may not be admissible at trial. However, courts have the discretion to enter a protective order against discovery in order to protect a person from annoyance, embarrassment, oppression or undue burden. The party seeking the protective order has the burden to show good cause. In the present case, Federal Rule of Evidence 412 should also be considered. Rule 412 aims to safeguard victims from the invasion of privacy associated with the public disclosure of intimate sexual details. It is not controlling with respect to persons who are not the victims of alleged misconduct, so it does not directly apply to Kmart's (D) sought protective order. Thus, the best grounds for entering a protective order is that there is no relationship between voluntary romantic and sexual activities of nonparty witnesses and the allegations of Stalnaker (P). The only possibly relevant information is Graves' (D) relationship with the nonparty witnesses. This might show that he encouraged or solicited that type of conduct in the workplace. Accordingly, the protective order is granted except to the limited question of whether the nonparty witnesses had romantic contact with Graves (D).

EDITOR'S ANALYSIS: Stalnaker (P) had already conceded that the information she sought should not be disseminated outside the parties and their attorneys. The court allowed a small part of the discovery sought, but ordered that this could not be disclosed to anyone outside the case. In this sense, Fed. R. Evid. 412 played a small role in the decision.

QUICKNOTES
FED. R. CIV. P. 26 - Protects work product revealing an attorney's mental processes absent a strong showing of necessity and unavailability.

PROTECTIVE ORDER - Court order protecting a party against potential abusive treatment through use of the legal process.

NOTES:

SCHLAGENHAUF v. HOLDER

Bus driver/bus company (D) v. Injured passengers (P)

279 U.S. 104 (1964).

NATURE OF CASE: Action to recover damages for negligence.

FACT SUMMARY: Passengers injured in a bus collision sued Greyhound, Schlagenhauf (D), the bus driver, and the owners of the trailer with which the bus collided. The trailer owners claimed the accident was due to Schlagenhauf's (D) negligence and moved for a physical and mental examination of him.

CONCISE RULE OF LAW: Under Federal Rule of Civil Procedure 35: (1) the rule which provides for physical and mental examinations of parties is applicable to defendants as well as plaintiffs; (2) though the person to be examined under the rule must be a party to the action, he need not be an opposing party vis-a-vis the movant; and (3) a person who moves for a mental or physical examination of a party who has not asserted her mental or physical condition either in support of or in defense of a claim must affirmatively show that the condition sought to be examined is really in controversy and that good cause exists for the particular examination requested.

FACTS: A bus collided with a tractor-trailer. The injured passengers brought a negligence action against Greyhound, owner of the bus (D), Schlagenhauf (D), the bus driver, Contract Carriers (D), owner of the tractor, and against the tractor driver and the trailer owner. Greyhound (D) cross-claimed against Contract (D) and the trailer owner. Contract (D) filed an answer to this cross-claim, stating that the collision was caused by Schlagenhauf's (D) negligence. Contract (D) petitioned for a mental and physical examination of Schlagenhauf (D) under Federal Rule of Civil Procedure 35. The district court judge granted the petition. Schlagenhauf (D) applied for a writ of mandamus to have the order requiring his (D) mental and physical examinations set aside.

ISSUES: (1) Would the application of the rule providing for physical and mental examinations of parties to defendants (Fed. R. Civ. P. 35) be an unconstitutional invasion of their privacy? (2) Must the party to be examined under the rule (Fed. R. Civ. P. 35) be an opposing party vis-a-vis the movant? (3) Must a person who moves for a mental or physical examination of a party (under Fed. R. Civ. P. 35) who has not asserted his mental or physical condition either in support of or in defense of a claim affirmatively show that the condition sought to be examined is really in controversy and that good cause exists for the particular examination requested?

HOLDING AND DECISION: (Goldberg, J.) (1) No. The rule which provides for physical and mental examinations of parties is Fed. R. Civ. P. 35. On its face, it applies to all parties to an action, and there is no basis for holding it applicable to plaintiffs and inapplicable to defendants. Issues cannot be resolved by a doctrine of favoring one class of litigants over another. In this case, the fact that Schlagenhauf (D) is a defendant does not make the rule inapplicable to him. (2) No. Rule 35 only requires that the person to be examined is a party to the action. It does not require that he be an opposing party, vis-a-vis the movant. Insistence that the movant have filed a pleading against the person to be examined would have the undesirable effect of an unnecessary proliferation of cross-claims and counterclaims and would not be in keeping with the aims of a federal discovery policy. Here, Schlagenhauf (D) was a party to this action by virtue of the original complaint. (3) Yes. Rule 35 expressly requires that the condition sought to be examined must be in controversy, and there must be good cause for the examination. These requirements are not mere formalities and are not met by mere conclusory allegations of the pleadings nor by mere relevance to the case. They require an affirmative showing by the movant that each condition sought to be examined is really and genuinely in controversy and that good cause exists for each examination. Here, Schlagenhauf (D) did not assert his mental or physical condition in support of or in defense of a claim. Hence, Contract (D), as movant, must make an affirmative showing that Schlagenhauf's (D) mental or physical condition was in controversy and that there was good cause for the examinations requested. Contract (D) requested examinations by an internist, an ophthalmologist, a neurologist, and a psychiatrist. Yet, the only allegations it made in respect to Schlagenhauf's (D) physical or mental condition were conclusory statements that he was not mentally or physically capable of driving a bus. The attorney's affidavit does have some additional statements about his vision and what an eye witness saw. There is nothing in the pleadings to support the examinations by the neurologist, internist, or psychiatrist. There was a specific allegation that Schlagenhauf's (D) vision was impaired. Were this the only exam requested, it would not be set aside. However, as the case must be remanded to the district court because of the other guidelines ordered, it would be appropriate for the district judge to reconsider this also in light of the guidelines set forth herein.

Continued on next page.

CONCURRENCE IN PART AND DISSENT IN PART: (Black, J.) The record plainly shows that there was a controversy as to Schlagenhauf's (D) mental and physical health and that "good cause" was shown for a physical and mental examination of him, unless failure to deny the allegations amounted to an admission that they were true. While the papers filed in connection with this motion were informal, there can be no doubt that other parties in the lawsuit specifically and unequivocally charged that Schlagenhauf (D) was not mentally or physically capable of operating a motor bus at the time of the collision, and that his negligent operation of the bus caused the resulting injuries and damage. In a collision case like this one, evidence as to very bad eyesight or impaired mental or physical health, which may affect the ability to drive, is obviously of the highest relevance.

DISSENT: (Douglas, J.) All relief requested under Rule 35 should be denied. The defendant is at the doctor's mercy. His report may confuse the jury or prevent a fair trial.

EDITOR'S ANALYSIS: Rule 35 provides that when the physical or mental condition of a party is at issue, the court, upon motion and for good cause, may order the party to submit to an examination by a physician. The party examined is, upon request, entitled to receive a copy of the written report of the examining physician. The rule provides that, by requesting and receiving a copy of the report, the party examined must, upon request, furnish copies of written reports made by his physicians.

QUICKNOTES

DISCOVERY - Pretrial procedure during which one party makes certain information available to the other.

FED. R. CIV. P. 35 - Provides that physical and mental examinations of all parties litigating the action are constitutional.

WRIT OF MANDAMUS - A court order issued commanding a public or private entity, or an official thereof, to perform a duty required by law.

NOTES:

HICKMAN v. TAYLOR
Representative of deceased (P) v. Tug owner (D)
392 U.S. 495 (1947).

NATURE OF CASE: Action for damages for wrongful death.

FACT SUMMARY: Five crew members drowned when a tug sank. In anticipation of litigation, the attorney for Taylor (D), the tug owner, interviewed the survivors. Hickman (P), as representative of one of the deceased, brought this action and tried by means of discovery to obtain copies of the statements Taylor's (D) attorney obtained from the survivors.

CONCISE RULE OF LAW: Material obtained by counsel in preparation for litigation is the work product of the lawyer, and while such material is not protected by the attorney-client privilege, it is not discoverable on mere demand without a showing of necessity or justification.

FACTS: Five of nine crew members drowned when a tug sank. A public hearing was held at which the four survivors were examined. Their testimony was recorded and was made available to all interested parties. A short time later, the attorney for Taylor (D), the tug owner, interviewed the survivors, in preparation for possible litigation. He also interviewed other persons believed to have information on the accident. Ultimately, claims were brought by representatives of all five of the deceased. Four were settled. Hickman (P), the fifth claimant, brought this action. He filed interrogatories asking for any statements taken from crew members as well as any oral or written statements, records, reports, or other memoranda made concerning any matter relative to the towing operation, the tug's sinking, the salvaging and repair of the tug, and the death of the deceased. Taylor (D) refused to summarize or set forth the material on the ground that it was protected by the attorney-client privilege.

ISSUE: Does a party seeking to discover material obtained by an adverse party's counsel in preparation for possible litigation have a burden to show a justification for such production?

HOLDING AND DECISION: (Murphy, J.) Yes. The deposition-discovery rules are to be accorded a broad and liberal treatment, since mutual knowledge of all the relevant facts gathered by both parties is essential to proper litigation. But discovery does have ultimate and necessary boundaries. Limitations arise upon a showing of bad faith or harassment or when the inquiry seeks material which is irrelevant or privileged. In this case, the material sought by Hickman (P) is not protected by the attorney-client privilege. However, such material as that sought here does constitute the work product of the lawyer. The general policy against invading the privacy of an attorney in performing his various duties is so well recognized and so essential to the

orderly working of our legal system that the party seeking work product material has a burden to show reasons to justify such production. Interviews, statements, memoranda, correspondence, briefs, mental impressions, *etc.*, obtained in the course of preparation for possible or anticipated litigation fall within the work product. Such material is not free from discovery in all cases. Where relevant and nonprivileged facts remain hidden in an attorney's file and where production of those facts is essential to the preparation of one's case, discovery may be had. But there must be a showing of necessity and justification. In this case, Hickman (P) seeks discovery of oral and written statements of witnesses whose identity is well known and whose availability to Hickman (P) appears unimpaired. Here no attempt was made to show why it was necessary that Taylor's (D) attorney produce the material. No reasons were given to justify this invasion of the attorney's privacy. Hickman's (P) counsel admitted that he wanted the statements only to help him prepare for trial. That is insufficient to warrant an exception to the policy of protecting the privacy of an attorney's professional activities.

CONCURRENCE: (Jackson, J.) A common law trial is and always should be an adversary proceeding. Discovery was hardly intended to enable a learned profession to perform its functions either without wits or on wits borrowed from the adversary. I can conceive of no practice more demoralizing to the Bar than to require a lawyer to write out and deliver to the adversary an account of what witnesses have told him.

EDITOR'S ANALYSIS: The *Hickman* decision left open a number of questions as to the scope of the work product doctrine and the showing needed to discover work product material. In 1970, Federal Rule of Civil Procedure 26(b)(3) was added to deal with the discovery of work product. It provides that documents and tangible things which were prepared in anticipation of litigation or for trial are discoverable only upon a showing that the party seeking such materials has substantial need of them and that he is unable without undue hardship to obtain the substantial equivalent of the materials by other means. The rule states that mental impressions, conclusions, opinions, or legal theories of an attorney or other representative of a party are to be protected against disclosure.

QUICKNOTES

ATTORNEY-CLIENT PRIVILEGE - A doctrine precluding the admission into evidence of confidential communications between an attorney and his client made in the course of obtaining professional assistance.

DEPOSITION - A pretrial discovery procedure whereby oral or written questions are asked by one party of a witness of the opposing party under oath in preparation for litigation.

DISCOVERY - Pretrial procedure during which one party makes certain information available to the other.

FED. R. CIV. P. 26 (b) (3) - Codifies the work product doctrine.

THOMPSON v. THE HASKELL CO.
Sexually-harassed employee (P) v. Employer (D)
65 F. Empl. Prac. Cas. (BNA) 1088 (M.D. Fl. 1994).

NATURE OF CASE: Motion for protective order in sexual harassment suit.

FACT SUMMARY: Thompson (P) sought to protect her psychologist's report from discovery.

CONCISE RULE OF LAW: Under exceptional circumstances, if it is impractical for the party seeking discovery to obtain facts or opinions on the same subject by other means, a party may, by interrogatories or by deposition, discover information by an expert who has been retained or specially employed by another party in anticipation of litigation and who is not to be called as a witness.

FACTS: Thompson (P) sued The Haskell Co. (D) and Zona (D), a supervisor of the Haskell Co. (D), alleging sexual harassment and that her employment with The Haskell Co. (D) was terminated when she refused to acquiesce to Zona's (D) advances. Thompson's (P) former counsel employed Dr. Lucas, a psychologist, to perform a diagnostic review and personality profile ten days after Thompson (P) was terminated. Thompson (P) sought an order to protect the psychological records possessed by Dr. Lucas.

ISSUE: May a party, under exceptional circumstances, obtain discovery of information by an opposing party's expert who has been retained or employed by a party in anticipation of litigation and who is not to be called as a witness?

HOLDING AND DECISION: (Snyder, Mag.J.) Yes. Under exceptional circumstances, a party may obtain discovery of information by an opposing party's expert who has been retained or employed by a party in anticipation of litigation and who is not to be called as a witness. Here, Dr. Lucas's report was made ten days after Thompson (P) was terminated and is the only evidence available which is probative of Thompson's (P) emotional state at that time. Motion denied.

EDITOR'S ANALYSIS: Thompson (P) did not file her complaint until several months after she was terminated. Thus, opposing counsel had no opportunity to obtain psychological information from Thompson (P) shortly after her termination which would be probative of her emotional state during that time. This factor provided the exceptional circumstance in the present case.

QUICKNOTES

DEPOSITION - A pretrial discovery procedure whereby oral or written questions are asked by one party of a witness of the opposing party under oath in preparation for litigation.

DISCOVERY - Pretrial procedure during which one party makes certain information available to the other.

EXPERT WITNESS - A witness providing testimony at trial who is specially qualified regarding the particular subject matter involved.

INTERROGATORY - A method of pretrial discovery in which written questions are provided by one party to another who must respond in writing under oath.

NOTES:

CHIQUITA INTERNATIONAL LTD. v. M/V BOLERO REEFER
Shipper (P) v. Cargo carrier (D)
1994 U.S. Dist. LEXIS 5820 (S.D. N.Y. 1994).

NATURE OF CASE: Motion to compel discovery.

FACT SUMMARY: International Reefer (D), a carrier, sought to compel discovery of a marine surveyor who had evaluated its loading cranes and side ports.

CONCISE RULE OF LAW: A nontestifying expert is immune from discovery unless exceptional circumstances apply.

FACTS: Shipper Chiquita International Ltd. (P) sued International Reefer Services, S.A. (D), a cargo carrier, for cargo loss and damage. Chiquita (P) alleged that loading cranes and side ports on International Reefer's (D) carrier failed to function properly, which prevented the carrier from shipping the full load of Chiquita (P) bananas to Germany and unloading them before spoilage in accord with their contract. International Reefer (D) requested an order compelling discovery from Winer, a marine surveyor Chiquita (P) had employed to inspect the carrier upon arrival in Germany. International Reefer (D) asserted that Winer was a fact witness rather than an expert and that even if Winer were a nontestifying expert exceptional circumstances existed to compel discovery. Chiquita (P) objected.

ISSUE: May a non-testifying expert be subject to discovery?

HOLDING AND DECISION: (Francis, Mag.J.) No. A nontestifying expert may not be subject to discovery unless exceptional circumstances apply. A fact witness is a witness whose information was obtained in the normal course of business; however, a nontestifying expert is a person hired to make an evaluation in connection with expected litigation. Winer was hired by Chiquita (P) to make an observation in anticipation of litigation; thus, he is a nontestifying expert. Because International Reefer (D) could have employed its own expert to examine its carrier, and Chicquita (P) did not prevent another expert from being retained, no exceptional circumstances apply here. Application for Winer's deposition is denied.

EDITOR'S ANALYSIS: It is often not clear whether a person is a fact witness or nontestifying expert; thus, this is a favorite topic for law school examinations. Another favorite topic is determining if exceptional circumstances apply which would warrant compelling discovery from a nontestifying expert.

QUICKNOTES

DEPOSITION - A pretrial discovery procedure whereby oral or written questions are asked by one party of a witness of the opposing party under oath in preparation for litigation.

DISCOVERY - Pretrial procedure during which one party makes certain information available to the other.

EXPERT WITNESS - A witness providing testimony at trial who is specially qualified regarding the particular subject matter involved.

NOTES:

THOMPSON v. DEPARTMENT OF HOUSING & URBAN DEVELOPMENT

*Public housing residents (P) v. Federal and city
government agencies (D)*
199 F.R.D. 168 (D. Md. 2001).

NATURE OF CASE: Motion by class plaintiffs to compel discovery requests.

FACT SUMMARY: In their racial discrimination suit against federal and city public housing authorities (D), Thompson (P) and other class plaintiffs sought to compel discovery of records going back 75 years.

CONCISE RULE OF LAW: When confronted with a difficult scope of discovery dispute, the parties themselves should confer in an effort to reach an acceptable compromise or narrow the scope of their disagreement.

FACTS: Thompson (P) and other residents of Baltimore's public housing developments filed a class action against the U.S. Department of Housing and Urban Development (D) and the Housing Authority of Baltimore (D)(HABC), alleging *de jure* racial segregation in Baltimore's public housing from 1933 through the present. Thompson (P) moved to compel HABC (D) to provide responsive answers to Rule 33 and Rule 34 discovery requests. The issue on the motion pertained to the fact that Rule 26(b)(1) restricts the scope of discovery to unprivileged facts relevant to "the claim or defense of any party" unless a court determines that there is "good cause" to permit broader discovery relevant to the subject matter of the action, but not more directly connected to the particular claims or defenses. The request here involved 75 years of information.

ISSUE: When confronted with a difficult scope of discovery dispute, should the parties themselves confer in an effort to reach an acceptable compromise or narrow the scope of their disagreement?

HOLDING AND DECISION: (Grimm, Mag.J.) Yes. When confronted with a difficult scope of discovery dispute, the parties themselves should confer in an effort to reach an acceptable compromise or narrow the scope of their disagreement. Here, since Thompson (P) and other members of the class, seek discovery of information going back 75 years, and the Department (D) objects on the grounds of burden, a possible solution may be to agree first to produce information going back five years. Then, depending on the results of a review of the more recent information, if more extensive disclosure can be justified, based on the results of the initial, more limited, less burdensome, examination, it should be produced. Both parties seem content to leave it to the court to sift through the 56-page complaint and the 74-page partial consent decree to determine what discovery should be allowed. Moreover, although counsel for the parties

undoubtedly have conferred in an effort to resolve or narrow the dispute, they have provided the court with nothing to show whether they have attempted to apply the Rule 26(b)(2) balancing factors to try to reach common ground, at least as to some of the areas of dispute. This will not do. The dispute is being returned by this court to the parties with guidance as to how they should meet and confer to attempt to resolve or narrow their differences by focusing their discussions not on their scope differences under Rule 26(b)(1), but instead on a particularized analysis of the burden/benefit factors of Rule 26(b)(2). In this regard, it seems clear that the challenged requests are too broad as stated and need to be narrowed by a good faith analysis of which claims that survived the partial consent decree will be furthered by the discovery sought.

EDITOR'S ANALYSIS: In *Thompson*, the court noted the propriety, in appropriate cases, of permitting a party to have access to some, but less than all, of the information they seek, with the understanding that, if following the initial, limited review, additional discovery would make sense under the Rule 26(b)(2) factors, it will be provided. Cost shifting or sharing, said the court, also should be considered.

QUICKNOTES

FED. R. CIV. P. 33 - Governs interrogatories to parties.

FED. R. CIV. P. 26 - Protects work product revealing an attorney's mental processes absent a strong showing of necessity and unavailability.

NOTES:

POOLE v. TEXTRON, INC.
Injured consumer (P) v. Golf cart manufacturer (D)
192 F.R.D. 494 (D. Md. 2000).

NATURE OF CASE: Motion for sanctions for discovery abuse.

FACT SUMMARY: When Textron, Inc. (D) committed numerous instances of discovery abuse, Poole (P) requested attorneys' fees and other expenses related to Textron's (D) violations.

CONCISE RULE OF LAW: A federal court has the latitude to fashion an "appropriate sanction," in addition to an award of expenses, for discovery abuse.

FACTS: Ryan Poole (P) sued Textron (D) for alleged defects in a golf car, which resulted in serious injuries to him. Poole (P) subsequently moved for sanctions against Textron (D) in the form of attorneys' fees and other expenses for a wide variety of discovery abuses on the part of Textron (D), including incomplete document production, failure to provide accurate interrogatory answers, lack of diligent search for documents and failure to provide a corporate designee able to address all specified areas of inquiry, refusal to answer questions at the deposition, lack of candor with the court and counsel, and attempt to conceal the existence of the 1998 GX-440 golf car in its possession.

ISSUE: Does a federal court have the latitude to fashion an "appropriate sanction," in addition to an award of expenses, for discovery abuse?

HOLDING AND DECISION: (Gauvey, Mag.J.) Yes. A federal court has the latitude to fashion an "appropriate sanction," in addition to an award of expenses, for discovery abuse. The rules do not limit a court to the award of expenses only. Nevertheless, an award of attorneys' fees appear to be the sanction most commonly imposed in reported decisions. Here, while counsel for Textron (D) signed the various discovery responses, counsel had not conducted the requisite "reasonable inquiry," and the quality of the responses suggest an improper purpose, specifically "to cause unnecessary delay or needless cost of litigation." There was no substantial justification for the certification in violation of the civil discovery rules. Furthermore, Textron's (D) responses *and* objections to Poole's (P) requests for admissions appeared crafted to sabotage the legitimate use of request for admissions. Under the plain language of the rule, a party must *either* lodge an objection *or* an answer to a request, but cannot do both. The conduct sanctionable violates Fed. Rule of Civil Proc. 37 and Fed Rule of Civil Proc. 26(g) as well. Here, there was no substantial justification for Textron's (D) non-disclosures, responses and objections, and there were no circumstances that make an award of expenses unjust. Hence, the court awards to Poole (P) $37,258.39 in expenses, including attorneys' fees.

EDITOR'S ANALYSIS: As pointed out in the *Poole* decision, a federal court has authority to redress discovery misconduct under the Federal Rules as well as under its inherent powers, and can impose a range of sanctions from award of expenses against both a party and its counsel to an entry of a default judgment. The sanctions depend on the nature of the discovery abuse.

QUICKNOTES
FED. R. CIV. P. 26 - Protects work product revealing an attorney's mental processes absent a strong showing of necessity and unavailability.

NOTES:

CHAPTER 8
RESOLUTION WITHOUT TRIAL

QUICK REFERENCE RULES OF LAW

1. **Default and Default Judgments.** A meritorious defense is not required to set aside a default entered after improper service. (Peralta v. Heights Medical Center)

2. **Third-Party Participation in Settlement: Facilitation, Encouragement, and Coercion.** Settlement of class action suits in state court may release exclusively federal claims pending in federal court. (Matsushita Elec. Industrial Co. v. Epstein)

3. **Contracting for Confidentiality.** Where a protective order or confidentiality agreement can be modified to place private litigants in a position they would otherwise reach only after repetition of another's discovery, modification can be denied only if it would tangibly prejudice substantial rights of the party opposing modification. (Kalinauskas v. Wong)

4. **Contracting for Private Adjudication: Arbitration and its Variants.** Parties may not be required to submit to arbitration unless they have received consideration for their promise to arbitrate. (Floss v. Ryan's Family Steak Houses, Inc.)

5. **Contracting for Private Adjudication: Arbitration and its Variants.** State contract law governs whether an arbitration agreement is valid. (Lyster v. Ryan's Family Steak Houses, Inc.)

6. **Contracting for Private Adjudication: Arbitration and its Variants.** Judicial review of arbitration proceedings is limited to whether the parties agreed to arbitration, whether the arbitration procedures provide a fair opportunity to be heard, and whether the arbitrators exceeded their powers. (Ferguson v. Writers Guild of America, West)

7. **Curtailed Adjudication: Summary Judgment.** The plain language of Federal Rule of Civil Procedure 56 (c) mandates the entry of summary judgment, after adequate time for discovery, against a party who fails to make a showing sufficient to establish the existence of an element essential to that party's case. (Celotex Corp. v. Catrett)

8. **Curtailed Adjudication: Summary Judgment.** Once a moving party has made a prima facie showing to support a motion for summary judgment, the motion will be granted unless the nonmoving party establishes specific facts showing a genuine issue for trial. (Bias v. Advantage International, Inc.)

9. **Judicial Management of Litigation.** A case may be dismissed for failure to comply with a court order if there is prejudice to the other party and lesser sanctions are unavailable. (Sanders v. Union Pacific Railroad Co.)

10. **Judicial Management of Litigation.** A trial judge has broad discretion to exclude evidence supporting a theory of recovery not raised in the complaint. (McKey v. Fairbairn)

PERALTA v. HEIGHTS MEDICAL CENTER, INC.
Employer/guarantor (P) v. Hospital (D)
485 U.S. 80 (1988).

NATURE OF CASE: Review of summary judgment dismissing bill of review.

FACT SUMMARY: A trial court refused to set aside a default entered after improper service when Peralta (P) could not show a meritorious defense to the action.

CONCISE RULE OF LAW: A meritorious defense is not required to set aside a default entered after improper service.

FACTS: Heights Medical Center, Inc. (D) sued Peralta (P) on a guarantee to pay medical expenses on an employee of Peralta (P). Peralta (P) was improperly served. Heights Medical (D) nonetheless entered a default on Peralta's (P) failure to respond and a judgment lien was placed on certain real estate belonging to Peralta (P). The property was sold at a marshal's sale at a large discount. Peralta (P), upon discovering the sale, filed an action to void the sale and have the default set aside, as the service was invalid. The trial court granted summary judgment, dismissing the action, holding that Peralta (P) had to show meritorious defense to the underlying action, which he could not do. The Texas Court of Appeals affirmed. The Supreme Court accepted review.

ISSUE: Is a meritorious defense required to set aside a default entered after improper service?

HOLDING AND DECISION: (White, J.) No. A meritorious defense is not required to set aside a default entered after improper service. It is basic to due process that before a judgment can be entered against a person, he must be given legally sufficient notice of the action and be given an opportunity to defend. It is no defense to a due process claim that the defendant would have lost on the merits. There are avenues that can be employed by a litigant in a losing posture, such as settling or impleading other parties. For the defendant to do this, he must have notice of the suit. Here, Peralta (P) was not given such notice, and due process therefore demands that the default be set aside. Reversed.

EDITOR'S ANALYSIS: Various avenues exist to challenge a default. The most direct manner is to move for relief in the same action in which the default is entered. However, most states place time limitations on this, as did Texas in this instance. This forced Peralta (P) to file a bill of review, a collateral proceeding.

QUICKNOTES

DEFAULT JUDGMENT - A judgment entered against a defendant due to his failure to appear in a court or defend himself against the allegations of the opposing party.

SERVICE OF PROCESS - The communication of reasonable notice of a court proceeding to a defendant in order to provide him with an opportunity to be heard.

SHERIFF'S SALE - A sale of property by a sheriff pursuant to a judgment.

NOTES:

MATSUSHITA ELECTRIC INDUSTRIAL CO. v. EPSTEIN
516 U.S. 367 (1996).

NATURE OF CASE: Appeal from dismissal of a class action for breach of fiduciary duty.

FACT SUMMARY: A class action suit against Matsushita (D) was settled in Delaware and purported to release pending federal claims against Matsushita (D) in a separate action.

CONCISE RULE OF LAW: Settlement of class action suits in state court may release exclusively federal claims pending in federal court.

FACTS: In 1990, Matsushita (D) made a tender offer for MCA (D), a Delaware corporation, and eventually acquired MCA (D). A class action was filed in Delaware state court against the directors of MCA (D) for failing to maximize shareholder value. While this action was pending, another suit was filed in federal court in California for violations of the Williams Act. The Securities Exchange Act of 1934 gives federal courts exclusive jurisdiction over these claims. The federal court failed to certify the class, and the decision was appealed. While the federal case was under appeal, the parties to the Delaware suit negotiated a settlement which included a global release of all claims arising out of the acquisition. The chancery court approved this settlement if the Delaware Supreme Court affirmed. Matshushita (D) invoked this settlement to the Ninth Circuit, which was considering the federal suit, but the Ninth Circuit held that the settlement could not preclude claims that were exclusively federal. The Supreme Court granted certiorari to clear up the issue.

ISSUE: May the settlement of class action suits in state court release exclusively federal claims pending in federal court?

HOLDING AND DECISION: (Thomas, J.) Yes. Settlement of class action suits in state court may release exclusively federal claims pending in federal court. The Full Faith and Credit Act mandates that the judicial proceedings of any state shall have the same full faith and credit in every United States court. Federal courts must accept the rules chosen by the state from which the judgment was taken in determining the effect of the state judgment. Judgments entered in class actions, like all other actions, are presumptively entitled to full faith and credit. Delaware courts have decided that a global release of claims precludes future federal court litigations of released claims. Thus, Delaware courts would give preclusive effect to a settlement, notwithstanding their lack of jurisdiction over federal claims. The only situation in which federal claims could not be released is if the state court did not have subject matter jurisdiction over the case. In the present case, the Delaware courts had proper jurisdiction over the action and understood that the global release approved in the settlement would release the federal claims. Therefore, the release must be given full effect. Reversed.

EDITOR'S ANALYSIS: The majority noted that it is an extremely rare occasion when a federal statute expressly or impliedly repeals the Full Faith and Credit Act. For an implicit repeal, the two statutes must cause an irreconcilable conflict. This has happened in only a few instances in history.

NOTES:

KALINAUSKAS v. WONG
Former employee (P) v. Employer (D)
151 F.R.D. 363 (D. Nev. 1993).

NATURE OF CASE: Motion for protective order.

FACT SUMMARY: Caesars Palace Hotel & Casino (D) sought to enforce a confidential settlement agreement with a former employee.

CONCISE RULE OF LAW: Where a protective order or confidentiality agreement can be modified to place private litigants in a position they would otherwise reach only after repetition of another's discovery, modification can be denied only if it would tangibly prejudice substantial rights of the party opposing modification.

FACTS: Kalinauskas (P) sued Desert Palace, Inc. (D), doing business as Caesars (D), for sexual discrimination. She sought to depose Thomas, a former Caesars (D) employee, who had sued Caesars (D) for sexual harassment the previous year. Thomas had settled her claim with Caesars (D) and agreed to a confidential settlement agreement which stated in part that Thomas "shall not discuss any aspect of plaintiff's employment at Caesars other than to state the dates of her employment and her job title." Caesars (D) sought a protective order to enforce the confidential settlement agreement and to bar Thomas's deposition. Kalinauskas (P) opposed the order.

ISSUE: May a protective order or confidentiality agreement be modified to place private litigants in a position they would otherwise reach only after repetition of another's discovery if modification would not tangibly prejudice substantial rights of the party opposing modification?

HOLDING AND DECISION: (Johnston, Mag.J.) Yes. A protective order or confidentiality agreement can be modified to place private litigants in a position they would otherwise reach only after repetition of another's discovery if modification would not tangibly prejudice substantial rights of the party opposing modification. Here, Kalinauskas's (P) claim duplicates Thomas's claim both factually and legally. Thus, to force Kalinauskas (P) to duplicate all of Thomas's work would be wasteful. The protective order is granted to the extent that during the deposition of Thomas no information regarding the settlement itself may be disclosed and is denied as to all other aspects. Protective order granted in part and denied in part.

EDITOR'S ANALYSIS: The party seeking to enforce a protective order against a party seeking discovery information has the burden of showing that allowing modification of the order would substantially prejudice that party's rights. As the case above indicates, this burden could be met by showing that an applicable privilege applies to the information sought to be disclosed or that the party would suffer potential injury or prejudice if the information were to be disclosed.

QUICKNOTES

DISCOVERY - Pretrial procedure during which one party makes certain information available to the other.

PROTECTIVE ORDER - Court order protecting a party against potential abusive treatment through use of the legal process.

NOTES:

FLOSS v. RYAN'S FAMILY STEAK HOUSES, INC.
Employees (P) v. Former employer (D)
211 F.3d 306 (6th Cir. 2000).

NATURE OF CASE: Appeal from the upholding of an arbitration agreement.

FACT SUMMARY: When Floss (P) and other employees sued their former employer, Ryan's Family Steak Houses, Inc. (D), for violation of federal statutes, Ryan's (D) filed a motion to compel arbitration.

CONCISE RULE OF LAW: Parties may not be required to submit to arbitration unless they have received consideration for their promise to arbitrate.

FACTS: Floss (P) and other employees brought suit against their former employer, Ryan's Family Steak Houses, Inc. (D), in federal district courts in different states, for violation of their rights under the Americans with Disabilities Act and the Fair Labor Standards Act. However, when applying for employment at Ryan's (D), Floss (P) and the other employees had signed a form indicating they would arbitrate all employee-related disputes. Ryan's (D) filed motions to compel arbitration. One federal district court upheld the arbitration agreements, while another federal district court did not. All parties appealed.

ISSUE: Must a party receive consideration for their promise to arbitrate?

HOLDING AND DECISION: (Gwin, Dist.J.) Yes. A party must receive consideration for their promise to arbitrate. Here, Ryan's (D) has pursued an acceptable objective (requiring an arbitration agreement as a condition of employment) in an unacceptable manner. An employer may enter an agreement with employees requiring the arbitration of all employment disputes, including those, as here, involving federal statutory claims. However, an employer cannot seek to do so in such a way that leaves employees with no consideration for their promise to submit their disputes to arbitration. Floss (P) and the other employees did not receive any consideration for their promise to arbitrate their disputes. Ryan's (D) relies upon a document entitled "Job Applicant Agreement to Arbitration of Employment-Related Disputes," however the employees agreement to arbitrate is not with Ryan's (D), but rather runs between the employee and a third-party arbitration service provider, Employment Dispute Services, Inc. (EDSI). Although Ryan's (D) is not explicitly identified as a party to the agreement, the agreement says the employee's potential employer is a third-party beneficiary of the employee's agreement to waive a judicial forum and arbitrate all employment-related disputes. The agreement gives EDSI complete discretion over arbitration rules and procedures and gives EDSI the unlimited right to modify the rules without the employee's consent. The arbitration agreements may not be enforced.

EDITOR'S ANALYSIS: In *Floss*, the court noted that even though arbitration is generally a suitable forum for resolving a particular statutory claim, the specific arbitral forum provided under an arbitration agreement must nevertheless allow for the effective vindication of that claim.

QUICKNOTES

ARBITRATION AGREEMENT - A mutual understanding entered into by parties wishing to submit to the decisionmaking authority of a neutral third party, selected by the parties and charged with rendering a binding decision amenable to those affected.

CONSIDERATION - Value given by one party in exchange for performance, or a promise to perform, by another party.

NOTES:

LYSTER v. RYAN'S FAMILY STEAK HOUSES, INC.

Employee (P) v. Former employer (D)

239 F.3d 943 (8th Cir. 2001).

NATURE OF CASE: Appeal from district court's refusal to compel arbitration.

FACT SUMMARY: When Lyster (P) sued her former employer, Ryan's Family Steak Houses, Inc. (D), for sexual harassment, Ryan's (D) filed a motion to compel arbitration.

CONCISE RULE OF LAW: State contract law governs whether an arbitration agreement is valid.

FACTS: Lyster (P) brought suit against her former employer, Ryan's Family Steak Houses, Inc. (D) for sexual harassment. Ryan's (D) moved to compel arbitration of the claims. The district court concluded that under the arbitration agreement between Lyster (P) and Ryan's (D), Lyster (P) was required to arbitrate her claim only if she filed her claim with the Equal Opportunity Employment Commission (EEOC) before she was terminated (which she did not) and denied Ryan's (D) motion. Ryan (D) appealed.

ISSUE: Does state contract law govern whether an arbitration agreement is valid?

HOLDING AND DECISION: (Jones, Dist.J.) Yes. State contract law governs whether an arbitration agreement is valid. Here, under the law of Missouri, Lyster's (P) claim was arbitrable and not an unconscionable adhesion contract. Under Missouri law, a contract is substantively unconscionable only if there is undue harshness in the terms of the contract. Lyster (P) executed a valid arbitration agreement. Thus, her claim of unlawful sexual harassment against Ryan's (D) falls within the scope of the agreement. Ryan's (D) is entitled to an order, pursuant to the Federal Arbitration Act, compelling Lyster (P) to pursue her claim in an arbitral, rather than a judicial, forum. Reversed.

EDITOR'S ANALYSIS: In *Lyster*, the court, while recognizing the potential that substantial arbitration fees *may* make an arbitration agreement unconscionable, pointed out that here Lyster (P) failed to establish on the record that undue harshness existed in the terms of this particular arbitration agreement in light of Missouri law governing unconscionability.

NOTES:

QUICKNOTES

PROCEDURAL UNCONSCIONABILITY - Rule of law whereby a court may excuse performance of a contract, or of a particular contract term, if it determines that such term(s) are unduly oppressive or unfair to one party to the contract, as a result of disparity in bargaining power during the formation of the contract.

FERGUSON v. WRITERS GUILD OF AMERICA, WEST
Screenwriter (P) v. Professional organization (D)
226 Cal. App.3d 1382 (1991).

NATURE OF CASE: Appeal of dismissal of action to set aside arbitration decision.

FACT SUMMARY: After a Writers Guild (D) arbitration proceeding supported a Guild (D) determination that Ferguson (P) should get only a partial writing credit on a film, Ferguson (P) sued to set aside the arbitration proceeding.

CONCISE RULE OF LAW: Judicial review of arbitration proceedings is limited to whether the parties agreed to arbitration, whether the arbitration procedures provide a fair opportunity to be heard, and whether the arbitrators exceeded their powers.

FACTS: A collective bargaining agreement gave the Writers Guild (D) the power to make determinations on writing credits for films. The agreement also provided that disputes could not be taken to court. Instead, any dispute had to be submitted to arbitration by the Guild (D). Anonymous arbitrators were chosen through a specified procedure. Their decision could be appealed to the Guild's (D) policy review board only for deviation from Guild (D) policy or procedure, not for matters of substance. Board approval of a determination was final. The Guild (D) gave Ferguson (P) partial credit on a film. Ferguson (P) initiated arbitration proceedings to have himself declared the sole writer. Ferguson (P) lost his arbitration and appealed to the review board on the substance of the dispute. After the review board declared the determination of partial credit final, Ferguson (P) sued in state court, urging the court to make its own determination and award him sole writing credit. In the alternative, Ferguson (P) asked the court to vacate the arbitration decision based on certain procedural defects and to require the Guild (D) to make a new determination of the writing credits. The Guild (D) argued that the collective bargaining agreement made disputes over writing credits nonjusticiable. The trial court dismissed Ferguson's (P) case, and he appealed.

ISSUE: Is judicial review of arbitration proceedings limited to whether the parties agreed to arbitration, whether the arbitration procedures provide a fair opportunity to be heard, and whether the arbitrators exceeded their powers?

HOLDING AND DECISION: (Klein, J.A.) Yes. Judicial review of arbitration proceedings is limited to whether the parties agreed to arbitration, whether the arbitration procedures provide a fair opportunity to be heard, and whether the arbitrators exceeded their powers. Courts accord considerable deference to the determination of arbitration review boards because of their expertise, which courts lack, in their specialized field. The Guild's (D) review board is such a body. Additionally, the principle of exhaustion of administrative remedies prevented Ferguson (P) from pursuing a judicial remedy for any alleged procedural defects in the Guild's (D) conduct of the arbitration and review, since he failed to raise them before the policy review board. Even if he had preserved the procedural defects issue, Ferguson's (P) claims were without merit. There was no material and prejudicial departure from the Guild's (D) procedures. Affirmed.

EDITOR'S ANALYSIS: The use of arbitration in place of judicial resolution has increased significantly in recent years. Parties often prefer arbitration because they can control the substantive and procedural rules which apply to their dispute, they can ensure having a fact finder with expertise in the area of the dispute, and they can save time and money as arbitration is often faster and cheaper. Moreover, while courts traditionally looked with disfavor on arbitration agreements, modern courts usually uphold arbitration agreements because they are a mechanism for reducing the increasingly heavy caseloads of civil courts.

QUICKNOTES
ADMINISTRATIVE REMEDIES - Relief that is sought before an administrative body as opposed to a court.

ARBITRATION - An agreement to have a dispute heard and decided by a neutral third party, rather than through legal proceedings.

NOTES:

CELOTEX CORP. v. CATRETT
Asbestos product manufacturer (D) v. Wife of decedent (D)
477 U.S. 317 (1986).

NATURE OF CASE: Appeal from reversal of summary judgment denying damages for asbestos exposure.

FACT SUMMARY: In Catrett's (P) action against Celotex Corp. (D) for the death of her husband as a result of his exposure to asbestos manufactured by Celotex (D), Celotex (D) moved for summary judgment, contending that Catrett (P) had failed to identify, in answering interrogatories specifically requesting such information, any witnesses who could testify about the decedent's exposure to Celotex's (D) asbestos.

CONCISE RULE OF LAW: The plain language of Federal Rule of Civil Procedure 56 (c) mandates the entry of summary judgment, after adequate time for discovery, against a party who fails to make a showing sufficient to establish the existence of an element essential to that party's case.

FACTS: Catrett (P) sued Celotex Corp. (D), alleging that the death of her husband resulted from his exposure to products containing asbestos manufactured by Celotex (D). At trial, Celotex (D) moved for summary judgment, contending that Catrett (P) had failed to identify, in answering interrogatories specifically requesting such information, any witnesses who could testify about the decedent's exposure to Celotex's (D) asbestos products. The district court granted Celotex's (D) motion because there was no showing that the decedent was exposed to Celotex's (D) product within the statutory period. Catrett (P) appealed.

ISSUE: Does the plain language of Federal Rule of Civil Procedure 56 (c) mandate the entry of summary judgment, after adequate time for discovery, against a party who fails to make a showing sufficient to establish the existence of an element essential to that party's case?

HOLDING AND DECISION: (Rehnquist, J.) Yes. The plain language of Federal Rule of Civil Procedure 56 (c) mandates the entry of summary judgment, after adequate time for discovery, against a party who fails to make a showing sufficient to establish the existence of an element essential to that party's case. In such a situation, there can be "no genuine issue as to any material fact," since a complete failure of proof concerning an essential element of the nonmoving party's case necessarily renders all other facts immaterial. Here, Catrett (P) failed to identify any witnesses who could testify about her husband's exposure to Celotex's (D) asbestos products. There was also no showing that the decedent was exposed to Celotex's (D) product within the statutory period. Catrett's (P) failure to show sufficient evidence to establish essential elements of her case makes summary judgment proper. Reversed and remanded.

CONCURRENCE: (White, J.) If respondent Catrett (P) had named a witness to support her claim, summary judgment could not have been granted without Celotex (D) somehow showing that the named witness' testimony raised no genuine issue of material fact.

DISSENT: (Brennan, J.) The nonmoving party may defeat a motion for summary judgment that asserts that the nonmoving party has no evidence by calling the court's attention to the supporting evidence in the record that was overlooked by the moving party.

EDITOR'S ANALYSIS: *Celotex* is an important case in two ways. First, it integrates the burden of proof borne by the parties at trial with the corresponding burdens on a summary judgment motion. Second, it hints at a larger, more significant role for summary judgment in deciding cases.

QUICKNOTES

FED. R. CIV. P. 56 - Provides that summary judgment be entered for a party who fails to make a showing sufficient to support a material element of its case.

MATERIAL FACT - A fact without the existence of which a contract would not have been entered.

SUMMARY JUDGMENT - Judgment rendered by a court in response to a motion by one of the parties, claiming that the lack of a question of material fact in respect to an issue warrants disposition of the issue without consideration by the jury.

NOTES:

BIAS v. ADVANTAGE INTERNATIONAL, INC.

Estate of basketball player (P) v. Business affairs
representative (D)
905 F.2d 1558 (1990).

NATURE OF CASE: Appeal of the granting of a motion for summary judgment.

FACT SUMMARY: Basketball star Leonard Bias (P) died from a cocaine overdose. When his estate sued Bias' business manager, Advantage International, Inc. (D) for failure to procure insurance for Bias (P) as it had promised to do, Advantage (D) argued that no insurer would have insured a cocaine user.

CONCISE RULE OF LAW: Once a moving party has made a prima facie showing to support a motion for summary judgment, the motion will be granted unless the nonmoving party establishes specific facts showing a genuine issue for trial.

FACTS: The estate of basketball star Leonard Bias (P) brought suit against Advantage International, Inc. (D) which was Bias' (P) management company, for failing to secure life insurance for Bias (P) as it had promised to do. Bias (P) died from a cocaine overdose without the one-million dollar life insurance policy which Advantage (D) had represented it had obtained. Advantage (D) moved for a summary judgment on the grounds that Bias' estate (P) did not suffer any damage from the failure of Advantage (D) to try to obtain life insurance for Bias (P) because even if they had attempted to obtain such a policy, they would not have been able to do so because of Bias' (P) known cocaine use. The district court agreed and granted the motion. Bias' estate (P) appealed.

ISSUE: Once a moving party has made a prima facie showing to support a motion for summary judgment, will the motion be granted unless the nonmoving party establishes specific facts showing a genuine issue for trial?

HOLDING AND DECISION: (Sentelle, Cir.J.) Yes. Once a moving party has made a prima facie showing to support a motion for summary judgment, the motion will be granted unless the nonmoving party establishes specific facts showing a genuine issue for trial. Here, Advatage (D) offered testimony of witnesses which clearly tended to show that Bias (P) was a cocaine user who would therefore have been uninsurable. Bias' estate (P) could have deposed these witnesses, or otherwise attempted to impeach their testimony, but failed to do so or even to try. Advantage (D) offered evidence that *every* insurance company inquires about prior drug use at *some point* in the application process. Bias' (P) evidence that some insurance companies existed in 1986 which did not inquire about prior drug use at certain particular stages in the application process does not

undermine Advantage's (D) claim that at some point *every* insurance company did inquire about drug use, particularly where a jumbo policy was involved. Bias' estate (P) failed to name a single particular company or provide other evidence that a single company existed which would have issued a jumbo policy in 1986 without inquiring about an applicant's drug use. Because Bias' estate (P) failed to do more than show that there was "some metaphysical doubt as to the material facts," the district court properly concluded there was no genuine issue of material fact as to the insurability of a drug user. Affirmed.

EDITOR'S ANALYSIS: In *Bias*, the court noted that, rather than presenting any evidence or questioning any witnesses, to try to establish a case on non-cocaine use, Bias's estate (P) relied instead "on bare arguments and allegations" or on evidence which did not actually create a genuine issue for trial.

QUICKNOTES

PRIMA FACIE - An action in which the plaintiff introduces sufficient evidence to submit an issue to the judge or jury for determination.

NOTES:

SANDERS v. UNION PACIFIC RAILROAD CO.
Employee (P) v. Employer (D)
154 F.3d 1037 (9th Cir. 1998).

NATURE OF CASE: Appeal from dismissal of personal injury lawsuit.

FACT SUMMARY: Sanders' (P) action was dismissed because his attorney failed to comply with a pretrial order.

CONCISE RULE OF LAW: A case may be dismissed for failure to comply with a court order if there is prejudice to the other party and lesser sanctions are unavailable.

FACTS: In 1995, Sanders (P) sued his employer, Union Pacific (D), following a work-related back injury. A trial date was set for November 19, 1996. A pretrial conference was scheduled for November 8, and an order was issued requiring that various motions be completed by then. The order indicated that failure to comply could result in sanctions. Some of the requirements demanded joint participation between the parties. However, Sanders's (P) attorney failed to comply with nearly all of the requirements, apparently because of his responsibilities in another case, but did not alert the court or Union Pacific (D). Following the pretrial conference, the court dismissed Sanders's (P) action with prejudice as a sanction for failure to comply with the pretrial order. Sanders (P) appealed.

ISSUE: May a case be dismissed for failure to comply with a court order if there is prejudice to the other party and lesser sanctions are unavailable?

HOLDING AND DECISION: (Per curiam) Yes. A case may be dismissed for failure to comply with a court order if there is prejudice to the other party and lesser sanctions are unavailable. In the present case, Sanders's (P) attorney had multiple failures with regard to the pretrial order of the court. This undoubtedly impaired Union Pacific's (D) efforts to prepare for trial. Furthermore, by neglecting to inform the court of the impending failures, Sanders's (P) counsel deprived the court of a chance to impose lesser sanctions. The attorney's conduct completely disrupted the trial calendar. In order to achieve justice for individual litigants, flagrant disobedience of orders cannot be tolerated. Sanders (P) was on notice, from the warning in the order, that dismissal could result from failure to comply. Thus, the court did not abuse its discretion in ordering dismissal with prejudice. Affirmed.

DISSENT: (Canby, J.) Dismissal in this case was too harsh and extreme given the fact that no repeated instances of dilatory behavior was involved and no inordinate delay resulted.

EDITOR'S ANALYSIS: The court seemed most concerned that the failure to comply with the order inconvenienced the court. It particularly pointed out that crowded calendars can overwhelm courts. However, the dismissal of this case almost certainly added another case to the docket: Sanders' (P) malpractice suit against his former attorney.

NOTES:

McKEY v. FAIRBAIRN
Lessee of premises (P) v. Agent of lessor (D)
345 F.2d 739 (D.C. Cir. 1965).

NATURE OF CASE: Appeal from directed verdict and denial of motion to amend.

FACT SUMMARY: Mrs. Littlejohn (P), a tenant, slipped on water which had leaked through the roof of an apartment she rented. The trial court denied her motion to amend her complaint to include certain housing regulations after her counsel had orally agreed with the judge that negligence was her theory of recovery.

CONCISE RULE OF LAW: A trial judge has broad discretion to exclude evidence supporting a theory of recovery not raised in the complaint.

FACTS: Mrs. Littlejohn (P) notified her landlord (D) of a leak in her apartment. Before repairs could be made, there was a heavy storm which resulted in her bedroom floor becoming wet from the leak in the roof. She twice mopped the room the following morning, but slipped and fell, sustaining certain injuries, when she returned to the bedroom. Mrs. Littlejohn (P) brought this action for damages, and at trial her counsel agreed with the trial judge's assessment of the case as one in negligence. Thereafter, Mrs. Littlejohn (P) moved to amend her complaint to include citations to certain allegedly relevant housing regulations, but the judge denied the motion and directed a verdict for the defendant. Plaintiff appealed.

ISSUE: Has a trial judge broad discretion to exclude evidence supporting a theory of recovery not raised in the complaint?

HOLDING AND DECISION: (Miller, J.) Yes. The questions on appeal are whether a directed verdict was error where evidence of a leak and a promise to repair it was offered and whether denial of the motion to amend to include housing regulations was error. The landlord did not have a duty to make the repairs alleged, so that a directed verdict on the issue of negligence liability was proper. Similarly, it was not error to refuse to allow McKey (P) to change her theory of recovery after the complaint was filed and answered. The trial court has broad discretion in the conduct of a trial, and this discretion was not abused in this case. A trial judge has broad discretion to exclude evidence supporting a theory of recovery not raised in the complaint, as a part of the conduct of the trial. Furthermore, since Mrs. Littlejohn entered a room where she knew there was a slippery wet spot, her own negligence contributed to the accident. Affirmed.

DISSENT: (Fahy, J.) Modification at trial is to be permitted to prevent manifest injustice. We have previously held that a landlord's duty to a tenant is covered in some part by the housing regulations. Modification should be permitted to allow McKey (P)

to include the regulations in the complaint as a basis for recovery. Furthermore, the issue of contributory negligence should be initially considered and answered by the district court, not by this court on appeal.

EDITOR'S ANALYSIS: Under Federal Rule of Civil Procedure 15, amendment of pleadings after responsive pleadings are served is permitted only by leave of the court or written consent of the adverse party. A party may proceed to trial of issues not raised by pleadings and later amend the pleadings to conform to the evidence, but trial of those unraised issues must be by "express or implied consent of the parties." McKey (P) was outside of all these possibilities in this case.

QUICKNOTES

AMENDMENT TO PLEADING - The modification of a pleading either as a matter of course upon motion to the court or by consent of both parties; a party is entitled to change its pleading once as a matter of course before a responsive pleading has been served.

DIRECTED VERDICT - A verdict ordered by the court in a jury trial.

FED. R. CIV. P. 15(a) - Sets forth the rule that a party may amend its pleading once as a matter of course at any time before a responsive pleading is served, or within 20 days if no responsive pleading is permitted and the action has not been placed on the trial calendar; otherwise a party may amend its pleading only by leave of court or written consent of the opposing party; a party is required to plead in response to an amended pleading within the time remaining for response to the original pleading or within ten days of service of the amended pleading, whichever is longer, unless otherwise stated by court order.

NOTES:

**CHAPTER 9
IDENTIFYING THE TRIER**

QUICK REFERENCE RULES OF LAW

1. **Judging Judges: Bias and Recusal.** The appearance of partiality, even in the absence of actual partiality, is sufficient grounds for recusal of a judge. (In re Boston's Children First)

2. **Applying the Historical Test to New Claims.** Plaintiffs in a fair representation suit against a union are entitled to a jury. (Chauffeurs, Teamsters & Helpers, Local No. 391 v. Terry)

3. **The Seventh Amendment and Changes in Judicial Procedure.** An equitable main claim cannot preclude a jury trial on a legal compulsory counterclaim. (Amoco Oil Co. v. Torcomian)

4. **Challenging Individual Jurors.** A juror must be excused for cause if they hold a belief which would impede them in giving due weight to the evidence and following the judge's instructions. (Thompson v. Altheimer & Gray)

IN RE BOSTON'S CHILDREN FIRST
Party seeking recusal of judge (P) v. Judge (D)
244 F.3d 164 (1st Cir. 2001).

NATURE OF CASE: Petition for writ of mandamus after judge refused to recuse herself.

FACT SUMMARY: When the district court judge made questionable public statements about a pending case, Boston's Children First (P) sought to have her recused.

CONCISE RULE OF LAW: The appearance of partiality, even in the absence of actual partiality, is sufficient grounds for recusal of a judge.

FACTS: Boston's Children First (P) filed suit to challenge Boston's elementary school student assignment process, claiming violations of state and federal law based on race. The plaintiff's attorney, in a newspaper interview for the *Boston Herald*, made provocative statements as to the district judge's handling of the case. In response to such statements, the judge herself gave a newspaper interview stating that, "This is a more complex case," than certain others. Based on those comments, Boston's Children First (P) moved that the judge recuse herself because "her impartiality might reasonably be questioned." The judge denied the request, and Boston's Children First (P) sought a writ of mandamus on the issue.

ISSUE: Does the appearance of partiality, even in the absence of actual partiality, constitute sufficient grounds for recusal of a judge?

HOLDING AND DECISION: (Torruella, C.J.) Yes. The appearance of partiality, even in the absence of actual partiality, is sufficient grounds for recusal of a judge. 28 U.S.C. § 455(a) requires any justice, judge, or magistrate of the United States to disqualify themselves in any proceeding in which their impartiality "might reasonably be questioned." This statute seeks to balance two competing policy considerations. First, that courts must not only be, *but seem to be*, free of bias or prejudice. Secondly, the fear that recusal on demand would provide litigants with a veto against unwanted judges. Here, the facts provide what an objective, knowledgeable member of the public would find to be a reasonable basis for doubting the judge's impartiality. Judge Gertner's comment—that the present case is "more complex" than some others—"could be construed" as a comment on the merits (whether it was or not) of the pending motions for preliminary injunction and class certification. In other words, by calling the instant case "more complex," Judge Gertner arguably suggested that Boston's Children First's (P) claims were less than meritorious and was perhaps signaling that relief was unlikely to be forthcoming. In highly newsworthy cases where tensions may be high, such as here, judges should be particularly cautious about commenting on pending litigation. The public might consider the judge's actions as expressing an undue degree of interest in the case and thus pay special attention to the language of such comments. The very rarity of judicial public statements, and the ease with which they may be avoided, make it more likely that a reasonable person will interpret such statements as evidence of bias. Writ of mandamus granted.

EDITOR'S ANALYSIS: As noted in the *In re Boston's Children First* case, the fact that the judge's public comments were made in response to what could be characterized as an attack by counsel on the procedures of her court, did not justify any comment by the judge beyond an explanation of those procedures.

QUICKNOTES

RECUSAL - Procedure whereby a judge is disqualified from hearing a case either on his own behalf, or on the objection of a party, due to some bias or interest in the subject matter of the suit.

WRIT OF MANDAMUS - A court order issued commanding a public or private entity, or an official thereof, to perform a duty required by law.

NOTES:

CHAUFFEURS, TEAMSTERS & HELPERS, LOCAL 391
v. TERRY
Labor union (D) v. Unhappy workers (P)
494 U.S. 558 (1990).

NATURE OF CASE: Review of order striking a jury demand.

FACT SUMMARY: Terry and several workers (P) in a fair representation suit against the Teamster's Union (D), contended that they were entitled to a jury.

CONCISE RULE OF LAW: Plaintiffs in a fair representation suit against a union are entitled to a jury.

FACTS: The Teamsters Union (D) instituted a grievance procedure against McLean Trucking on behalf of certain workers. Following the conclusion of the procedure, Terry (P) and several workers, unhappy with the result, filed an action against the Union (D), contending that the Union (D) breached its duty of fair representation. The Union (D) moved to strike Terry's (P) jury demand, contending that Terry (P) was not entitled to a trial by jury. The district court granted the motion, but the Fourth Circuit reversed. The U.S. Supreme Court granted review.

ISSUE: Are plaintiffs in a fair representation suit against a union entitled to a jury?

HOLDING AND DECISION: (Marshall, J.) Yes. Plaintiffs in a fair representation suit against a union are entitled to a jury. In deciding whether the Seventh Amendment guarantees a right to a jury trial, a court must examine the issues being litigated and the remedy sought. Here, the two issues are subject to trial. One is whether McLean breached a collective bargaining agreement, and the other is whether the Union (D) breached its duty of fair representation. The first issue is similar to a breach of contract action, which is an action at law contending a right to a jury. The second is similar to breach of fiduciary duty, an equitable action. Consequently, the issues to be tried are both legal and equitable. However, the remedy sought is back pay, which is akin to money damages. These are historically recovered at law, and this Court thinks that this tips the scales in favor of the action in question being more akin to one at law than one in equity, thus implicating the Seventh Amendment. Affirmed.

CONCURRENCE: (Brennan, J.) The only relevant factor for Seventh Amendment issues should be nature of the remedy sought.

CONCURRENCE: (Stevens, J.) An action against a union for breaching its duty of fair representation is more akin to a malpractice action, which is historically an action at law.

DISSENT: (Kennedy, J.) The Court correctly identified the type of action as akin to breach of fiduciary duty. However, this should be the stopping point, at which the issue should have been decided.

EDITOR'S ANALYSIS: The Seventh Amendment necessarily involves an historical analysis. The amendment guarantees a jury in actions "at common law." This has been interpreted to mean that actions implicate the amendment, but equitable ones do not. As many types of actions prevalent today did not exist in 1791, when the amendment was adopted, courts must analogize to determine whether a particular action is more like one at law, for which the right for a jury trial exists, or in equity, which traditionally is heard by a judge alone.

QUICKNOTES

ACTION AT LAW - Lawsuit in a which a plaintiff seeks legal remedies such as damages.

EQUITABLE ACTION (ACTION IN EQUITY) - Lawsuit in which a plaintiff seeks equitable remedies.

MONEY DAMAGES - Monetary compensation sought by, or awarded to, a party who incurred loss as a result of a breach of contract or tortious conduct on behalf of another party.

NOTES:

AMOCO OIL CO. v. TORCOMIAN
Franchisor (P) v. Franchisee (D)
722 F.2d 1099 (3d. Cir. 1983).

NATURE OF CASE: Appeal from judgment in ejectment action.

FACT SUMMARY: The trial court refused a jury to the defendants in an ejectment action involving a counterclaim for damages.

CONCISE RULE OF LAW: An equitable main claim cannot preclude a jury trial on a legal compulsory counterclaim.

FACTS: Torcomian (D) took over a service station and sought to become a franchisee of Amoco (D). While the negotiations proceeded, Torcomian (D) ran the station, but never executed the agreement due to a dispute. Subsequently, Amoco (P) brought a suit requesting ejectment of Torcomian (D) from the service station and lost profits as a result of alleged wrongful possession. At the beginning of trial, Amoco (P) attempted to orally amend its complaint to delete the portions that sought money damages to foreclose Torcomian's (D) right to a jury trial. Torcomian (D) filed a counterclaim for a breach of contract and sought damages. The trial court refused to order a jury trial and ruled for Amoco (P). Torcomian (D) appealed.

ISSUE: Can an equitable main claim preclude a jury trial on a legal compulsory counterclaim?

HOLDING AND DECISION: (Becker, Cir.J.) No. An equitable main claim cannot preclude a jury trial on a legal compulsory counterclaim. It has long been settled that joinder of an equitable claim to a legal claim does not defeat the Seventh Amendment's requirement of a jury trial. Therefore, if there were any legal claims present in the instant case, the district court erred in not allowing a jury trial. On the surface, Amoco's (P) complaint appears to present a number of legal claims. Ejectment has long been regarded as a legal claim and damages were sought as a form of relief. Federal law unequivocally holds actions seeking ejectment as legal, not equitable. Furthermore, Torcomian's (D) counterclaim seeking damages for breach of contract is plainly a legal claim. Therefore, it was error the trial court to refuse a jury trial. This error would be harmless if Amoco (P) would have been entitled to a directed verdict anyway. However, in the present case, the disposition of the claims rested largely on issues of credibility. Thus, a directed verdict could not have been properly granted by the district court. Accordingly, the judgment must be vacated and the case remanded for a new trial.

EDITOR'S ANALYSIS: Amoco (P) had tried to argue that two Pennsylvania cases had found that ejectment type cases were equitable injunctions against continued use of property. The court found Amoco's (P) interpretation of these cases to be both dubious and beside the point. The characterization of a claim as legal or equitable must be made by recourse to federal law.

QUICKNOTES

EJECTMENT - An action to oust someone in possession of real property unlawfully and to restore possession to the party lawfully entitled to it.

EQUITABLE ACTION (ACTION IN EQUITY) - Lawsuit in which a plaintiff seeks equitable remedies.

SEVENTH AMENDMENT - Provides that no fact, tried by a jury shall be otherwise re-examined in any court of the United States, other than according to the rules of the common law.

NOTES:

THOMPSON v. ALTHEIMER & GRAY
Employee (P) v. Employer (D)
248 F.3d 621 (7th Cir. 2003).

NATURE OF CASE: Appeal from a defense jury verdict.

FACT SUMMARY: In an employment discrimination case, when the judge refused to strike a juror who stated that the fact she was a business owner "will definitely sway my judgment," the losing party argued that the judge erred in not striking the juror for cause.

CONCISE RULE OF LAW: A juror must be excused for cause if they hold a belief which would impede them in giving due weight to the evidence and following the judge's instructions.

FACTS: Thompson (P) sued her employer, Altheimer & Gray (D), under Title VII of the Civil Rights Act, charging racial discrimination. During voir dire, the juror Leiter stated that she was currently the owner of a business and that, "I feel that as an employer and owner of a business that will definitely sway my judgment in this case." When asked by the judge whether she would be able to apply the law as instructed, she replied "I think my experience will cloud my judgment, but I can do my best." The judge refused to grant Thompson's (P) attorney's request to strike Leiter for cause, and she remained on the jury. The case was tried, and the jury returned a verdict for Altheimer & Gray (D). Thompson (P) appealed, arguing that Leiter should have been struck for cause.

ISSUE: Must a juror be excused for cause if they hold a belief which would impede them in giving due weight to the evidence and following the judge's instructions?

HOLDING AND DECISION: (Posner, Cir.J.) Yes. A juror must be excused for cause if they hold a belief which would impede them in giving due weight to the evidence and following the judge's instructions. When the juror Leiter said she believed that some people sue their employer just because they have not received a promotion or a raise or some other benefit, she was not manifesting bias. She was simply expressing a prior belief. The question here was not whether Leiter's belief that some claims against employers are spurious was true or false (it was clearly true), but rather whether this belief would somehow impede her in giving due weight to the evidence and following the judge's instructions. In the instant case, that question was not adequately explored by the judge. Had the judge pushed Leiter and had she finally given unequivocal assurances that he deemed credible, his ruling could not be disturbed. But he failed to do that. Furthermore, the denial of the right to an unbiased tribunal is one of those trial errors that is not excused by being shown to have been harmless. Reversed and remanded.

CONCURRENCE: (Wood, Cir.J.) It occasionally happens that not all peremptories are used. If there are left-over peremptories and the plaintiff has failed to convince the court to strike a certain juror for cause, it is at least imaginable that a decision not to use an available peremptory challenge on that juror might amount to a waiver of the right to assert that the juror should not have sat.

EDITOR'S ANALYSIS: In *Thompson*, the court stressed that it was pertinent to note that no issue of credibility was presented and no argument that the juror Leiter was not telling the truth. The issue was interpretive: did she manifest a degree of bias such that the judge abused his discretion in failing to strike her for cause.

QUICKNOTES
PEREMPTORY CHALLENGE - The exclusion by a party to a lawsuit of a prospective juror without the need to specify a particular reason.

VOIR DIRE - Examination of potential jurors on a case.

NOTES:

CHAPTER 10
TRIAL

QUICK REFERENCE RULES OF LAW

1. **The Limits of Rational Inference.** A plaintiff has the burden of presenting evidence that it is more probable than not that the defendant is liable in order to overcome a motion for a directed verdict for the defendant. (Reid v. San Pedro, Los Angeles & Salt Lake Railroad)

2. **Judgment as a Matter of Law (Directed Verdict).** Where evidence is so insubstantial that if a verdict is rendered for one of the parties, the other would be entitled to a new trial, it is up to the judge to direct a verdict according to the court's view of all the evidence. (Pennsylvania Railroad v. Chamberlain)

3. **New Trial — Flawed Verdicts.** Where nothing indicates that the jury was not properly presented with correct evidence, the judge may not nullify the jury verdict by granting a new trial so long as the evidence admits of the conclusion made by the jury. (Lind v. Schenley Industries)

4. **The Limits of the Law's Control: The Jury as a Black Box.** The admission of juror testimony to impeach a jury verdict is prohibited. (Peterson v. Wilson)

REID v. SAN PEDRO, LOS ANGELES & SALT LAKE RAILROAD

Cattle owner (P) v. Railroad company (D)

39 Utah 617, 118 P. 1009 (1911).

NATURE OF CASE: Appeal from award of damages for negligence.

FACT SUMMARY: Reid (P) gave evidence showing that his cow was killed by San Pedro's (D) train either because San Pedro (D) neglected to repair a fence or because Reid (P) neglected to close a gate allowing the cow to get to the tracks.

CONCISE RULE OF LAW: A plaintiff has the burden of presenting evidence that it is more probable than not that the defendant is liable in order to overcome a motion for a directed verdict for the defendant.

FACTS: Reid (P) was permitted by a landowner to graze certain cows on the landowner's property adjacent to train tracks. One of Reid's (P) cows found its way to the tracks and was struck by one of San Pedro's (D) trains and killed. The cow could have had access to the tracks either by going through a portion of the fence negligently left unrepaired by San Pedro (D) or by going through a gate which could have been negligently left open by Reid (P). There was no direct evidence as to which caused the accident. The jury brought in a verdict for Reid (P) upon which judgment was entered, and San Pedro (D) appealed.

ISSUE: Has a plaintiff the burden of presenting evidence that it is more probable than not that the defendant is liable in order to overcome a motion for a directed verdict for the defendant?

HOLDING AND DECISION: (McCarty, J.) Yes. The evidence presented in this case admits of two readings: one that San Pedro (D) was negligent and one that Reid (P) was negligent. Neither of these propositions is stronger than the other under the facts as known by the court and the jury. Where the undisputed evidence of the plaintiff, from which the existence of an essential fact is sought to be inferred, points with equal force to two things, one of which renders the defendant liable and the other not, the plaintiff must fail. Thus, a plaintiff has the burden of presenting evidence that it is more probable than not that the defendant is liable in order to overcome a motion for a directed verdict for the defendant. In this case, a verdict for San Pedro (D) should have been directed by the trial court. Reversed.

EDITOR'S ANALYSIS: As the plaintiff is the master of his lawsuit, it is incumbent upon him to show that the defendant is responsible for whatever injury has been sustained. There must be more than a possibility of the defendant's liability, there must be a probability. Where it is equally possible that defendant is not responsible after the plaintiff has presented all of his evidence, the defendant is entitled to be dismissed from the lawsuit.

QUICKNOTES

BURDEN OF PERSUASION - The duty of a party to introduce evidence to support a fact that is in dispute in an action.

DIRECTED VERDICT - A verdict ordered by the court in a jury trial.

RELEVANT EVIDENCE - Evidence having any tendency to prove or disprove a disputed fact.

NOTES:

PENNSYLVANIA RAILROAD CO. v. CHAMBERLAIN
Railroad company (D) v. Estate of brakeman (P)
288 U.S. 333 (1933).

NATURE OF CASE: Appeal of an action for negligent homicide.

FACT SUMMARY: When deceased was killed while routing railroad cars, Chamberlain (P) sued Pennsylvania Railroad Co. (D) for negligently bringing about a collision. Three eyewitnesses testified there was no such collision and one witness gave testimony which would have given equal inferential support for both collision and noncollision.

CONCISE RULE OF LAW: Where evidence is so insubstantial that if a verdict is rendered for one of the parties, the other would be entitled to a new trial, it is up to the judge to direct a verdict according to the court's view of all the evidence.

FACTS: Chamberlain (P) sued Pennsylvania Railroad Co. (D) to recover for the death of a brakeman who was killed while routing train cars in a railroad yard. The complaint alleged that certain railroad cars were negligently brought into collision with the cars the deceased was riding on causing him to fall off and be run over. There was corroborated testimony by three eyewitnesses that there was no such collision. Bainbridge, a witness for Chamberlain (P), testified that a loud crash occurred before the accident. He also stated that he stood about 900 feet away from the body of the deceased, was not paying particular attention, and loud crashes were not an unusual event. The trial court entered a directed verdict for Pennsylvania Railroad Co. (D). Reversed on appeal. Certiorari granted.

ISSUE: Should a judge refrain from ordering a directed verdict where the evidence, taken in toto, would require a new trial to be ordered for one party should the other manage to prevail with the jury?

HOLDING AND DECISION: (Sutherland, J.) No. Where there is a true conflict of testimony, evidence must be left to the jury. Here, there was no such conflict. There was an inference drawn from Bainbridge's testimony that there had been a collision, but the testimony gave equal support to an inference that there was no collision. Argument that a collision took place is mere speculation in light of the witness' limited observations. Bainbridge's testimony was so insubstantial that it did not justify submission to the jury as there was no evidence that a jury could have properly proceeded to a verdict for the party offering it as proof. Judgment of appellate court reversed. District court judgment affirmed.

EDITOR'S ANALYSIS: This case points up the distinctly minority rule for determining the propriety of a motion for directed verdict.

In most jurisdictions, the trial court may look only to the evidence presented by the party against whom a directed verdict is sought to determine whether as a matter of law the evidence is insufficient to support such party's case. In Chamberlain, and a minority of jurisdictions, however, the trial court may look to all the evidence presented by both sides to determine whether "reasonable minds could differ" as to the ultimate disposition of the case. Note, of course, that this "minority view" is the majority view for determining the right to a new trial—a fact which gives rise to substantial criticism of the rule as too liberal (since the effect of a new trial is somewhat less drastic than that of a directed verdict).

QUICKNOTES
DIRECTED VERDICT - A verdict ordered by the court in a jury trial.

NOTES:

LIND v. SCHENLEY INDUSTRIES

Sales negotiator (P) v. Employer company (D)

278 F.2d 79 (3d Cir. 1960).

NATURE OF CASE: Appeal from granting of judgment notwithstanding the verdict and, in the alternative, a new trial.

FACT SUMMARY; Although a jury awarded Lind (P) damages in his breach of contract suit against his employer, Schenley Industries, Inc. (D), the trial judge set aside the award as being against the weight of the evidence.

CONCISE RULE OF LAW: Where nothing indicates that the jury was not properly presented with correct evidence, the judge may not nullify the jury verdict by granting a new trial so long as the evidence admits of the conclusion made by the jury.

FACTS: Lind (P) sued his employer Schenley Industries, Inc. (D), alleging that Schenley (D) had breached its oral promise to give him an increase in pay and a share of commissions. Lind (P) and his secretary testified to such promises. Schenley's (D) agents denied making the promises. The jury found that a contract was created and awarded damages to Lind (P). The trial judge granted Schenley's (D) motion for judgment notwithstanding the verdict and, alternatively, for a new trial. Lind (P) appealed.

ISSUE: Where nothing indicates that the jury was not properly presented with correct evidence, may the judge nullify the jury verdict by granting a new trial if the evidence admits of the conclusion made by the jury?

HOLDING AND DECISION: (Biggs, C.J.) No. The jury found the testimony of the plaintiff and his secretary credible. The judge disagreed. The evidence given as to what Lind (P) had received as a result of his negotiations demonstrates that the jury's finding was not against the weight of the evidence, however. Furthermore, there was evidence enough to sustain the finding that the contract was not too indefinite to be sustainable. Where nothing indicates that the jury was not properly presented with the correct evidence, the judge may not nullify the jury verdict by granting a new trial if the evidence admits of the conclusion made by the jury. Reversed.

DISSENT: (Hastie, J.) The judge may not substitute his own verdict for that of the jury. But he may avoid what in his professionally trained and experienced judgment is an unjust verdict by vacating it and causing the matter to be tried again. Here, there was a sharp conflict of testimony as to the offers and promises. It was not an abuse of discretion to grant the new trial.

EDITOR'S ANALYSIS: A reversal of an order granting a new trial requires an abuse of discretion by the granting judge. Showing an abuse of discretion is not an easy proposition, but it is possible. Where the new trial is granted despite a logically defensible jury verdict based on properly admitted correct evidence, such an abuse is shown.

QUICKNOTES

DIRECTED VERDICT - A verdict ordered by the court in a jury trial.

FED. R. CIV. P. 50 - Provides that a party which has lost an adjudication may make all its post-trial notions at once.

NOTES:

PETERSON v. WILSON
Employee (P) v. Employer (D)
141 F.3d 573 (5th Cir. 1998).

NOTES:

NATURE OF CASE: Appeal from judgment in a retrial of wrongful termination action.

FACT SUMMARY: The trial court ordered a new trial on its own motion after meeting with a jury after their verdict.

CONCISE RULE OF LAW: The admission of juror testimony to impeach a jury verdict is prohibited.

FACTS: Peterson (P) filed suit in district court after he was fired as grant director at Texas Southern University (D). After a trial, a jury awarded Peterson (P) $187,000. The defendants moved for a new trial. Four months later, the district court granted the new trial, but its order revealed that it did so because comments made by the jurors after the verdict indicated that they had disregarded the court's instructions. The case was re-tried and Peterson's (P) claims were rejected by the second jury. Peterson (P) appealed the grant of a new trial.

ISSUE: Is the admission of juror testimony to impeach a jury verdict prohibited?

HOLDING AND DECISION: (Wiener, J.) Yes. The admission of juror testimony to impeach a jury verdict is prohibited. A jury's verdict can be disregarded if it is against the great weight of the evidence. However, in the present case, the district court clearly granted the new trial due to its meeting with jurors following the verdict and the comments made at that time. This post verdict, ex parte meeting was impermissible. FRE 606(b) provides that jurors may not testify as to statements made in deliberations or concerning the mental process of decision making. The only exception is for extraneous and outside influences on the jury. This reflects a conscious decision to disallow juror testimony as to their fidelity to the court's instructions. Given this rule, the court's granting of a new trial in the present case was clearly erroneous. The only reason given for granting the new trial was the comments made by the jurors after the verdict. Therefore, the judgment in the second trial must be vacated and the results of the first trial reinstated.

EDITOR'S ANALYSIS: The court also awarded Peterson (P) his costs and attorney's fees incurred in both trials and on appeal. The decision also found that the original verdict was not against the weight of the evidence, even if the district court had used this legal reason for granting the new trial. The exception to the rule in this case is a situation where the jurors are influenced by evidence that is brought illegally into the jury room.

CHAPTER 11
APPEAL

QUICK REFERENCE RULES OF LAW

1. **Appellate Jurisdiction and the Final Judgment Rule.** An interlocutory appeal under Rule 54(b) of the Federal Rules of Civil Procedure is limited expressly to multiple claims actions. (Liberty Mutual Insurance Co. v. Wetzel)

2. **Exceptions to the Final Judgment Rule: Practical Finality.** Under the collateral order doctrine, a prejudgment order may be appealed only when it conclusively determines the disputed question, resolves an important issue completely separable from the merits of the action, and is effectively unreviewable on appeal from a final judgment. (Lauro Lines, s.r.l. v. Chasser)

3. **Scope of Review: Law and Fact.** Under Federal Rule of Civil Procedure 52(a), a finding is clearly erroneous only when, although there is evidence to support it, the reviewing court, on the entire evidence, is left with the definite and firm conviction that a mistake has been made. (Anderson v. Bessemer City)

LIBERTY MUTUAL INS. CO. v. WETZEL
Insurer (D) v. Employer insured (P)
424 U.S. 737 (1976).

NATURE OF CASE: Appeal from finding of liability for violation of Title VII of the Civil Rights Act of 1964.

FACT SUMMARY: Wetzel (P) alleged that Liberty Mutual's (D) employee insurance benefits and maternity leave regulations discriminated against women in violation of Title VII of the Civil Rights Act of 1964.

CONCISE RULE OF LAW: An interlocutory appeal under Rule 54(b) of the Federal Rules of Civil Procedure is limited expressly to multiple claims actions.

FACTS: Wetzel (P) filed a complaint which asserted that Liberty Mutual's (D) employee insurance benefits and maternity leave regulations discriminated against women in violation of Title VII of the Civil Rights Act of 1964. Wetzel's (P) complaint sought several forms of relief, including monetary damages, attorney fees, and injunctive relief. On January 9, 1974, after finding no issues of material fact in dispute, the district court granted partial summary judgment for Wetzel (P) on the issue of liability only. On February 20, 1974, the district court issued an order of final judgment as to Liberty Mutual's (D) liability, but granted none of the relief requested in Wetzel's (P) complaint. The court of appeals held that it had jurisdiction over Liberty Mutual's (D) appeal under 28 U.S.C. § 1291 and affirmed the judgment of the district court.

ISSUE: Is an interlocutory appeal under Rule 54(b) of the Federal Rules of Civil Procedure limited expressly to multiple claims actions?

HOLDING AND DECISION: (Rehnquist, J.) Yes. Rule 54(b) is limited expressly to multiple claims actions in which one or more, but less than all, of the multiple claims have been finally decided and are found otherwise to be ready for appeal. Here, Wetzel's (P) complaint set forth a single claim, which advanced a single legal theory which was applied to only one set of facts. Even if the district court's order was a declaratory judgment on the issue of liability, it still left unresolved Wetzel's (P) requests for an injunction, for compensatory and exemplary damages, and for attorney fees. Although it might be argued that the order of the district court, insofar as it failed to include the injunctive relief requested, was an interlocutory order refusing an injunction within the meaning of § 1292(a)(1), even if this would have allowed the obtaining of a review in the court of appeals, there was no denial of any injunction sought. Nor was the order appealable under § 1292(b). There can be no assurance that had the requirements of § 1292(b) been complied with, the court of appeals would have exercised its discretion to entertain the interlocutory appeal. The district court's order is therefore not appealable pursuant to 28 U.S.C. § 1291. Reversed.

EDITOR'S ANALYSIS: The basic rationale for the policy in federal courts of requiring final judgments is one based upon a cost-benefit analysis. If the trial judge turns out to have been correct, the cost of allowing an interlocutory appeal is the cost of an unnecessary extra appeal. Conversely, if the trial judge turns out to have been wrong in his or her judgment, the cost of not allowing an interlocutory appeal is the sum expended for an unnecessary or an unnecessarily long trial. However, because trial judges are affirmed far more often than they are reversed, the federal policy seems to be logical.

QUICKNOTES

FED. R. CIV. P. 54 - Sets forth the provisions regarding judgments and costs.

INTERLOCUTORY APPEAL - The appeal of an issue that does not resolve the disposition of the case, but is essential to a determination of the parties' legal rights.

NOTES:

LAURO LINES S.R.L. v. CHASSER
Ship company (D) v. Passenger (P)
490 U.S. 495 (1989).

NATURE OF CASE: Interlocutory appeal of a denial of a motion to dismiss action for damages for personal injuries.

FACT SUMMARY: After the district court denied Lauro's (D) motion for dismissal based on a forum-selection clause which purportedly limited Chasser (P) to suing in Naples, Italy, Lauro (D) sought to overturn the denial on interlocutory appeal.

CONCISE RULE OF LAW: Under the collateral order doctrine, a prejudgment order may be appealed only when it conclusively determines the disputed question, resolves an important issue completely separable from the merits of the action, and is effectively unreviewable on appeal from a final judgment.

FACTS: Chasser (P) and the other plaintiffs were passengers aboard Lauro's (D) ship, the Achille Lauro, when it was hijacked in the Mediterranean Sea by terrorists. Lauro (D) moved to dismiss Chasser's (P) personal injury suit on the ground that a forum-selection clause printed on the passenger tickets limited any passenger to suing in Naples, Italy. The district court denied the motion, holding that the ticket did not give passengers reasonable notice that they were giving up the right to sue in the United States. The court of appeals dismissed Lauro's (D) appeal, finding that the district court's order was interlocutory and not appealable. Lauro (D) appealed to the U.S. Supreme Court.

ISSUE: Is a prejudgment order subject to interlocutory appeal when it can be effectively reviewed on appeal from a final judgment?

HOLDING AND DECISION: (Brennan, J.) No. Under the collateral order doctrine, a prejudgment order may be appealed only when it conclusively determines the disputed question, resolves an important issue completely separable from the merits of the action, and is effectively unreviewable on appeal from a final judgment. An order is "effectively" unreviewable on final judgment when the order involves an asserted right the practical value of which would be destroyed if it were not vindicated before trial. Thus, interlocutory appeal is allowed when the defendant asserts a right that is not an ultimate right upon which the suit is brought. Here, Lauro (D) only asserted a right not to be sued in a particular forum. This right was not lost. Lauro (D) could assert the forum-selection clause in appealing any unfavorable final judgment. If an appeals court agreed with Laurel's (D) position, it could vacate trial judgment and limit the refiling of the case in Naples. Affirmed.

CONCURRENCE: (Scalia, J.) Implicit in the Court's ruling is that Lauro's (D) right of forum selection is not important enough to require vindication on interlocutory appeal.

EDITOR'S ANALYSIS: Where a criminal defendant asserts a right not to be tried, an order denying that right is reviewable on interlocutory appeal. In civil cases, a partial list of orders reviewable on interlocutory appeal includes denial of a motion to dismiss based on a claim of absolute or qualified official immunity, an order denying a party leave to proceed in forma pauperis, an order requiring class action defendants to bear the cost of notifying members of the plaintiff class, and an order vacating attachment of a vessel.

QUICKNOTES

COLLATERAL ORDER - Doctrine pursuant to which an appeal from an interlocutory order may be brought in order to hear and determine claims which are collateral to the merits of the case and which could not be granted adequate review on appeal.

IN FURMA PAUPERIS - Permission to proceed with litigation without incurring fees or costs.

INTERLOCUTORY APPEAL - The appeal of an issue that does not resolve the disposition of the case, but is essential to a determination of the parties' legal rights.

JUDGMENT ON THE MERITS - A determination of the rights of the parties to litigation based on the presentation evidence, barring the party from initiating the same suit again.

NOTES:

ANDERSON v. BESSEMER CITY
Sex discrimination claimant v. Municipality (D)
470 U.S. 564 (1985).

NATURE OF CASE: Appeal of finding of discriminatory intent in action brought under Title VII of the Civil Rights Act of 1964.

FACT SUMMARY: In Anderson's (P) action against Bessemer City (D) for discrimination in an action brought under Title VII of the Civil Rights Act of 1964, Anderson (P), a woman applying for a job as a Recreation Director for Bessemer City (D), alleged that she had been denied the position because of her sex, and that the district court's finding of discriminatory intent in Anderson's (P) action was a factual finding that could be overturned on appeal only if it was clearly erroneous.

CONCISE RULE OF LAW: Under Federal Rule of Civil Procedure 52(a), a finding is clearly erroneous only when, although there is evidence to support it, the reviewing court, on the entire evidence, is left with the definite and firm conviction that a mistake has been made.

FACTS: In Anderson's (P) action against Bessemer City (D) for discrimination in an action brought under Title VII of the Civil Rights Act of 1964, Anderson (P), a woman, alleged that she had been denied a position as Recreation Director in a city athletic program because of her sex. After a two-day trial, the court issued a memorandum of decision setting forth its finding that Anderson (P) had been denied the position because of her sex and that male members of the Bessemer City (D) hiring commission for the position had been biased against Anderson (P) because she was a woman. The City (D) appealed and the Fourth Circuit reversed, holding that the lower court's findings were clearly erroneous. Anderson (P) appealed.

ISSUE: Under Federal Rule of Civil Procedure 52(a), is a finding clearly erroneous only when, although there is evidence to support it, the reviewing court, on the entire evidence, is left with the definite and firm conviction that a mistake has been made?

HOLDING AND DECISION: (White, J.) Yes. Under Federal Rule of Civil Procedure 52(a), a finding is clearly erroneous only when, although there is evidence to support it, the reviewing court, on the entire evidence, is left with the definite and firm conviction that a mistake has been made. Application of the foregoing principles to the facts of this case lays bare the errors committed. The Fourth Circuit improperly conducted what amounted to a de novo weighing of the evidence in the record. The district court's findings were based on essentially undisputed evidence and from the evidence, the court determined that Anderson's (P) more varied educational and employment background and her extensive experience in variety of civil activities left her better qualified to implement such a rounded program than the other job applicants. Our determination that the findings of the district court regarding Anderson's (P) qualifications, the conduct of her interview, and the bias of the male committee members were not clearly erroneous leads this Court to conclude that the court's finding that Anderson (P) was discriminated against on account of her sex was also not clearly erroneous. Reversed and remanded.

EDITOR'S ANALYSIS: *Anderson v. Bessemer City* grows out of a practice that has its roots in the distinction between law and equity. Because cases in equity were considered only on a written record and the appellate court was able to read the record as the trial court, the rule evolved in equity that the appellate court reviewed equity decisions de novo. That standard came to dominate appellate review not just of decisions in equity, but of all decisions by a judge sitting without a jury.

QUICKNOTES
FED. R. CIV. P. 52(a) - Requires that findings of fact not be set aside unless clearly erroneous.

NOTES:

**CHAPTER 12
RESPECT FOR JUDGMENTS**

QUICK REFERENCE RULES OF LAW

1. **Precluding the "Same" Claim: Efficiency.** Claim preclusion bars a second suit where the first suit arose out of the same transaction. (Frier v. City of Vandalia)

2. **Consistency — The Logical Implications of the Former Judgment.** Res judicata bars a counterclaim when its prosecution would nullify rights established by a prior action. (Martino v. McDonald's System, Inc.)

3. **Between the "Same" Parties.** A person is in privity with another if he is so identified in interest with the other that he represents the same legal right. (Searle Brothers v. Searle)

4. **After a Judgment "on the Merits."** A judgment rendered by a court lacking subject matter jurisdiction does not have claim preclusive effect in subsequent proceedings. (Gargallo v. Merrill Lynch, Pierce, Fenner & Smith)

5. **An Issue "Actually Litigated and Determined."** The doctrine of estoppel by verdict allows a judgment in a prior action to operate as a complete bar to those facts or issues actually litigated and determined in the prior action. (Illinois Central Gulf Railroad v. Parks)

6. **Between Which Parties?: The Precluder.** A trial judge has broad discretion to permit the offensive use of collateral estoppel to establish an element of a plaintiff's case where it is not unfair to the defendant. (Parklane Hosiery Co. v. Shore)

7. **Between Which Parties?: The Precluder.** Where prior judicial determinations on a particular matter are inconsistent, the doctrine of collateral estoppel will not bar relitigation of that matter. (State Farm Fire & Casualty Co. v. Century Home Components)

8. **Full Faith and Credit as a Bar to Collateral Attack.** The principles of res judicata and full faith and credit preclude relitigation of judgments of a foreign state when the parties have appeared and have fully and fairly litigated the issues. (Durfee v. Duke)

9. **The Reopened Judgment as an Alternative to Collateral Attack.** Independent actions pursuant to Rule 60(b) are reserved for cases of injustice sufficiently gross to demand departure from adherence to the doctrine of res judicata. (United States v. Beggerly)

FRIER v. CITY OF VANDALIA
Owner of towed car (P) v. Municipality (D)
770 F.2d 699 (7th Cir. 1985).

NATURE OF CASE: Appeal of dismissal of action for deprivation of property without due process under color of law.

FACT SUMMARY: After Frier (P) lost his state court suit against Vandalia (D) for replevin of his car, he then sued Vandalia (D) in federal court under 42 U.S.C. § 1983 for depriving him of his car without due process under color of law.

CONCISE RULE OF LAW: Claim preclusion bars a second suit where the first suit arose out of the same transaction.

FACTS: Vandalia (D) police had a garage tow Frier's (P) car because it was parked in traffic. Frier (P) did not receive a citation or a hearing either before the car was towed or after he refused to pay to retrieve it. Frier (P) sued Vandalia (D) and the garage in state court for replevin of his car. After a trial, the court decided that Vandalia (D) had the right to tow Frier's (P) car because it was obstructing traffic. Therefore, the court did not issue the writ of replevin. Frier (P) then filed a 42 U.S.C. § 1983 suit in federal court, seeking equitable relief and compensatory and punitive damages from Vandalia (D) for depriving him of his car without due process under color of law. The district court dismissed Frier's (P) suit for failure to state a claim, and Frier (P) appealed, arguing that he was not precluded from filing a federal suit under a different legal theory than the one he on which he based his state court action.

ISSUE: Does claim preclusion bar a second suit where the first suit arose out of the same transaction?

HOLDING AND DECISION: (Easterbrook, Cir.J.) Yes. Claim preclusion bars a second suit where the first suit arose out of the same transaction. Claim preclusion, also called res judicata, is designed to impel parties to consolidate all closely related matters in the same suit. First, this prevents oppression of defendants through multiple cases. Second, when the facts and issues of all theories of liability are closely related, there is no good reason to incur the cost of litigation more than once. Frier (P) could have sued in his state court action for both replevin, to get his car back, and under § 1983, for damages. Both theories alleged the same conduct: that Vandalia (D) towed and detained his cars without lawful process, i.e., without a determination of a parking violation. Thus, claim preclusion bars Frier's (P) federal suit. The district court, though it properly dismissed the case, should not have reached the merits. Affirmed.

CONCURRENCE: (Swygert, Sr.Cir.J.) Frier's (P) suit should properly have been dismissed on summary judgment, but not for claim preclusion. Illinois law, applicable in this case, follows the narrower, traditional rule of claim preclusion, not the broader Restatement rule applied by the majority. Under the traditional rule, one suit bars a second where the evidence necessary to sustain a second verdict would have sustained the first, *i.e.,* where the causes of action are based on a common core of operative facts. To prevail on his replevin claim, Frier (P) would have had to prove a superior right to possession of the car, which turned on whether he had parked illegally. However, under § 1983, the legality of Frier's (P) parking was irrelevant. The issues as to § 1983 were whether Frier (P) had notice that he would be towed for parking where he did, and whether he had a fair hearing on the detaining of his car. The fact that Frier (P) could have brought the two causes of action in the same suit is irrelevant under the traditional rule of claim preclusion.

EDITOR'S ANALYSIS: Judge Easterbrook and Judge Swygert agree that under the "same transaction" rule Frier's (P) second suit was barred by claim preclusion or res judicata. However, Judge Swygert applied the narrower, traditional, "core of operative facts" rule to reach the opposite result on the claim preclusion issue. The federal courts and most states follow the "same transaction" rule, which is codified in the Restatement (Second) of Judgments § 24 (1982).

QUICKNOTES
CLAIM - The demand for a right to payment or equitable relief; the fact or facts giving rise to such demand.

42 U.S.C. § 1983 - The Civil Rights Act; usually invoked when a party commences suit based on the alleged state's violation of the party's civil rights.

RES JUDICATA - The rule of law that a final judgment by a court precludes subsequent litigation between the parties regarding the same cause of action.

NOTES:

MARTINO v. McDONALD'S SYSTEM, INC.
Franchise owner (P) v. Fast food company (D)
598 F.2d 1079 (7th Cir. 1979), cert. denied, 444 U.S. 966 (1979).

NATURE OF CASE: Appeal from summary judgment in antitrust action.

FACT SUMMARY: Martino (P) alleged that a franchise and lease agreement between Martino (P) and McDonald's (D) violated provisions of the Sherman Antitrust Act.

CONCISE RULE OF LAW: Res judicata bars a counterclaim when its prosecution would nullify rights established by a prior action.

FACTS: In 1962, Martino (P) entered into a franchise and lease agreement with McDonald's (D), which specified that neither Martino (P) nor a member of his immediate family would acquire a financial interest in a competing self-service food business without the written consent of McDonald's (D). In 1968, Martino's (P) son purchased a Burger Chef franchise in Pittsburg, Kansas. After McDonald's (D) brought suit for breach of contract, Martino (P) and McDonald's (D) entered into a consent agreement which provided for the sale of Martino's (P) franchise back to McDonald's (D). In 1975, Martino (P) brought this action, alleging that the enforcement of the restriction on acquisition in the franchise and lease agreements violated the Sherman Act. The district court held that both res judicata and the compulsory counterclaim rule of the Federal Rules of Civil Procedure barred Martino (P) from suing for antitrust violations.

ISSUE: Does res judicata bar a counterclaim when its prosecution would nullify rights established by a prior action?

HOLDING AND DECISION: (Pell, J.) Yes. Because the earlier action between Martino (P) and McDonald's (D) was terminated by a consent judgment before an answer was filed, Federal Rule of Civil Procedure 13(a), which bars compulsory counterclaims that are not raised at the proper time, is not applicable here. However, the res judicata effect of the earlier consent judgment is a bar to raising the antitrust claim in this action. The conclusion of the earlier contract lawsuit with a consent judgment does not prevent the earlier judgment from having a res judicata effect, because that judgment was accompanied by judicial findings of fact and conclusions of law that go to the merits of the controversy. It is an accepted general rule that when facts form the basis of both a defense and a counterclaim, the defendant's failure to allege these facts as a defense or a counterclaim does not preclude him from relying on those facts in an action subsequently brought by him against the plaintiff. However, an exception to this general rule provides that res judicata bars a counterclaim when its prosecution would nullify rights established by the prior action. In this case, the doctrine of res judicata bars

Martino (P) from waging this direct attack on the rights established by the prior judgment. Affirmed.

EDITOR'S ANALYSIS: Because Martino (P) had not entered pleadings in the action which ended in the consent judgment, it was necessary here to consider the relationship between res judicata and counterclaims. The same process must be undertaken in jurisdictions which have no rule governing compulsory counterclaims.

QUICKNOTES

COMPULSORY COUNTERCLAIM - An independent cause of action brought by a defendant to a lawsuit in order to oppose or deduct from the plaintiff's claim that arises out of the same transaction or occurrence that is the subject matter of the plaintiff's claim and does.

COUNTERCLAIM - An independent cause of action brought by a defendant to a lawsuit in order to oppose or deduct from the plaintiff's claim.

RES JUDICATA - The rule of law that a final judgment by a court precludes subsequent litigation between the parties regarding the same cause of action.

NOTES:

SEARLE BROS. v. SEARLE
Father-son partnership (P) v. Wife (D)
588 P.2d 689 (Utah 1978).

NATURE OF CASE: Appeal from decision barring claim of interest in real property.

FACT SUMMARY: Searle Bros. (P) claimed an undivided one-half interest in Slaugh House, which had been awarded to Searle (D) in a divorce proceeding.

CONCISE RULE OF LAW: A person is in privity with another if he is so identified in interest with the other that he represents the same legal right.

FACTS: Edlean Searle (D) sued Woodey Searle for divorce. During that proceeding, the court determined that a piece of property known as the "Slaugh House," which was recorded in Woodey's name, was part of the marital property and subsequently awarded the entire property to Edlean Searle (D). Woodey had argued that he had a half interest in the property and that the other half was owned by a partnership with his sons as partners. Searle Bros. (P), the partnership, then sued Edlean Searle (D), claiming an undivided one-half interest in Slaugh House. The trial court held that res judicata and collateral estoppel barred the action by Searle Bros. (P).

ISSUE: Is a person in privity with another if he is so identified in interest with the other that he represents the same legal right?

HOLDING AND DECISION: (Ellett, C.J.) Yes. A divorce decree, like other final judgments, is conclusive as to parties and their privies and operates as a bar to any subsequent action. The legal definition of a person in privity with another is a person so identified in interest with another that he represents the same legal right. This includes a mutual or successive relationship to rights in property. Here, Searle Bros.' (P) interest was neither mutual nor successive. Searle Bros. (P) claims no part of the interest owned by Woodey Searle, but asserts its own, independent, and separate partnership interest in 50% of the property involved. Collateral estoppel may not be applied against Searle Bros. (P) because it was not a partner to the first suit, and there is insufficient evidence in the record to show that the interest of the partnership in the Slaugh House was ever litigated. Reversed.

DISSENT: (Crockett, J.) The doctrine of collateral estoppel should bar the suit by Searle Bros. (P). It is plain that the members of the family were actively involved in the divorce action, which involved whatever interest any of them had in the family assets. Further, Searle Bros. (P) was fully aware of the adverse claims being asserted to the Slaugh House.

EDITOR'S ANALYSIS: It is possible for both res judicata and collateral estoppel to apply here. Res judicata requires that the causes of action be identical, and it is generally assumed that different parties automatically have different causes of action. However, if Searle Bros. (P) were in privity with the parties to the earlier divorce action, the requirements for res judicata are met.

QUICKNOTES

CLAIM - The demand for a right to payment or equitable relief; the fact or facts giving rise to such demand.

COLLATERAL ESTOPPEL - A doctrine whereby issues litigated and determined in a prior proceeding are binding upon all subsequent litigation between the parties regarding that issue.

ISSUE - A fact or question that is disputed between two or more parties.

RES JUDICATA - The rule of law that a final judgment by a court precludes subsequent litigation between the parties regarding the same cause of action.

NOTES:

GARGALLO v. MERRILL LYNCH, PIERCE, FENNER & SMITH

Client (P) v. Broker (D)

918 F.2d 658 (6th Cir. 1990).

NATURE OF CASE: Appeal from dismissal of action for securities violations.

FACT SUMMARY: Gargallo's (P) federal court action was dismissed because in a previous state court case, his counterclaim involving the same issues was rejected.

CONCISE RULE OF LAW: A judgment rendered by a court lacking subject matter jurisdiction does not have claim preclusive effect in subsequent proceedings.

FACTS: Gargallo (P) had a brokerage account with Merrill Lynch (D). When the investments went poorly, Gargallo (P) ended up owing Merrill Lynch (D) $17,000. The broker (D) brought suit in Ohio state court for collection of the debt and Gargallo (P) filed a counterclaim alleging that the losses were caused by violation of federal securities law. The Ohio court dismissed the counterclaim with prejudice for Gargallo's (P) failure to comply with discovery requests and orders. Gargallo (P) then filed a complaint in U.S. district court. The court dismissed the action on res judicata grounds, finding that the claims were the same as those dismissed by the Ohio court. Gargallo (P) appealed.

ISSUE: Does a judgment rendered by a court lacking subject matter jurisdiction have claim preclusive effect in subsequent proceedings?

HOLDING AND DECISION: (Ryan, J.) No. A judgment rendered by a court lacking subject matter jurisdiction does not have claim preclusive effect in subsequent proceedings. The doctrine of res judicata provides that a final judgment by a court is conclusive of the rights, questions and facts at issue with respect to the parties in all other actions. In the present case, it is clear that Gargallo's (P) federal court complaint alleges the same violations that were alleged in the state court counterclaim. Ordinarily, federal courts are required to give state court judgments the same preclusive effect such judgment would have in a state court. Ohio subscribes to the position that res judicata does not apply where the original court did not have subject matter jurisdiction over the issue. In the present case, Ohio did not have jurisdiction over Gargallo's (P) allegations of securities violations by Merrill Lynch (D). Thus, the dismissal should not have been given preclusive effect in federal district court. Reversed and remanded.

EDITOR'S ANALYSIS: The decision did not directly address the issue that Gargallo's (P) state court counterclaim was not really decided on the merits. It was dismissed because of failure to abide by discovery requirements. However, it would still have been subject to res judicata if the state court had had subject matter jurisdiction.

QUICKNOTES

RES JUDICATA - The rule of law that a final judgment by a court precludes subsequent litigation between the parties regarding the same cause of action.

SUBJECT MATTER JURISDICTION - A court's ability to adjudicate a specific category of cases based on the subject matter of the dispute.

28 U.S.C. § 1738A - Federal law governing the enforcement and modification of foreign decrees and the treatment of concurrent proceedings. Only custody determinations made consistent with its provisions are to be given full faith and credit by states. It preempts conflicting state law and requires that a custody determination be made in the child's home state.

NOTES:

ILLINOIS CENTRAL GULF RAILROAD v. PARKS
Railroad company (D) v. Injured car occupants (P)
181 Ind. App. 141, 390 N.E.2d 1078 (1979).

NATURE OF CASE: Interlocutory appeal from denial of motion for summary judgment.

FACT SUMMARY: Parks (P) was injured when his car collided with an Illinois Central (D) train.

CONCISE RULE OF LAW: The doctrine of estoppel by verdict allows a judgment in a prior action to operate as a complete bar to those facts or issues actually litigated and determined in the prior action.

FACTS: Parks (P) and his wife were injured when their car collided with an Illinois Central (D) train. Parks' (P) wife recovered $30,000 on her claim for damages for personal injuries, but judgment was rendered for Illinois Central (D) on Parks' (P) own claim for damages for loss of services and loss of consortium. Parks (P) then sued Illinois Central (D) to recover damages for his own injuries. On Illinois Central's (D) motion for summary judgment, the trial court held that Parks' (P) claim was not barred by res judicata, and that the prior action did not collaterally estop Parks (P) on the issue of contributory negligence.

ISSUE: Does the doctrine of estoppel by verdict allow a judgment in a prior action to operate as a complete bar to those facts or issues actually litigated and determined in the prior action?

HOLDING AND DECISION: (Lybrook, J.) Yes. The doctrine of estoppel by verdict allows the judgment in a prior action to operate as an estoppel as to those facts or questions actually litigated and determined in the prior action. Where a prior judgment may have been based upon either or any of two or more distinct facts, a party desiring to plead the judgment as an estoppel by verdict must show the actual basis for the prior judgment. Here, the basis for the prior judgment against Parks (P) could have been predicated on a finding by the jury that either Parks (P) had sustained no damages, or that his own negligence was a proximate cause of his damages. Illinois Central (D) failed to show that the judgment against Parks (P) in the prior action was based upon a finding that Parks (P) was contributorily negligent in the accident. Affirmed.

EDITOR'S ANALYSIS: The doctrine of collateral estoppel is reflective of a policy that the needs of judicial finality and efficiency outweigh the possible gains of fairness or accuracy which would result from the continued litigation of an issue that had been decided in prior judicial proceedings. There is a strong policy favoring consistency of judicial rulings in both state and federal courts.

QUICKNOTES

COLLATERAL ESTOPPEL - A doctrine whereby issues litigated and determined in a prior proceeding are binding upon all subsequent litigation between the parties regarding that issue.

NOTES:

PARKLANE HOSIERY CO. v. SHORE
Hosiery company (D) v. Shareholder (P)
439 U.S. 322 (1979).

NATURE OF CASE: Review of denial of relitigation of issue determined in a separate case.

FACT SUMMARY: Shore (P) sought rescission of a merger on the ground that Parklane (D), a party to the merger, had issued a false and misleading proxy statement, and in a separate action filed by the Securities Exchange Commission (SEC), the district court found the proxy statement to be false, so Shore (P) moved for partial summary judgment in this action on that issue, alleging that Parklane (D) was collaterally estopped from relitigating the issue.

CONCISE RULE OF LAW: A trial judge has broad discretion to permit the offensive use of collateral estoppel to establish an element of a plaintiff's case where it is not unfair to the defendant.

FACTS: Shore (P) brought a shareholder's class action against Parklane (D) alleging that Parklane (D) had issued a materially false and misleading proxy statement in violation of §§ 14(a), 10(b), and 20(a) of the Securities Exchange Act. Shore (P) sought rescission of merger to which Parklane (D) was a party because of the proxy statement, which related to the merger. Before trial, however, the Securities Exchange Commission filed suit on the same basis seeking injunctive relief. The court in that suit found the statement false and misleading and entered a declaratory judgment to that effect. Shore (P) then moved for partial summary judgment on the issue of falsity, alleging that Parklane (D) was collaterally estopped from relitigating the issue. The district court denied the motion, but the court of appeals reversed. The U. S. Supreme Court granted certiorari.

ISSUE: Has a trial judge broad discretion to permit the offensive use of collateral estoppel to establish an element of a plaintiff's case where it is not unfair to the defendant?

HOLDING AND DECISION: (Stewart, J.) Yes. The defensive use of collateral estoppel to prevent relitigation of issues previously litigated and lost by a plaintiff against another defendant has been upheld by this Court. But the present case involves the offensive use of collateral estoppel to prevent relitigation of issues by a defendant against whom a different plaintiff has obtained a ruling. It is argued that such offensive use will not promote judicial economy because plaintiffs can await a ruling in another matter without intervening, and then be relieved of making proofs if the issue is resolved to their satisfaction, but not be foreclosed from raising it again if it is not. Here, however, it is doubtful that Shore (P) could have joined in the SEC injunction suit, so that this argument is inapplicable. Another argument is that a defendant may have little incentive to defend in an action for small or nominal

damages, and should not be subjected to unforeseeable future suits against which he will not be adequately able to defend. But here, Parklane (D) had as strong an incentive offensive use of collateral estoppel to establish an element of a plaintiff's case where it is not unfair to the defendant. Under these circumstances, it is not unfair to use collateral estoppel against Parklane (D), who had a full and fair opportunity to litigate its claims.

EDITOR'S ANALYSIS: In a separate part of the opinion, the Court found that the offensive use of collateral estoppel in this case would violate Parklane's (D) right to a jury trial in the legal action as opposed to the SEC's equitable suit. This Seventh Amendment right did not, however, affect the propriety of use of collateral estoppel offensively where not unfair to the defendant if the jury trial right was not at issue.

QUICKNOTES

JOINDER OF PARTIES - The joining of parties in one lawsuit.

OFFENSIVE COLLATERAL ESTOPPEL - A doctrine that may be invoked by a plaintiff whereby a defendant is prohibited from relitigating issues litigated and determined in a prior proceeding against another plaintiff.

NOTES:

STATE FARM FIRE & CASUALTY CO. v.
CENTURY HOME COMPONENTS
Insurance company (P) v. Builder of prefab housing (D)
275 Or. 97, 550 P.2d 1185 (1976).

NATURE OF CASE: Appeal from award of damages for negligence.

FACT SUMMARY: State Farm (P) and many others claimed that Century Home (D) had been negligent by allowing a fire to erupt and spread, causing damage to property.

CONCISE RULE OF LAW: Where prior judicial determinations on a particular matter are inconsistent, the doctrine of collateral estoppel will not bar relitigation of that matter.

FACTS: Over 50 separate actions for damages were filed against Century Home (D) to recover losses from a fire. Three of the actions proceeded separately through trial to final judgment. One judgment was awarded in favor of Century Home (D), and judgment was twice awarded to separate claimants. State Farm (P), who was not a party to any of the previous actions, sought to utilize the prior claimants' judgments to establish conclusively Century Home's (D) negligence and its responsibility for any losses caused by the fire. The trial court held that Century Home (D) was collaterally estopped from any further contesting its liability.

ISSUE: Where prior judicial determinations on a particular matter are inconsistent, does the doctrine of collateral estoppel bar relitigation of that matter?

HOLDING AND DECISION: (Holman, J.) No. In every situation where collateral estoppel is asserted by a person who was neither a party nor in privity with a party to the prior case, it is essential to determine that no unfairness will result to the prior litigant if the estoppel is applied. Where outstanding judicial determinations are inconsistent on the matter sought to be precluded, it would be patently unfair to estop a party by the judgment it lost. The question of whether preclusion would be fair under all the circumstances is independent of, and in addition to, whether a party had a full and fair opportunity to present its case in the action resulting in the adverse judgment. Here, because the prior determinations are basically inconsistent, it would be unfair to preclude Century Home (D) from relitigating the issue of liability. Reversed and remanded.

EDITOR'S ANALYSIS: The Restatement position regarding mutuality of estoppel is consistent with the view taken in this case. It allows relitigation of an issue when "the determination relied on as preclusive was itself inconsistent with another determination of the same issue." Restatement of the Law (Second) Judgments (Tent. Draft No. 2 1975). The Restatement would also allow relitigation of an issue in cases where preclusion would complicate the determination of issues in subsequent actions, prejudice the interests of another party, or where the person seeking preclusion could have joined in the initial action.

QUICKNOTES
COLLATERAL ESTOPPEL - A doctrine whereby issues litigated and determined in a prior proceeding are binding upon all subsequent litigation between the parties regarding that issue.

MUTUALITY OF ESTOPPEL - Doctrine pursuant to which a court may not consider a judgment final as to one party to a cause of action if it is not final as to the other.

NOTES:

DURFEE v. DUKE
Landowner (D) v. Title claimant (P)
375 U.S. 106 (1963).

NATURE OF CASE: On writ of certiorari in action to quiet title to land.

FACT SUMMARY: Duke (P), having lost a quiet title action brought in the Nebraska court by Durfee (D), brought an additional quiet title action regarding the same land in a Missouri court.

CONCISE RULE OF LAW: The principles of res judicata and full faith and credit preclude relitigation of judgments of a foreign state when the parties have appeared and have fully and fairly litigated the issues.

FACTS: Durfee (D) brought an action against Duke (P) in a Nebraska court to quiet title to land situated on the Missouri River at the Missouri-Nebraska boundary line. The Nebraska court had subject matter jurisdiction only if the land was in Nebraska. Duke (P) appeared in the Nebraska court and finally litigated the issues, including the court's jurisdiction. Both the Nebraska trial and appellate courts found for Durfee (D) and held that the Nebraska court had subject matter jurisdiction based on their finding that the land was in Nebraska. Duke (P) then brought this action in a Missouri court to quiet title on the same land. Because of diversity of citizenship, the action was removed to the federal district court. That court held that, although the disputed land was in Missouri, since the Nebraska litigation had adjudicated and determined all the issues, the judgment of the Nebraska court was res judicata and binding. Duke (P) argued that the Nebraska judgment was not conclusive on the merits in the Missouri court since Nebraska had no jurisdiction over Missouri land. The appellate court reversed, holding that the court was not obliged to give full faith and credit to the Nebraska judgment and that res judicata was inapplicable because the controversy involved land and the Missouri court was therefore free to retry the issue of the Nebraska court's jurisdiction over the subject matter.

ISSUE: Once a matter has been fully and fairly litigated and judicially determined, does the principle of res judicata preclude the same issue being retried by the same parties in another state?

HOLDING AND DECISION: (Stewart, J.) Yes. The constitutional command of full faith and credit requires that judicial proceedings shall have the same full faith and credit in every court with the United States as they have by law or usage in the courts of the state from which they are taken. Full faith and credit as well as the principle of res judicata therefore preclude relitigation of judgments of a foreign state when the parties have appeared and have fully and fairly litigated the issues. Here, it is not questioned that the Nebraska courts would give full res judicata effect to the Nebraska judgment quieting title in Durfee (D) and therefore the

Missouri court was limited to inquiring only whether the jurisdictional issues had been fully and fairly litigated by the parties and finally determined in the Nebraska courts. The underlying rationale is the doctrine of jurisdictional finality which holds that one trial of an issue is enough. The principles of res judicata apply to questions of jurisdiction of the subject matter as well as to other issues. Also public policy demands that there be an end to litigations, that those who have voluntarily, fully, and fairly contested an issue should be bound by the result. This rule applies to real as well as personal property. While there are the exceptions of federal preemption and sovereign immunity, these overriding considerations are not present here. The judgment of the court of appeals is reversed and that of the district court is affirmed.

CONCURRENCE: (Black, J.) The dispute in this case is as to whether the tract of land in question is in Nebraska or in Missouri. The Nebraska Supreme Court has held that it is in that state and the majority today has agreed that the determination in that suit bars a second suit brought in Missouri. I concur in the holding, but with the understanding that the Nebraska decision would be binding in the event of an authoritative determination by an original suit between the two states or by state compact.

EDITOR'S ANALYSIS: Following the principle of collateral attack, a judgment may always be attacked either in the state where rendered, or in any other state or forum, on the basis of lack of jurisdiction. Lack of subject matter jurisdiction is never waived and hence a collateral attack may be made for the first time when the judgment is accorded res judicata effect in some other action. However, collateral attack is available only to a party who did not appear in the original action. No such attack is permitted by a party who raised and litigated the jurisdictional defect in the original action (or merely appeared and therefore could have raised it). In such a case, the first court's findings as to its jurisdiction—no matter how erroneous—are themselves entitled to res judicata and cannot be relitigated.

QUICKNOTES

FULL FAITH AND CREDIT - Doctrine that a judgment by a court of one state shall be given the same effect in another state.

ISSUE - A fact or question that is disputed between two or more parties.

RES JUDICATA - The rule of law that a final judgment by a court precludes subsequent litigation between the parties regarding the same cause of action.

UNITED STATES v. BEGGERLY
Government (D) v. Alleged property owner (P)
524 U.S. 38 (1998).

NATURE OF CASE: Appeal from dismissal of action to set aside settlement in prior quiet title litigation.

FACT SUMMARY: Beggerly (P) sought to set aside an earlier judgment based on a settlement.

CONCISE RULE OF LAW: Independent actions pursuant to Rule 60(b) are reserved for cases of injustice sufficiently gross to demand departure from adherence to the doctrine of res judicata.

FACTS: In 1979, the United States (D) brought a quiet title action in Mississippi against Beggerly (P) over certain real property. The issue was whether the land in question had been deeded prior to the date of the Louisiana Purchase in 1803. If not, the United States (D) would own it and not have to purchase it from Beggerly (P). During discovery, Beggerly (P) sought proof of title. A search by government officials of public records revealed nothing that proved a land grant prior to 1803. On the eve of trial, the case was settled for a modest sum and judgment entered based on the agreement. However, Beggerly (P) continued to search for information and in 1991, a specialist claimed to have found a grant in 1781. Beggerly (P) then filed a complaint seeking to set aside the settlement and award damages. The district court dismissed the case on jurisdictional grounds but the court of appeals reversed, deciding that it qualified as an independent action under Fed. R. Civ. P. 60(b).

ISSUE: Are independent actions pursuant to Rule 60(b) reserved for cases of injustice sufficiently gross to demand departure from adherence to the doctrine of res judicata?

HOLDING AND DECISION: (Rehnquist, J.) Yes. Independent actions pursuant to Rule 60(b) are reserved for cases of injustice sufficiently gross to demand departure from adherence to the doctrine of res judicata. Prior to the adoption of the Federal Rules of Civil Procedure, the availability of relief from a judgment turned on whether the court was still in the same term in which the challenged judgment was entered. The 1946 amendment to Rule 60 made clear that all old forms of relief from a judgment were abolished except for the independent action. However, an independent action is only available to prevent a grave miscarriage of justice. In the present case, it is obvious that Beggerly's (P) allegations do not come close to meeting this standard. Beggerly (P) only alleges that the government (D) failed to thoroughly search its record. It would surely result in no grave injustice to allow the settlement and judgment in the prior litigation to stand. Therefore, the court of appeals is reversed.

EDITOR'S ANALYSIS: The decision noted that the alleged failure to furnish relevant information could possibly fit under Rule 60(b)(3). This subsection provides for a one-year limit on motions. Given that the time limit had long expired, the court declined to fully rule on this possibility.

QUICKNOTES

RES JUDICATA - The rule of law that a final judgment by a court precludes subsequent litigation between the parties regarding the same cause of action.

NOTES:

CHAPTER 13
JOINDER

QUICK REFERENCE RULES OF LAW

1. **Claims by the Defendant: Counterclaims.** A claim for the amount of a debt owed pursuant to a transaction which is the subject of a truth-in-lending suit brought in federal court is a compulsory counterclaim of such suit. (Plant v. Blazer Financial Services)

2. **Joinder of Parties: By Plaintiffs.** Permissive joinder of parties is to be broadly granted under Federal Rule of Civil Procedure 20 where each party seeks relief arising out of the same transaction or series of transactions and a common question of fact or law will arise in the action. (Mosely v. General Motors Corp.)

3. **By Defendants: Third-Party Claims.** A defendant may assert a claim against anyone not a party to the original action if that third party's liability is in some way dependent upon the outcome of the original action. (Price v. CTB, Inc.)

4. **More Complex Litigation.** In a diversity case, the federal court does not have ancillary jurisdiction over the plaintiff's claims against a third-party defendant who is a citizen of the same state. (Owen Equipment & Erection Co. v. Kroger)

5. **Compulsory Joinder.** Joint tortfeasors are not necessary parties under Fed. R. Civ. P. 19. (Temple v. Synthes Corp.)

6. **Compulsory Joinder.** A tenant under a lease which violates a clause in another tenant's lease from a common landlord is not an indispensable party under Federal Rule of Civil Procedure 19 to a suit by such other tenant against that landlord. (Helzberg's Diamond Shops v. Valley West Des Moines Shopping Center)

7. **Intervention.** A party may intervene in an action under Federal Rule of Civil Procedure 24(a)(2) if he has an interest upon which the disposition of that action will have a significant legal effect. (Natural Resources Defense Council v. United States Nuclear Regulatory Commission)

8. **Intervention.** A party may not be bound by a judgment rendered in an action in which he was not a party, even if he had knowledge of the action. (Martin v. Wilks)

9. **Interpleader.** A party has an unconditional right to intervene if the party can prove a risk of practical impairment of a relevant interest, timely application, and lack of adequate representation. (Cohen v. The Republic of the Philippines)

10. **Statutory Requirements.** Class certification prerequisites under Rule 23 must be rigorously analyzed by the court. (Communities for Equity v. Michigan High School Athletic Assn.)

11. **Statutory Requirements.** The presence of counterclaims requiring individual defenses can be the basis for denying class certification under Rule 23(b)(3). (Heaven v. Trust Company Bank)

12. **The Class Action and the Constitution: Representative Adequacy.** There must be adequate representation of the members of a class action or the judgment is not binding on the parties not adequately represented. (Hansberry v. Lee)

13. **The Class Action and the Constitution: Jurisdiction.** A state may exercise jurisdiction over absent plaintiffs in a classification suit even if the plaintiffs have no contacts with that state. (Phillips Petroleum v. Shutts)

14. Settlement of Class Actions and the "Settlement Class": Settlement and Dismissal. Rule 23 requirements for class certification must be met even if the certification is for settlement only. (Amchem Products, Inc. v. Windsor)

PLANT v. BLAZER FINANCIAL SERVICES, INC.
Borrower (P) v. Lender (D)
598 F.2d 1357 (1979).

NATURE OF CASE: Appeal from ruling finding a counter-claim compulsory.

FACT SUMMARY: Plant (P) was a debtor of Blazer (D) who sued Blazer (D) for violations of the Truth-In-Lending Act, and Blazer (D) asserted a counterclaim on the debt owing which Plant (P) sought to dismiss.

CONCISE RULE OF LAW: A claim for the amount of a debt owed pursuant to a transaction which is the subject of a truth-in-lending suit brought in federal court is a compulsory counterclaim of such suit.

FACTS: Plant (P) executed a note for $2,520 to be paid to Blazer (D) in monthly installments. No payments were made. Plant (P) brought suit in federal court alleging violations of the Truth-In-Lending Act by Blazer (D) for failure to disclose a limitation on an after-acquired security interest. Blazer (D) sought to interpose a counterclaim for the amount of the note which Plant (P) challenged as not compulsory and an improper permissive counterclaim, as no diversity or federal question existed. The district court ruled the counterclaim compulsory, and Plant (P) appealed.

ISSUE: Is a claim for the amount of debt owed pursuant to a transaction which is the subject of a truth-in-lending suit brought in federal court a compulsory counterclaim?

HOLDING AND DECISION: (Roney, J.) Yes. Rule 13(a) of the Federal Rules of Civil Procedure provides that a counterclaim is compulsory if it "arises out of the transaction or occurrence" which is the subject matter of the plaintiff's claim. Four inquiries are designed to provide an answer: (1) Are the issues of fact and law the same? (2) Would res judicata bar a subsequent suit on the counterclaim? (3) Is the same evidence involved? (4) Is the counterclaim logically related to the main claim? All need not be satisfied. Under the last, or logical relation test, it is clear that the same operative facts give rise to both claims here. A claim for the amount of a debt owed pursuant to a transaction which is the subject of a truth-in-lending suit brought in federal court is a compulsory counterclaim of such suit. Other district courts are in accord. Had Congress intended to insulate truth-in-lending recoveries from counterclaims of creditors, it could have done so. Affirmed.

EDITOR'S ANALYSIS: A compulsory counterclaim falls under a federal court's ancillary jurisdiction. Unlike a permissive counter-claim, it needs no independent basis for jurisdiction. The policy of avoiding multiple litigation is served by allowing courts to resolve all matters which are substantially enough related to an action properly brought.

QUICKNOTES

ANCILLARY JURISDICTION - Authority of a federal court to hear and determine issues related to a case over which it has jurisdiction, but over which it would not have jurisdiction if such claims were brought independently.

COMPULSORY COUNTERCLAIM - An independent cause of action brought by a defendant to a lawsuit in order to oppose or deduct from the plaintiff's claim that arises out of the same transaction or occurrence that is the subject matter of the plaintiff's claim and does.

FED. R. CIV. P. 13 (a) - Lays out the requirements for a compulsory counterclaim.

RES JUDICATA - The rule of law that a final judgment by a court precludes subsequent litigation between the parties regarding the same cause of action.

NOTES:

MOSLEY v. GENERAL MOTORS CORP.
Class action plaintiffs (P) v. Car company (D)
497 F.2d 1330 (8th Cir. 1974).

NATURE OF CASE: Appeal from order requiring severance of joint action.

FACT SUMMARY: Mosley (P) and nine others brought this class action against GM (D) for various acts of race and sex discrimination, and the district court ordered the 10 plaintiffs to bring 10 separate actions due to the wide variety of the claims and the unmanageability of the joint proceeding.

CONCISE RULE OF LAW: Permissive joinder of parties is to be broadly granted under Federal Rule of Civil Procedure 20 where each party seeks relief arising out of the same transaction or series of transactions and a common question of fact or law will arise in the action.

FACTS: Mosley (P) and nine other plaintiffs brought this class action against GM (D) alleging various different acts which in some cases they contended constituted racial discrimination and in others sex discrimination. They filed complaints individually with the Equal Employment Opportunity Commission (EEOC), and the EEOC notified each of their right to bring a civil action in federal court. At that point the plaintiffs joined in bringing the class action. The district court ordered that each plaintiff bring a separate action, separately filed, due to the differing types of claims alleged and the unmanageability of the joint proceeding. The judge found that there was no right to relief arising out of the same transaction or series of transactions or a common question of fact or law as required by Fed. R. Civ. P. 20. Mosley (P) appealed.

ISSUE: Is permissive joinder to be broadly granted under Fed. R. Civ. P. 20 where each party seeks relief arising out of the same transaction or series of transactions and a common question of fact or law will arise in the action?

HOLDING AND DECISION: (Ross, J.) Yes. The purpose of Fed. R. Civ. P. 20 is to promote trial convenience and expedite the final determination of disputes. The rules permit the trial judge, however, to order separate trials within his discretion if such an order will prevent delay or prejudice. Reversal of such an order depends upon an abuse of that discretion. In this case, a series of "logically related" events occurred, which has been held to constitute a single series of transactions as required. Furthermore, the rights asserted depend on a common question of law. The district court abused its discretion, therefore, in ordering the separate trials. Permissive joinder is to be broadly granted under Fed. R. Civ. P. 20 where each party seeks relief arising out of the same transaction or series of transactions and a common question of fact or law will arise in the action. Reversed.

EDITOR'S ANALYSIS: It is not often easy to determine what is a single series of transactions when distinct events have taken place. However, a series of employment or advancement decisions together appearing like a policy of discrimination is the kind of matter that Fed. R. Civ. P. 20 seeks to have determined in one action. It is when the rights of the parties suffer at the expense of judicial economy that Fed. R. Civ. P. 20(b) can be involved to require separate trials, rather than when the judge finds the case "unmanageable."

QUICKNOTES

FED. R. CIV. P. 20 - Provides that parties requesting relief for injuries arising from the same transaction or common question of law or fact be permitted to consolidate their actions into a single one

PERMISSIVE JOINDER - The joining of parties or claims in a single suit if the claims against the parties arise from the same transaction or occurrence or involve common issues of law or fact; such joinder is not mandatory.

NOTES:

PRICE v. CTB, INC.
Chicken farmer (P) v. Construction contractor (D)
168 F.Supp.2d 1299 (M.D. Ala. 2001).

NATURE OF CASE: Motion to dismiss an impleaded party.

FACT SUMMARY: When Price (P) sued Latco (D) for faulty construction of a chicken house, Latco (D), in turn, impleaded ITW (D), the manufacturer of the nails, on theories of statutory and common law indemnity.

CONCISE RULE OF LAW: A defendant may assert a claim against anyone not a party to the original action if that third party's liability is in some way dependent upon the outcome of the original action.

FACTS: Price (P), a chicken farmer, hired Latco (D) to build a chicken house. Alleging defective construction, Price (P) sued CTB (D), which equips poultry houses, and Latco (D) who was the original defendant in the underlying suit concerning the quality of construction workmanship. Latco (D), in turn, moved to implead ITW (D), alleging that ITW (D), a nail manufacturer, defectively designed the nails used in the construction. The specific causes of action against ITW (D) included (1) breach of warranty, (2) Alabama's extended manufacturer's liability doctrine, and (3) common law indemnity. ITW (D) moved that it be dismissed from the suit on the grounds that it had been improperly impleaded under Rule 14 of the Federal Rules of Civil Procedure.

ISSUE: May a defendant assert a claim against anyone not a party to the original action if that third party's liability is in some way dependent upon the outcome of the original action?

HOLDING AND DECISION: (DeMent, Dist.J.) Yes. A defendant may assert a claim against anyone not a party to the original action if that third party's liability is in some way dependent upon the outcome of the original action. Under the doctrine of implied contractual indemnity, Alabama courts recognize that a manufacturer of a product has impliedly agreed to indemnify the seller when (1) the seller is without fault, (2) the manufacturer is responsible, and (3) the seller has been required to pay a monetary judgment. Here, under Latco's (D) theory, should it be found liable for its construction of the chicken houses, it can demonstrate that the true fault lies with the nail guns and the nails manufactured by ITW (D). Accordingly, Alabama law provides Latco (D) a cause of action under common law indemnity against ITW (D). Although the doctrine permits recovery only when the party to be indemnified is without fault, whether such a factual scenario will be proven at trial is irrelevant for present purposes. The only issue presently is whether there is a legal basis to implead ITW (D), *not* whether ITW (D) is, in fact, liable to Latco (D). Since Federal Rule of Civil Procedure 14 permits Latco (D) to implead any party who "may be liable," it follows that the court must permit development of the factual record so the extent of that liability may be determined. Furthermore, it is well established that a properly impleaded claim may serve as an anchor for separate and independent claims under Rule 18(a). In short, Latco (D) has properly impleaded ITW (D) under Rule 14(a). ITW's (D) motion to dismiss is denied.

EDITOR'S ANALYSIS: In *Price*, the court noted that there is a limitation on the general rule of permitting a defendant to assert a claim against anyone not a party to the original action if that third party's liability is in some way dependent upon the outcome of the original action. Even though it may arise out of the same general set of facts as the main claim, a third party claim will not be permitted when it is based upon a separate and independent claim. Rather, the third party liability must in some way be derivative of the original claim; a third party may be impleaded only when the original defendant is trying to pass all or part of the liability onto that third party.

QUICKNOTES

FED. R. CIV. P. 14 - Permits the impleader of a party who is or may be liable in order to determine the rights of All parties in one proceeding.

NOTES:

OWEN EQUIPMENT & ERECTION v. KROGER
Crane company (D) v. Wife of electrocuted decedent (P)
437 U.S. 365 (1978).

NATURE OF CASE: Action for damages for wrongful death.

FACT SUMMARY: Kroger (P) brought a wrongful death action in federal court against a defendant of diverse citizenship and then amended her complaint to include an impleaded third-party defendant, Owen (D), even though they were citizens of the same state.

CONCISE RULE OF LAW: In a diversity case, the federal court does not have ancillary jurisdiction over the plaintiff's claims against a third-party defendant who is a citizen of the same state.

FACTS: Kroger's (P) husband was electrocuted when the boom of a steel crane owned and operated by Owen (D), and next to which he was walking, came too close to a high tension electric power line of the Omaha Public Power District (OPPD). Kroger (P) brought a wrongful death action against OPPD in federal court in Nebraska, she being a resident of Iowa. However, OPPD filed a third-party complaint against Owen (D), alleging its negligence had caused the electrocution. Eventually, OPPD's motion for summary judgment was granted, and Owen (D) was the only defendant left in the case. During trial, it was discovered that Owen (D), a Nebraska corporation, had its principal place of business in Iowa and was therefore a citizen of the same state as Kroger (P). The district court denied Owen's (D) motion to dismiss the complaint for lack of jurisdiction, and the jury returned a verdict in favor of Kroger (P). The court of appeals affirmed.

ISSUE: Can a federal court exercise ancillary jurisdiction over a plaintiff's claims against a third-party defendant who is a citizen of the same state in a diversity case?

HOLDING AND DECISION: (Stewart, J.) No. The concept of ancillary jurisdiction is not so broad as to permit a federal court in a diversity case to exercise jurisdiction over the plaintiff's claims against a third-party defendant who is a citizen of the same state. 28 U.S.C. § 1332(a)(1) requires complete diversity of citizenship. To allow ancillary jurisdiction in a case like this would be to allow circumvention of that requirement by the simple expedient of suing only those defendants who were of diverse citizenship and waiting for them to implead nondiverse defendants. Reversed.

DISSENT: (White, J.) Section 1332 requires complete diversity only between the plaintiff and those parties he actually brings into the suit, which would not include Owen (D) in this case. Beyond that, I would hold the district court has the power to entertain all claims among the parties arising from the same nucleus of operative fact as the plaintiff's original, jurisdiction-conferring claim against the original defendant. Thus, ancillary jurisdiction existed in this case.

EDITOR'S ANALYSIS: Rule 14 of the Federal Rules of Civil Procedure is the one which permits ancillary jurisdiction. In amending it, the Advisory Committee stated that any attempt by a plaintiff to amend his complaint to assert a claim against an impleaded third party would be unavailing, by majority view, where the third party could not have been joined by the plaintiff originally due to jurisdictional limitations. Congress reenacted § 1332 without relevant change and with knowledge of the aforementioned view. The majority opinion took this as evidence of congressional approval of that view.

QUICKNOTES

ANCILLARY JURISDICTION - Authority of a federal court to hear and determine issues related to a case over which it has jurisdiction, but over which it would not have jurisdiction if such claims were brought independently.

FED. R. CIV. P. 14 - Permits the impleader of a party who is or may be liable in order to determine the rights of All parties in one proceeding.

28 U.S.C. § 1332 - Governs the requirements for diversity jurisdiction.

NOTES:

TEMPLE v. SYNTHES CORP.

Medical implant user (P) v. Implant manufacturer (D)
498 U.S. 5, rehg. denied, 498 U.S. 1092 (1990).

NATURE OF CASE: Appeal of dismissal with prejudice of action for damages for products liability, medical malpractice, and negligence.

FACT SUMMARY: Temple's (P) federal suit against Synthes (D), the manufacturer of a plate implanted in Temple's (P) back, was dismissed when Temple (P) failed to join the doctor and the hospital responsible for installing the plate.

CONCISE RULE OF LAW: Joint tortfeasors are not necessary parties under Federal Rule of Civil Procedure 19.

FACTS: A plate and screw device implanted in Temple's (P) back malfunctioned. Temple (P) filed a federal court products liability action against Synthes (D), the manufacturer of the device. Temple (P) also filed a state court medical malpractice and negligence action against the doctor who implanted the device and the hospital where the operation was performed. Synthes (D) filed a motion to dismiss the federal lawsuit under Fed. R. Civ. P. 19 for Temple's (P) failure to join necessary parties. The district court agreed that the doctor and the hospital were necessary parties and gave Temple (P) 20 days to join them. When Temple (P) did not, the court dismissed the suit with prejudice. The court of appeals affirmed, finding that Rule 19 allowed the district court to order joinder in the interest of complete, consistent, and efficient settlement of controversies. It further found that overlapping, separate lawsuits would have prejudiced Synthes (D) because Synthes (D) might claim the device was not defective but that the doctor and the hospital were negligent, and the doctor and the hospital might claim the opposite. Temple (P) appealed, arguing that joint tortfeasors are not necessary parties under Rule 19.

ISSUE: Are joint tortfeasors necessary parties under Fed. R. Civ. P. 19?

HOLDING AND DECISION: (Per curiam) No. Joint tortfeasors are not necessary parties under Fed. R. Civ. P. 19. It has long been the rule that joint tortfeasors need not be named as defendants in a single lawsuit. Rule 19 does not change that principle. The Advisory Committee Notes to Rule 19(a) state that a tortfeasor with the usual joint and several liability is merely a permissive party. There is a public interest in avoiding multiple lawsuits. However, since the requirements of Rule 19(a) have not been met, the district court had no authority to order dismissal. Reversed and remanded.

EDITOR'S ANALYSIS: The function of compulsory joinder, codified in Fed. R. Civ. P. 19, is to bring all affected parties into the same lawsuit. Joinder is often required where the suit involves jointly-held rights or liabilities, where more than one party claims the same property, or where granting relief necessarily would affect the rights of parties not in the lawsuit. Though there is a strong interest in "complete, consistent, and efficient settlement of controversies," compulsory joinder is limited. There is a strong tradition of allowing the parties themselves to determine who shall be a party, what claims shall be litigated, and what litigation strategies shall be followed.

QUICKNOTES

COMPULSORY JOINDER - The joining of parties to a lawsuit that is mandatory if complete relief cannot be afforded to the parties in his absence or his absence will result in injustice.

FED. R. CIV. P. 19 - Sets forth the rules governing joinder.

JOINDER - The joining of claims or parties in one lawsuit.

JOINT TORTFEASORS - Two or more parties that either act in concert, or whose individual acts combine to cause a single injury, rendering them jointly and severally liable for damages incurred.

NECESSARY PARTIES - Parties whose joining in a lawsuit is essential to the disposition of the action.

NOTES:

HELZBERG'S DIAMOND SHOPS v. VALLEY WEST DES MOINES SHOPPING CENTER

Jewelry stores (P) v. Shopping center (D)
564 F.2d 816 (8th Cir. 1977).

NATURE OF CASE: Appeal from denial of motion to dismiss for failure to join an indispensable party.

FACT SUMMARY: Helzberg's (P) brought this suit to enjoin Valley West (D), Helzberg's (P) commercial landlord, from breaching their lease agreement by leasing more than two full-line jewelry stores in the mall where Helzberg's (P) leasehold was located, and Valley West (D) unsuccessfully moved to dismiss on the ground that Helzberg's (P) failed to join the full-line jewelry store tenant, Lord's.

CONCISE RULE OF LAW: A tenant under a lease which violates a clause in another tenant's lease from a common landlord is not an indispensable party under Federal Rule of Civil Procedure 19 to a suit by such other tenant against that landlord.

FACTS: Helzberg's (P), a full-line jewelry store, leased space in Valley West's (D) shopping center to operate their store. The lease agreement provided that no more than two such stores would be allowed to rent space other than Helzberg's (P) in the mall. Valley West (D), however, leased space to a third such store, Lord's. Helzberg's (P) brought this action to enjoin such a lease, and Valley West (D) moved to dismiss on the ground that Lord's was not joined and was an indispensable party. Helzberg's (P) brought suit in district court in Missouri and could not obtain personal jurisdiction over Lord's, which had no Missouri contacts. The district court denied Valley West's (D) motion, and Valley West (D) appealed.

ISSUE: Is a tenant under a lease which violates a clause in another tenant's lease from a common landlord an indispensable party under Fed. R. Civ. P. 19 to a suit brought by such other tenant against that landlord?

HOLDING AND DECISION: (Alsop, J.) No. Fed. R. Civ. P. 19 defines an indispensable party as one in whose absence complete relief cannot be accorded, or claims an interest related to the subject of the action and whose absence will impair or impede his ability to protect that interest or force him to risk multiple or inconsistent obligations. Valley West (D) contends that Lord's and Valley West's (D) rights under their contract cannot be adjudicated in Lord's absence. However, the determination that may result in this action is that Valley West (D) may be forced to terminate that contract, in which case Lord's will still be empowered to assert its rights under the contract for that eventuality. The claim that Valley West (D) may be subjected then to inconsistent obligations following another contract action also fails. Valley West's (D) inconsistent obligations will result from

their voluntary execution of two lease agreements with inconsistent obligations required under them. The litigation here can proceed without Lord's, which is not an indispensable party under these circumstances. A tenant under a lease which violates a clause in another tenant's lease is not an indispensable party under Fed. R. Civ. P. 19 to a suit by such other tenant against their common landlord. Affirmed.

EDITOR'S ANALYSIS: In federal practice, the court will balance the prejudice to an absent party against the desirability of ruling on a meritorious claim. The judge can shape the relief granted under his equitable powers so as to avoid any such prejudice so long as he renders an effective judgment.

QUICKNOTES

COMPULSORY JOINDER - The joining of parties to a lawsuit that is mandatory if complete relief cannot be afforded to the parties in his absence or his absence will result in injustice.

FED. R. CIV. P. 19 - Governs compulsory party joinder.

INDISPENSABLE PARTY - Parties whose joining in a lawsuit is essential for the adequate disposition of the action and without whom the action cannot proceed.

NOTES:

NATURAL RESOURCES DEFENSE COUNCIL v.
UNITED STATES NUCLEAR REGULATORY COMMISSION
Federal regulatory agency (D) v. Federal commission (P)
578 F.2d 1341 (10th Cir. 1978).

NATURE OF CASE: Appeal of denial of motion to intervene.

FACT SUMMARY: The American Mining Congress (AMC) and Kerr-McGee (KM) appealed the denial of their motion to intervene in an action brought by the Natural Resources Defense Council (NRDC) (P) against the Nuclear Regulatory Commission (NRC) (D) seeking a declaration that state-granted nuclear power operation licenses are subject to the requirement of filing an environmental impact statement and seeking an injunction of the grant of one such license by the New Mexico Environmental Improvement Agency (NMEIA).

CONCISE RULE OF LAW: A party may intervene in an action under Federal Rule of Civil Procedure 24(a)(2) if he has an interest upon which the disposition of that action will have a significant legal effect.

FACTS: The NRC (D) is permitted by federal law to give the several states the power to grant licenses to operate nuclear power facilities. The NRC (D) is empowered to grant such licenses subject to a requirement that such "major federal action" be preceded by the preparation of an environmental impact statement. The NRC (D) entered into an agreement with NMEIA permitting it to issue a license, which it did, to United Nuclear without preparing an impact statement. NRDC (P) brought this action seeking a declaration that state-granted licenses are the product of "major federal action" and subject to the statement requirement and seeking an injunction against the issuance of the license. United Nuclear intervened without objection. KM, a potential recipient of an NMEIA license, and AMC, a public interest group, sought to intervene, but their motions were denied. Both appealed.

ISSUE: May a party intervene in an action under Fed. R. Civ. P. 24(a)(2) if he has an interest upon which the disposition of that action will have a significant legal effect?

HOLDING AND DECISION: (Doyle, J.) Yes. Fed. R. Civ. P. 24(a) gives a party the right to intervene when he has a sufficiently protectable interest related to the property or transaction which is the subject of the action and the disposition will "as a practical matter, impair or impede his ability to protect that interest." The argument that the effect upon the movant's right must be a res judicata effect is unpersuasive. The effect must "as a practical matter" impair or impede the ability to protect the right. A party may thus intervene in an action under Fed. R. Civ. P. 24(a)(2) if he has an interest upon which the disposition of that action will have a significant legal effect. It need not be a strictly legal effect. KM and AMC each have rights, not protected by other parties to the litigation, which will be thus effected, and they must be allowed to intervene. Reversed and remanded.

EDITOR'S ANALYSIS: Fed. R. Civ. P. 24(a) covers the intervention of right, while Rule 24(b) sets forth criteria for permissive intervention. Intervention is permissive if there is a common question of law or fact or if a statute gives a conditional right to intervene. In either case, an intervenor has the same status in the litigation as an original party, but he cannot raise any new issues. Ancillary jurisdiction attaches over the intervenor.

QUICKNOTES

FED. R. CIV. P. 24 - Governs permissive intervention and intervention as a matter of right.

NOTES:

MARTIN v. WILKS
Firefighters (P) v. Court (D)
490 U.S. 755 (1989).

NATURE OF CASE: Review of reversal of dismissal of reverse discrimination action.

FACT SUMMARY: Several white firefighters challenged affirmative action plans mandated by a consent decree which was entered in an action of which they had knowledge but had not intervened.

CONCISE RULE OF LAW: A party may not be bound by a judgment rendered in an action in which he was not a party, even if he had knowledge of the action.

FACTS: As part of a discrimination action, a consent decree was rendered between the City of Birmingham, Alabama, and a class of black firefighters. As part of the decree, the City instituted an affirmative action program. Subsequent to this, a group of white firefighters filed a reverse discrimination action. The district court dismissed, holding that because the white firefighters had notice of the prior action but had elected not to intervene, the matter was res judicata as to them. The Eleventh Circuit reversed, and the U.S. Supreme Court granted review.

ISSUE: May a party be bound by a judgment rendered in an action in which he was not a party, if he had knowledge of the action?

HOLDING AND DECISION: (Rehnquist, C.J.) No. A party may not be bound by a judgment rendered in an action in which he was not a party, even if he had knowledge of the action. It is a principle of general application that one is not bound by an in personam judgment in a litigation in which he is not designated as a party or has not been made a party by service of process. The argument asserted by those defending the consent decree is that by knowing about the underlying action and failing to intervene, the plaintiffs herein waived that objection to being bound. This is incorrect. A party seeking a judgment binding on another cannot obligate that person to intervene; he must be joined. This was the position taken by the Eleventh Circuit, and it was correct in so doing. Affirmed.

DISSENT: (Stevens, J.) In no sense were the white firefighters herein "bound" by the consent decree; rather it was the City that was so bound. The district court properly dismissed the action because the City was fulfilling its legal obligations, not because the white firefighters were somehow bound by the consent decree.

EDITOR'S ANALYSIS: Joinder is governed by Fed. R. Civ. P. 19. The rule distinguishes between parties that should be joined and

parties that must be joined. Parties may be joined either as defendants or as involuntary plaintiffs.

QUICKNOTES

COMPULSORY JOINDER - The joining of parties to a lawsuit that is mandatory if complete relief cannot be afforded to the parties in his absence or his absence will result in injustice.

FED. R. CIV. P. 19 - Governs compulsory party joinder.

INTERVENTION - The method by which a party, not an initial party to the action, is admitted to the action in order to assert an interest in the subject matter of a lawsuit.

PERMISSIVE JOINDER - The joining of parties or claims in a single suit if the claims against the parties arise from the same transaction or occurrence or involve common issues of law or fact; such joinder is not mandatory.

RES JUDICATA - The rule of law that a final judgment by a court precludes subsequent litigation between the parties regarding the same cause of action.

NOTES:

COHEN v. THE REPUBLIC OF THE PHILIPPINES
Painting consignee (P) v. Sovereign country (D)
146 F.R.D. 90 (S.D.N.Y. 1993).

NATURE OF CASE: Motion to intervene in ownership dispute.

FACT SUMMARY: Imelda Marcos (D) sought to intervene in an interpleader action before the court to determine who legally owned several paintings.

CONCISE RULE OF LAW: A party has an unconditional right to intervene if the party can prove a risk of practical impairment of a relevant interest, timely application, and lack of adequate representation.

FACTS: Cohen (P) had in his possession four paintings valued at approximately five million dollars which were received on consignment from Braemer (D), Marcos's agent, whom she had entrusted to run her New York home. Braemer (D) demanded return of the paintings, but Cohen (P) refused and brought an interpleader action to determine the ownership of the paintings, naming the Republic of the Philippines (D) and Braemer (D) as defendants. Marcos sought leave to intervene in the interpleader action to assert her claim to the paintings. The Philippine government (D) objected and asserted that existing parties would be prejudiced.

ISSUE: Does a party have an unconditional right to intervene if the party can prove a risk of practical impairment of a relevant interest, timely application, and lack of adequate representation?

HOLDING AND DECISION: (Conner, J.) Yes. A party has an unconditional right to intervene if the party can prove a risk of practical impairment of a relevant interest, timely application, and lack of adequate representation pursuant to Fed. R. Civ. P. 24(a)(2). Here, Marcos made her claim before the proceedings reached an advanced stage; thus, her claim is timely. Marcos's affidavit indicates that her interests will be impaired if she is not permitted to intervene as she risks losing her interest in the paintings. Marcos's interest is not being represented by either existing party; thus, it is not presently protected. Motion to intervene is granted.

EDITOR'S ANALYSIS: A party who possesses property that is the subject of multiple claims may bring an interpleader action in federal court. There are two types of federal interpleader actions: statutory interpleader and rule interpleader. Statutory interpleader actions have more generous subject matter jurisdiction and venue provisions.

QUICKNOTES

FED. R. CIV. P. 24 - Governs permissive intervention and intervention as a matter of right.

INTERPLEADER - An equitable proceeding whereby a person holding property, which is subject to the claims of multiple parties, may require such parties to resolve the matter through litigation.

INTERVENTION - The method by which a party, not an initial party to the action, is admitted to the action in order to assert an interest in the subject matter of a lawsuit.

NOTES:

COMMUNITIES FOR EQUITY v. MICHIGAN HIGH SCHOOL ATHLETIC ASSN.

Public interest group (P) v. School organization (D)
1999 U.S. Dist. Lexis 5780 (W.D. Mich. 1999).

NATURE OF CASE: Motion for class certification.

FACT SUMMARY: Communities for Equity (P) sought to bring a class action on behalf of girl athletes who had allegedly been discriminated against in Michigan.

CONCISE RULE OF LAW: Class certification prerequisites under Rule 23 must be rigorously analyzed by the court.

FACTS: The Communities for Equity (P) brought suit against the Michigan High School Athletic Association (MSHAA) for allegedly excluding girls from equal treatment in interscholastic athletics. They proposed a class action on behalf of all present and future female students enrolled in MHSAA schools who participate, or are deterred from participating, in athletics. This class would involve thousands of students and would-be athletes.

ISSUE: Must class certification prerequisites under Rule 23 be rigorously analyzed by the court?

HOLDING AND DECISION: (Enslen, C.J.) Yes. Class certification prerequisites under Rule 23 must be rigorously analyzed by the court. A class action is not maintainable merely because the complaint parrots the legal requirements of Rule 23. The court should probe behind the pleadings before making the certification determination. In the present case, the vast number of class members satisfies the numerosity requirement since joinder would be impractical. The commonality requirement provides that there must be common questions of law and fact. If separate proofs are needed to establish liability, there is no commonality. Here, there is one overarching question: whether the MHSAA acts in a manner consistent with Title IX and the Equal Protection Clause. The typicality requirement demands the closest attention in this case. The members of the class must have suffered the same type of injury. The various discrete harms alleged by the class are suffered by all the members: inequitable facilities, scheduling and rules. That there is some distinction between the particular claims is insignificant. The final requirement is that the class members and their counsel provide fair and adequate representation to the class. The representative must have common interests with the unnamed members of the class and must vigorously prosecute the interests of the class. The only potential problem to this requirement is that potential conflicts could arise between athletes in different sports. However, this could be solved by the creation of sub-classes. Therefore, the proposed class should be certified because it meets all of the requirements of Rule 23.

EDITOR'S ANALYSIS: The court rejected the MHSAA's (D) argument that a class was unnecessary because relief granted to the named plaintiffs would benefit the class. The class was certified pursuant to Rule 23(b)(2). This would allow for injunctive relief.

QUICKNOTES

CLASS ACTION - A suit commenced by a representative on behalf of an ascertainable group that is too large to appear in court, who shares a commonality of interests and who will benefit from a successful result.

FED. R. CIV. P. 23 - Sets forth the requirements in order to maintain a class action suit.

NOTES:

HEAVEN v. TRUST COMPANY BANK
Lessee (P) v. Lessor (D)
118 F.3d 735 (11th Cir. 1997).

NATURE OF CASE: Appeal from denial of class certification.

FACT SUMMARY: Heaven (P brought suit against Sun Trust (D) for failure to comply with strict disclosure requirements, seeking to certify a class under Federal Rule of Civil Procedure 23.

CONCISE RULE OF LAW: The presence of counterclaims requiring individual defenses can be the basis for denying class certification under Rule 23(b)(3).

FACTS: Heaven (P) leased a car from Sun Trust (D) and signed a preprinted lease form. Subsequently, Heaven (P) claimed that Sun Trust (D) failed to comply with the strict disclosure requirements of the Consumer Leasing Act. Heaven (P) sought to certify a class action pursuant to Rule 23. Sun Trust (D) counterclaimed that the individual defendants had defaulted on the terms of the lease agreements and made false statements in the applications. The district court ruled that while Heaven (P) had established the four requirements of Rule 23(a), certification had to be denied because the counterclaims would involve individual defenses under Rule 23(b). Heaven (P) appealed.

ISSUE: Can the presence of counterclaims requiring individual defenses be the basis for denying class certification under Rule 23(b)(3)?

HOLDING AND DECISION: (Burns, J.) Yes. The presence of counterclaims requiring individual defenses can be the basis for denying class certification under Rule 23(b)(3). In the present case, the counterclaims asserted by Sun Trust (D) were compulsory because debt counterclaims must be brought in Truth in Lending cases. Although Heaven (P) argues that counterclaims cannot be the basis for denying class certification, there is no such universal rule. Since individual defenses to the counterclaims would require the court to engage in multiple separate factual determinations, the district court properly considered this a factor against certification. The court also properly determined that some defendants whose exposure to counterclaims would exceed the amount they might recover for Sun Trust's (D) alleged violations would not be in a better position due to the class action. Given these factors, class certification was a very close call in this case. This court is unable to find that the district court abused its discretion in denying certification. Under that standard of review, the denial must be affirmed.

EDITOR'S ANALYSIS: The district court also noted that the class certification was a close call. One way around the dilemma of this case would have been for the district court to decline jurisdiction over the counterclaims. District courts may decline to exercise supplemental jurisdiction if there are compelling reasons, such as it would make a class action unmanageable.

QUICKNOTES

FED. R. CIV. P. 23 - Sets forth the requirements in order to maintain a class action suit.

NOTES:

HANSBERRY v. LEE
Black land purchaser (D) v. Party to covenant (P)
11 U.S. 32 (1940).

NATURE OF CASE: A class action to enforce a racially restrictive covenant.

FACT SUMMARY: Lee (P) sought to enjoin a sale of land to Hansberry (D) on the grounds that the sale violated a racially restrictive covenant.

CONCISE RULE OF LAW: There must be adequate representation of the members of a class action or the judgment is not binding on the parties not adequately represented.

FACTS: Hansberry (D), a black, purchased land from a party who had signed a restrictive covenant forbidding the sale of the land to blacks. Lee (P), one of the parties who signed the covenant, sought to have the sale enjoined because it breached the covenant. Lee (P) contended that the validity of the covenant was established in a prior case in which one of the parties was a class of landowners involved with the covenant. To be valid, 95% of the landowners had to sign the covenant, and the trial court in the prior case held that 95% of the landowners had signed the covenant. That case was appealed, and the Illinois Supreme Court upheld the decision, even though they found that 95% of the landowners had not signed the covenant, but they held that since it was a class action, all members of the class would be bound by the decision of the court. Hansberry (D) claimed that he and the party selling him the house were not bound by the res judicata effect of the prior decision, as they were not parties to the litigation. The lower court held that the decision of the Illinois Supreme Court would have to be challenged directly in order that it be set aside or reversed. Otherwise, their decision was still binding. The case was appealed to the United States Supreme Court.

ISSUE: For a judgment in a class action to be binding, must all of the members of the class be adequately represented by parties with similar interests?

HOLDING AND DECISION: (Stone, J.) Yes. It is not necessary that all members of a class be present as parties to the litigation to be bound by the judgment if they are adequately represented by parties who are present. In regular cases, to be bound by the judgment the party must receive notice and an opportunity to be heard. If due process is not afforded the individual, then the judgment is not binding. The class action is an exception to the general rule. Because of the numbers involved in class actions, it is enough if the party is adequately represented by a member of the class with a similar interest. Hansberry (D) was not adequately represented by the class of landowners. Their interests were not similar enough to even be considered

members of the same class. Lee (P) and the landowners were trying to restrict blacks from buying any of the land, and Hansberry (D) was a black attempting to purchase land. When there is such a conflicting interest between members of a class, there is most likely not adequate representation of one of the members of the class. There must be a similarity of interest before there can even be a class. Since there was no similarity of interests between Lee (P) and Hansberry (D), Hansberry (D) could not be considered a member of the class and so the prior judgment was not binding on Hansberry (D). Hansberry (D) was not afforded due process because of the lack of adequate representation. The judgment is reversed.

EDITOR'S ANALYSIS: Rule 23(c)(3) requires that the court describe those whom the court finds to be members of the class. The court is to note those to whom notice was provided and also those who had not requested exclusion. These members are considered members of the class and are bound by the decision of the court whether it is in their favor or not. The federal rules allow a member of the class to request exclusion from the class, and that party will not be bound by the decision of the court. Since a party must receive notice of the class action before he can request exclusion from the class, the court must determine if a party received sufficient notice of the action or if sufficient effort was made to notify him of the action. The rules state if the court finds that the party did have sufficient notice and was considered a member of the class, he is bound by the decision.

QUICKNOTES

CLASS ACTION - A suit commenced by a representative on behalf of an ascertainable group that is too large to appear in court, who shares a commonality of interests and who will benefit from a successful result.

COVENANT - A written promise to do, or to refrain from doing, a particular activity.

FED. R. CIV. P. 23 - Sets forth the requirements in order to maintain a class action suit.

PHILLIPS PETROLEUM v. SHUTTS
Gas and oil company (D) v. Class of lessees (P)
472 U.S. 797 (1985).

NATURE OF CASE: Appeal of a judgment in a class action suit.

FACT SUMMARY: Shutts (P) filed a class action suit against Phillips Petroleum (D) for allegedly underpaying royalties on gas leases.

CONCISE RULE OF LAW: A state may exercise jurisdiction over absent plaintiffs in a classification suit even if the plaintiffs have no contacts with that state.

FACTS: Phillips Petroleum (D) had gas and mineral leases with numerous individuals. Royalties were based on the selling price of the final product. When prices were raised, Phillips (D) would often pay royalties at a lower price. Shutts (P) filed a class action suit on behalf of over 33,000 individuals, seeking damages. A Kansas court certified the class. Letters were sent to all members of the plaintiff class. A plaintiff had the right to opt out of the class or be bound by the judgment. About 3,000 opted out. A judgment for the plaintiffs was entered. The Kansas Supreme Court rejected an appeal by Phillips (D) claiming that Kansas could not exercise jurisdiction over plaintiffs not residents of Kansas. Phillips (D) appealed to the U.S. Supreme Court.

ISSUE: May a state exercise jurisdiction over absent plaintiffs in a class action suit, if the plaintiffs have no contacts with that state?

HOLDING AND DECISION: (Rehnquist, J.) Yes. A state may exercise jurisdiction over absent plaintiffs in a class action suit even if the plaintiffs have no contacts with that state. The "minimum contacts" rule is a matter of personal liberty, not state sovereignty. It exists to protect defendants from being hauled into a distant forum unfairly. A plaintiff in a class action suit is in a much different position. He is in no danger of a loss of freedom or assets and, in fact, can sit back and let others do the work for him. His ability to opt out of the class further protects him; he is not forced to enter a class unwillingly. Affirmed.

EDITOR'S ANALYSIS: The Court stated in this opinion that minimum contacts is an issue of liberty, not sovereignty. This issue has been touched upon since *Pennoyer v. Neff.* The Court here held that the opt-out procedure was a sufficient protection of personal liberty.

AMCHEM PRODUCTS, INC. v. WINDSOR
Asbestos producer (D) v. Class action plaintiffs (P)
521 U.S. 591 (1997).

NATURE OF CASE: Appeal from reversal of class certification in mass tort action.

FACT SUMMARY: The district court certified a class (P) of persons exposed to asbestos products in order to effect a settlement of the case.

CONCISE RULE OF LAW: Rule 23 requirements for class certification must be met even if the certification is for settlement only.

FACTS: All of the asbestos exposure cases pending in federal courts were transferred and consolidated for pretrial proceedings to a single district court. Following this consolidation, the parties began settlement negotiations. The defendants' steering committee (D) made an offer to settle all pending and future asbestos cases by providing a fund from which to pay claims. Eventually, a settlement was reached for pending cases. A second settlement for potential plaintiffs was then reached. The parties then sought certification of this class of potential plaintiffs for purposes of settlement only. Nine lead plaintiffs were named who were designed to be representative of a class of all persons and family members who had been exposed to asbestos products but had not yet filed suit. The district court approved the settlement, certified the class (P), and enjoined class members from filing additional suits. Objectors raised numerous challenges to the settlement, claiming that it unfairly disadvantaged those without current problems. The court of appeals reversed the certification on the grounds that Rule 23 requirements were not met. The defendants appealed.

ISSUE: Must Rule 23 requirements for class certification be met even if the certification is for settlement only?

HOLDING AND DECISION: (Ginsburg, J.) Yes. Rule 23 requirements for class certification must be met even if the certification is for settlement only. Rule 23 authorizing class actions has several requirements that must be satisfied. These standards are designed to protect absent class members. They may not be disregarded simply because a court believes that a settlement is fair. First of all, common questions of law or fact must predominate over questions affecting individual members. The district court's reliance on the claimants' interest in a compensation scheme does not meet this requirement. A compensation scheme is a matter for legislative consideration. Secondly, the named parties in a class action must fairly and adequately protect the interests of the class. The district court failed to break the class into subclasses. Thus, the named parties had diverse medical conditions and diverse interests that could cause conflicts of interest. Furthermore, there are impediments to

the provision of adequate notice because there are persons in the class who may not even know of their exposure to asbestos yet. The only proper accommodation that should be made to settlement-only class certification is that the problems of trial administration should be ignored. Accordingly, in the present case, the class was improperly certified because the requirements of Rule 23 were not satisfied. Affirmed.

CONCURRENCE AND DISSENT: (Breyer, J.) The need for settlement in mass tort cases is greater than the majority suggests. Also, settlement-related issues should be given more weight for purposes of determining whether common issues predominate. The settlement is something that should help the class meet the Rule 23 requirements.

EDITOR'S ANALYSIS: Settlement classes have become more and more common since the advent of Rule 23, which does not make provision for such classes. Many commentators have called for revision to Rule 23 to address the reality of settlement classes. However, others have objected on the basis that settlement classes invite collusion among class counsel and the defense.

QUICKNOTES

FED. R. CIV. P. 23 - Sets forth the requirements in order to maintain a class action suit.

NOTES:

GLOSSARY
COMMON LATIN WORDS AND PHRASES ENCOUNTERED IN THE LAW

A FORTIORI: Because one fact exists or has been proven, therefore a second fact that is related to the first fact must also exist.

A PRIORI: From the cause to the effect. A term of logic used to denote that when one generally accepted truth is shown to be a cause, another particular effect must necessarily follow.

AB INITIO: From the beginning; a condition which has existed throughout, as in a marriage which was void ab initio.

ACTUS REUS: The wrongful act; in criminal law, such action sufficient to trigger criminal liability.

AD VALOREM: According to value; an ad valorem tax is imposed upon an item located within the taxing jurisdiction calculated by the value of such item.

AMICUS CURIAE: Friend of the court. Its most common usage takes the form of an amicus curiae brief, filed by a person who is not a party to an action but is nonetheless allowed to offer an argument supporting his legal interests.

ARGUENDO: In arguing. A statement, possibly hypothetical, made for the purpose of argument, is one made arguendo.

BILL QUIA TIMET: A bill to quiet title (establish ownership) to real property.

BONA FIDE: True, honest, or genuine. May refer to a person's legal position based on good faith or lacking notice of fraud (such as a bona fide purchaser for value) or to the authenticity of a particular document (such as a bona fide last will and testament).

CAUSA MORTIS: With approaching death in mind. A gift causa mortis is a gift given by a party who feels certain that death is imminent.

CAVEAT EMPTOR: Let the buyer beware. This maxim is reflected in the rule of law that a buyer purchases at his own risk because it is his responsibility to examine, judge, test, and otherwise inspect what he is buying.

CERTIORARI: A writ of review. Petitions for review of a case by the United States Supreme Court are most often done by means of a writ of certiorari.

CONTRA: On the other hand. Opposite. Contrary to.

CORAM NOBIS: Before us; writs of error directed to the court that originally rendered the judgment.

CORAM VOBIS: Before you; writs of error directed by an appellate court to a lower court to correct a factual error.

CORPUS DELICTI: The body of the crime; the requisite elements of a crime amounting to objective proof that a crime has been committed.

CUM TESTAMENTO ANNEXO, ADMINISTRATOR (ADMINISTRATOR C.T.A.): With will annexed; an administrator c.t.a. settles an estate pursuant to a will in which he is not appointed.

DE BONIS NON, ADMINISTRATOR (ADMINISTRATOR D.B.N.): Of goods not administered; an administrator d.b.n. settles a partially settled estate.

DE FACTO: In fact; in reality; actually. Existing in fact but not officially approved or engendered.

DE JURE: By right; lawful. Describes a condition that is legitimate "as a matter of law," in contrast to the term "de facto," which connotes something existing in fact but not legally sanctioned or authorized. For example, de facto segregation refers to segregation brought about by housing patterns, etc., whereas de jure segregation refers to segregation created by law.

DE MINIMUS: Of minimal importance; insignificant; a trifle; not worth bothering about.

DE NOVO: Anew; a second time; afresh. A trial de novo is a new trial held at the appellate level as if the case originated there and the trial at a lower level had not taken place.

DICTA: Generally used as an abbreviated form of obiter dicta, a term describing those portions of a judicial opinion incidental or not necessary to resolution of the specific question before the court. Such nonessential statements and remarks are not considered to be binding precedent.

DUCES TECUM: Refers to a particular type of writ or subpoena requesting a party or organization to produce certain documents in their possession.

EN BANC: Full bench. Where a court sits with all justices present rather than the usual quorum.

EX PARTE: For one side or one party only. An ex parte proceeding is one undertaken for the benefit of only one party, without notice to, or an appearance by, an adverse party.

EX POST FACTO: After the fact. An ex post facto law is a law that retroactively changes the consequences of a prior act.

EX REL.: Abbreviated form of the term ex relatione, meaning, upon relation or information. When the state brings an action in which it has no interest against an individual at the instigation of one who has a private interest in the matter.

FORUM NON CONVENIENS: Inconvenient forum. Although a court may have jurisdiction over the case, the action should be tried in a more conveniently located court, one to which parties and witnesses may more easily travel, for example.

GUARDIAN AD LITEM: A guardian of an infant as to litigation, appointed to represent the infant and pursue his/her rights.

HABEAS CORPUS: You have the body. The modern writ of habeas corpus is a writ directing that a person (body) being detained (such as a prisoner) be brought before the court so that the legality of his detention can be judicially ascertained.

IN CAMERA: In private, in chambers. When a hearing is held before a judge in his chambers or when all spectators are excluded from the courtroom.

IN FORMA PAUPERIS: In the manner of a pauper. A party who proceeds in forma pauperis because of his poverty is one who is allowed to bring suit without liability for costs.

INFRA: Below, under. A word referring the reader to a later part of a book. (The opposite of supra.)

IN LOCO PARENTIS: In the place of a parent.

IN PARI DELICTO: Equally wrong; a court of equity will not grant requested relief to an applicant who is in pari delicto, or as much at fault in the transactions giving rise to the controversy as is the opponent of the applicant.

IN PARI MATERIA: On like subject matter or upon the same matter. Statutes relating to the same person or things are said to be in pari materia. It is a general rule of statutory construction that such statutes should be construed together, i.e., looked at as if they together constituted one law.

IN PERSONAM: Against the person. Jurisdiction over the person of an individual.

IN RE: In the matter of. Used to designate a proceeding involving an estate or other property.

IN REM: A term that signifies an action against the res, or thing. An action in rem is basically one that is taken directly against property, as distinguished from an action in personam, i.e., against the person.

INTER ALIA: Among other things. Used to show that the whole of a statement, pleading, list, statute, etc., has not been set forth in its entirety.

INTER PARTES: Between the parties. May refer to contracts, conveyances or other transactions having legal significance.

INTER VIVOS: Between the living. An inter vivos gift is a gift made by a living grantor, as distinguished from bequests contained in a will, which pass upon the death of the testator.

IPSO FACTO: By the mere fact itself.

JUS: Law or the entire body of law.

LEX LOCI: The law of the place; the notion that the rights of parties to a legal proceeding are governed by the law of the place where those rights arose.

MALUM IN SE: Evil or wrong in and of itself; inherently wrong. This term describes an act that is wrong by its very nature, as opposed to one which would not be wrong but for the fact that there is a specific legal prohibition against it (malum prohibitum).

MALUM PROHIBITUM: Wrong because prohibited, but not inherently evil. Used to describe something that is wrong because it is expressly forbidden by law but that is not in and of itself evil, e.g., speeding.

MANDAMUS: We command. A writ directing an official to take a certain action.

MENS REA: A guilty mind; a criminal intent. A term used to signify the mental state that accompanies a crime or other prohibited act. Some crimes require only a general mens rea (general intent to do the prohibited act), but others, like assault with intent to murder, require the existence of a specific mens rea.

MODUS OPERANDI: Method of operating; generally refers to the manner or style of a criminal in committing crimes, admissible in appropriate cases as evidence of the identity of a defendant.

NEXUS: A connection to.

NISI PRIUS: A court of first impression. A nisi prius court is one where issues of fact are tried before a judge or jury.

N.O.V. (NON OBSTANTE VEREDICTO): Notwithstanding the verdict. A judgment n.o.v. is a judgment given in favor of one party despite the fact that a verdict was returned in favor of the other party, the justification being that the verdict either had no reasonable support in fact or was contrary to law.

NUNC PRO TUNC: Now for then. This phrase refers to actions that may be taken and will then have full retroactive effect.

PENDENTE LITE: Pending the suit; pending litigation underway.

PER CAPITA: By head; beneficiaries of an estate, if they take in equal shares, take per capita.

PER CURIAM: By the court; signifies an opinion ostensibly written "by the whole court" and with no identified author.

PER SE: By itself, in itself; inherently.

PER STIRPES: By representation. Used primarily in the law of wills to describe the method of distribution where a person, generally because of death, is unable to take that which is left to him by the will of another, and therefore his heirs divide such property between them rather than take under the will individually.

PRIMA FACIE: On its face, at first sight. A prima facie case is one that is sufficient on its face, meaning that the evidence supporting it is adequate to establish the case until contradicted or overcome by other evidence.

PRO TANTO: For so much; as far as it goes. Often used in eminent domain cases when a property owner receives partial payment for his land without prejudice to his right to bring suit for the full amount he claims his land to be worth.

QUANTUM MERUIT: As much as he deserves. Refers to recovery based on the doctrine of unjust enrichment in those cases in which a party has rendered valuable services or furnished materials that were accepted and enjoyed by another under circumstances that would reasonably notify the recipient that the rendering party expected to be paid. In essence, the law implies a contract to pay the reasonable value of the services or materials furnished.

QUASI: Almost like; as if; nearly. This term is essentially used to signify that one subject or thing is almost analogous to another but that material differences between them do exist. For example, a quasi-criminal proceeding is one that is not strictly criminal but shares enough of the same characteristics to require some of the same safeguards (e.g., procedural due process must be followed in a parol hearing).

QUID PRO QUO: Something for something. In contract law, the consideration, something of value, passed between the parties to render the contract binding.

RES GESTAE: Things done; in evidence law, this principle justifies the admission of a statement that would otherwise be hearsay when it is made so closely to the event in question as to be said to be a part of it, or with such spontaneity as not to have the possibility of falsehood.

RES IPSA LOQUITUR: The thing speaks for itself. This doctrine gives rise to a rebuttable presumption of negligence when the instrumentality causing the injury was within the exclusive control of the defendant, and the injury was one that does not normally occur unless a person has been negligent.

RES JUDICATA: A matter adjudged. Doctrine which provides that once a court of competent jurisdiction has rendered a final judgment or decree on the merits, that judgment or decree is conclusive upon the parties to the case and prevents them from engaging in any other litigation on the points and issues determined therein.

RESPONDEAT SUPERIOR: Let the master reply. This doctrine holds the master liable for the wrongful acts of his servant (or the principal for his agent) in those cases in which the servant (or agent) was acting within the scope of his authority at the time of the injury.

STARE DECISIS: To stand by or adhere to that which has been decided. The common law doctrine of stare decisis attempts to give security and certainty to the law by following the policy that once a principle of law as applicable to a certain set of facts has been set forth in a decision, it forms a precedent which will subsequently be followed, even though a different decision might be made were it the first time the question had arisen. Of course, stare decisis is not an inviolable principle and is departed from in instances where there is good cause (e.g., considerations of public policy led the Supreme Court to disregard prior decisions sanctioning segregation).

SUPRA: Above. A word referring a reader to an earlier part of a book.

ULTRA VIRES: Beyond the power. This phrase is most commonly used to refer to actions taken by a corporation that are beyond the power or legal authority of the corporation.

ADDENDUM OF FRENCH DERIVATIVES

IN PAIS: Not pursuant to legal proceedings.

CHATTEL: Tangible personal property.

CY PRES: Doctrine permitting courts to apply trust funds to purposes not expressed in the trust but necessary to carry out the settlor's intent.

PER AUTRE VIE: For another's life; in property law, an estate may be granted that will terminate upon the death of someone other than the grantee.

PROFIT A PRENDRE: A license to remove minerals or other produce from land.

VOIR DIRE: Process of questioning jurors as to their predispositions about the case or parties to a proceeding in order to identify those jurors displaying bias or prejudice.

CASENOTE LEGAL BRIEFS